RAISED WITH CHRIST

HOW THE **RESURRECTION** CHANGES EVERYTHING

ADRIAN WARNOCK

CROSSWAY

WHEATON, ILLINOIS

Cover design: Dual Identity inc.

First printing, 2010

Printed in the United States of America

Italics in biblical quotes indicate emphasis added.

Trade paperback ISBN: 978-1-4335-0716-8

PDF ISBN: 978-1-4335-0717-5

Mobipocket ISBN: 978-1-4335-0718-2

ePub ISBN: 978-1-4335-2261-1

Library of Congress Cataloging-in-Publication Data
Warnock, Adrian, 1971–
   Raised with Christ : how the Resurrection changes everything / Adrian Warnock
      p. cm.
   Includes bibliographical references.
   ISBN: 978-1-4335-0716-8 (tpb)
   1. Jesus Christ—Resurrection. I. Title
BT482.W37   2010
236'.8—dc22   2009022138

Crossway is a publishing ministry of Good News Publishers.

VP		20	19	18	17	16	15	14	13	12	11	10
15	14	13	12	11	10	9	8	7	6	5	4	3	2

"Jesus is alive! And, as my friend Adrian Warnock will help you learn, this fact changes everything for everyone."

MARK DRISCOLL, Founding Pastor, Mars Hill Church; President, The Resurgence; President, The Acts 29 Church Planting Network

"The resurrection of Jesus Christ from the dead separates Christianity from all mere religion—whatever its form. Christianity without the literal, physical resurrection of Jesus Christ from the dead is merely one religion among many. Adrian Warnock points us all to the centrality of the resurrection for every dimension of the Christian life. Adrian is a first-rate communicator and a man whose life demonstrates the joy of Christ's resurrection. You will be greatly blessed by this book."

AL MOHLER, President, The Southern Baptist Theological Seminary

"Adrian Warnock presents a beautiful picture of why the resurrection matters to each of us. In *Raised with Christ*, the resurrection of Jesus is unleashed to its exalted place where it supplies our new birth, surrounds our new life, and empowers our new mission. With great clarity, Adrian teaches how the resurrection of Christ matters every day."

ED STETZER, President, LifeWay Research

"*Raised with Christ* is wonderfully accessible to ordinary Christians because Adrian Warnock is, in his own words, an ordinary Christian. Those who follow his popular blog will recognize his sincere and straightforward style, as he explains why the resurrection is not merely a dry doctrine about a past event but a promise that the life of the risen Christ can transform our lives today."

NANCY PEARCEY, author, *Total Truth*

"Adrian Warnock rightly highlights the common neglect of the resurrection and helpfully shows why this matters. Come and share the excitement of his own rediscovery of this central event of our faith."

TIM CHESTER, The Crowded House and the Northern Training Institute

"Adrian has helpfully drawn the spotlight back to a strangely under-emphasized element of evangelical faith. He writes winsomely and with fitting enthusiasm. I hope many will find their way to a fuller grasp of the gospel through this highly accessible book."

JOEL VIRGO, Lead Pastor, Church of Christ the King, Brighton

"Finally, a new generation of readers has a clear and highly readable book on the resurrection of Jesus Christ. In *Raised with Christ*, Christians are in for a delightful surprise as they grasp anew all the benefits which flow from Jesus' resurrection—what an awesome difference it can make in our lives, our churches, and our communities! Thank you, Adrian, for helping to open our eyes to all the glories and the blessings of Christ's resurrection and the power, present and future, which proceeds from it."

JONI EARECKSON TADA, Joni and Friends International Disability Center

"An important reminder—for members and leaders in Christ's Church—that the celebration of Jesus' resurrection isn't just for Easter. It's for every day of our lives. Since Jesus rose from the dead, everything he said and did is not only true, it has a profound impact on how we are to live. This book not only reminds us of that, it also points us toward meaningful application of this life-changing event."

ELLIOT GRUDEM, Senior Minister, Christ the King Presbyterian Church, Raleigh, NC

"This book faithfully expounds the Bible's teaching on Christ's resurrection and ours and applies the power of Christ's resurrection to our lives here and now. Read it and know better the immeasurable greatness of God's power toward us who believe."

BOBBY JAMIESON, Assistant Editor, 9Marks

"This is an excellent, ground-breaking book that fills a huge gap in our understanding and experience as Christians. It is high time the doctrine of the resurrection was put back on the map. Adrian has done us a great service in writing this timely book."
MARK STIBBE, Father's House Trust, www.fathershousetrust.com

"Every so often, a book is written that reawakens our soul to some gloriously powerful aspect of the full gospel. The resurrection is such a truth, and this is such a book. Adrian Warnock has been a part of the church I lead since 1995 and has served on our leadership team for more than ten years. It is my delight that he has written this engaging volume on such a life-transforming truth. If you want to know why the resurrection is crucial to your faith, if you want to know where the power for a transformed life comes from, then read this hugely accessible book and gain fresh insight into the most powerful event that has ever happened, the resurrection."
TOPE KOLEOSO, Pastor, Jubilee Church, London

"Adrian Warnock is brilliantly obsessed with the resurrection! He believes that Jesus Christ being raised from death is the only way to have hope that goes beyond the grave. In this punchy and accessible book, Adrian helps us to look forward expectantly to a life of eternal future joy, united with God, and in this life, to experience the Holy Spirit and preach the good news in the power of the resurrection. I'm thankful to Adrian for reorienting me to this essential ingredient of life and belief. You will be too."
MARCUS HONEYSETT, author, *Finding Joy*

"Books are often dull, repetitive, or have nothing new to say. *Raised with Christ* is different. It is well-written, well-researched, and well-worth reading. Read this book and Adrian will excite your heart, stretch your mind, and bless your soul with the fantastic, life-changing truth of Christ conquering death. I'm excited to promote this book."
JONATHAN CARSWELL, founder of The 10 Group of Companies
(incorporating www.10ofthose.com)

"This is an excellent book on a much neglected subject. We Christians need to learn again to be Easter people, and Adrian has done us all a great service in producing this book."
SAM ALLBERRY, author, *Lifted*

"Packed with gems and clear, heart-affecting theology, this is a plum pudding of a book that the church badly needs."
MICHAEL REEVES, Theological Advisor, UCCF

"Adrian Warnock has a passion to put the resurrection back in the center of our proclamation. He understands that without a risen Savior there is no credibility to Jesus' claims, no salvation through his death, no reason for Christian living, no explanation of the church's existence, and no hope of eternal life. This book challenged me to reexamine my own preaching to see whether there was enough of Christ risen in it."
LIAM GOLIGHER, Senior Minister, Duke Street Church, London

"Congenital heretics, in every generation, take a fiendish delight in warping the gospel. The gospel is centered upon two great facts—Christ's crucifixion and stand-in death for us to expunge our guilt, and Christ's return from the grave in his body to secure our salvation and the renewal of all things. The latter is criminally neglected in much preaching and writing. Few books exist that can inspire and excite both preachers and general readers alike concerning the importance of the resurrection as this one does. Warnock's bang-up-to-date, big-picture approach is a gold mine of glittering insights, designed to shatter our dulled over-familiarity and rekindle an awed sense of wonder."
GREG HASLAM, Senior Minister, Westminster Chapel, London

"Adrian has provided us with a thorough, thoughtful, and inspiring study of the resurrection. It left me better informed, more eager to live the life, and more thankful to God for the basis of my faith: a risen Lord Jesus and an empty tomb!"
DAVID STROUD, UK Team Leader, Newfrontiers; author, *Planting Churches, Changing Communities*

To my wonderful wife
Andrée

CONTENTS

FOREWORD

THE EARLY BELIEVERS were not only accused of turning the world upside down but also of saying there was another king called Jesus (Acts 17:7) who was the Savior of the world and the Son of God—a dangerous message to proclaim in an empire where Caesar also rejoiced in the titles "savior of the world" and "son of god" and did not welcome another making similar claims.

Happily for Caesar, the one whom the Christians talked about as the world's Savior had already been dealt with in far-off Palestine. Pilate, the procurator of Judea, had crucified him, so no problems there! Dead pretenders to the throne hardly pose a threat!

The strange thing was that his being dead didn't seem to bother the Christians since they claimed that he was alive again! The apostle Paul even argued that it was Jesus' resurrection from the dead that designated him "Son of God in power" (Romans 1:4). They were not claiming that a corpse was strangely resuscitated or that Jesus of Nazareth somehow survived crucifixion. They were certainly not saying that though he was physically dead, his teachings lived on so we could still follow his dream.

Their claim was far greater. They were saying that Jesus had been exonerated by Israel's God. He wasn't simply breathing again; he was vindicated as a Savior and Lord with unique and global power.

Christ's resurrection had massive implications for his followers. Through their faith in him, they had become incorporated into Christ himself. Paul's favorite phrase for a Christian was one who is "in Christ"; so Christ's resurrection implied *their* resurrection. They were raised with him (Ephesians 2:6).

The Jews had for some time been anticipating a national "resurrection," particularly since Ezekiel had vividly described his vision of a valley full of dead bones that were breathed upon by the Holy Spirit and suddenly came alive as a mighty army (Ezekiel 37). Sadly, their interpretation of the vision had usually been in political terms focused on Israel's national well-being, especially as it related to Rome's domination of their lives.

They actually dreamed of having a Messiah like David. His own personal charisma would resurrect Israel and give them famous victories. Just as David emerged from nowhere, defeated Goliath, and became first a national hero, then an invincible king who thrashed the Philistines, so the Jews were anticipating the arrival of a similar figure who would resurrect Israel as a nation enjoying phenomenal success and military conquest. The dead nation would come alive again under its messianic leader, which would have international ramifications.

Indeed, the kingdom of the Messiah would not only extend to the borders of Israel but far beyond them. He would have international authority, and all nations would acknowledge Israel's king. Staggeringly, their hopes went even further. His reign would usher in a new age that would never end. The one who came would sit on David's throne and reign forever (Isaiah 9:7).

Sometimes the crowds wondered if Jesus of Nazareth might be the one. He had demonstrated amazing power, especially when he miraculously fed five thousand. After that extraordinary sign, they even tried to force the issue and "make him king" (John 6:15).

Such hopes were, of course, thoroughly dashed when Jesus of Nazareth was taken and crucified. Messiahs don't get crucified! It seemed that they would have to wait for another who would bring deliverance and extend his rule over the nations. The international kingdom of Israel's God and his Messiah would have to wait for another generation. The resurrection of the people of God into a great army was still on hold.

Saul of Tarsus would certainly have thought the same until that historic day on the Damascus road when he discovered to his amazement that Jesus of Nazareth, the dead impostor, was very much alive and full of power and that this messianic vision was not on hold after all! He truly was Lord of all, and as an international king he appointed Paul as his new ambassador to represent him among the nations, stand before kings, and bring the Gentiles out of darkness into light and from the power of Satan to God (Acts 26:16–18).

Paul and his fellow believers were to go and tell the world that

Israel's long-awaited Messiah had indeed come, had died for their sins, but was now truly alive, the Lord of all and the King of the nations. The church was to herald this truth to the ends of the earth. The Scriptures had been fulfilled—God had indeed come in power.

What a refreshing wake-up call Adrian's fine book provides in restating the vital place of Christ's resurrection. I count it an honor to provide some words of introduction. May Adrian's volume greatly serve the twenty-first-century church by inspiring this generation to a new awareness of the resurrection and enthronement of their glorified Lord.

Terry Virgo,
Founder and Leader,
Newfrontiers

PREFACE

THIS BOOK IS ABOUT THE resurrection of Jesus and its effects on us today. If, like me, you have wondered why Christians often seem to talk more about the events of Good Friday than Easter Sunday, this book is for you. Although we talk about the death of Jesus often, for some reason we have tended to only mention the resurrection at Easter time. Christians sometimes even say Jesus died to save us without mentioning that he also rose for our salvation. It's time to redress the balance a bit and talk more about Jesus' death *and* resurrection.

For Christians all over the world, every Sunday is Resurrection Sunday. We meet each week, among other things, in order to celebrate the glorious, wondrous fact that Jesus rose from the dead. Jesus' resurrection really did change everything. It changed the cross from a tragedy into a triumph, and it changed the Roman Empire into a Christian state. This was the most powerful divine event in the history of creation, and it ushered in a new age of the Holy Spirit's activity and power in saving and transforming lives.

When considering if Christianity is true, it all boils down to whether Jesus rose from the dead. The lives of Christians today demonstrate that the resurrection is still changing people. It changes fear into love, despair into joy. The resurrection changes people from being spiritually dead to being alive to God. It changes guilty condemnation into a celebration of forgiveness and freedom. It changes anxiety into a hope that goes beyond the grave. It can change our sinful hearts so they want to follow the Lord Jesus, and the power of the resurrection is relentlessly killing sin in every true Christian. Because we neglect to emphasize this truth, many Christians have a meager expectation of the extent to which we can today experience resurrection life and victory over sin. The resurrection is far from being something we only benefit from in the future!

John MacArthur[1] claimed:

> The Resurrection is the ground of our assurance, it is the basis for all
> our future hopes, and it is the source of power in our daily lives here
> and now. It gives us courage in the midst of persecution, comfort in the
> midst of trials, and hope in the midst of this world's darkness.[2]

It is no accident that many of these things that MacArthur credits to
the resurrection are elsewhere also attributed to the activity of the Holy
Spirit—namely assurance (Romans 8:16–24), a source of power in our
daily lives (Romans 8:4), and a comfort (John 14:16, 26).

Through his resurrection Jesus became "a life-giving Spirit"
(1 Corinthians 15:45), a whole new kind of human being, and enabled
us to share in this new life. Also, it was only because of his resurrection
and ascension that he was able to send the Holy Spirit into the world to
carry out his special work in Christians (John 7:39; Acts 2:33). What the
Spirit does for believers today is only possible as a result of the resurrection. Not only that, but Paul tells us in three places that Christians have
already been raised with Christ:

> If then you have been raised with Christ, seek the things that are above,
> where Christ is, seated at the right hand of God. (Colossians 3:1)

> We were buried therefore with him by baptism into death, in order
> that, just as Christ was raised from the dead by the glory of the Father,
> we too might walk in newness of life. (Romans 6:4)

> God . . . made us alive together with Christ—by grace you have been
> saved—and raised us up with him. (Ephesians 2:5–6)

Christians have therefore already been changed by Jesus' resurrection. Jesus really is alive today. Because of this Christians are also alive
in a whole new way. The same power that raised Christ from the dead is
living in every true Christian. God wants us not just to believe in Jesus'
resurrection but to be transformed by it and to receive the power we
need to live the way we know we ought. If you already follow Jesus, then

---

[1]Radio preacher, pastor of Grace Community Church in Sun Valley, California, and the leader of Grace
to You ministries; see http://gty.org.
[2]John MacArthur's Preface, in Gerard Chrispin, *The Resurrection: The Unopened Gift* (Epsom, UK:
Day One, 2002), 6.

this book aims to help you love him more. For all of us, the questions, *did Jesus rise from the dead?* and *what are the implications of his resurrection?* are the most important ones we will ever answer.

My hope is that you will not find this a complicated book. I write as an ordinary Christian, and not a theologian. My goal is that each of us can explore what the resurrection means and how we are affected today by what happened two thousand years ago.

As we begin, I pray that God himself will help each of us to better understand this wonderful subject and to live in light of the resurrection of Jesus Christ.

ACKNOWLEDGMENTS

THANKS TO ALL THE PEOPLE AT Crossway for their wonderful support, help, and friendship. No author could hope for a better publisher. In particular, Justin Taylor has been a great encouragement at every stage of the process, and Ted Griffin edited the manuscript with skill and sensitivity. The book is definitely much better for it.

This book would never have happened if not for my Web site, adrianwarnock.com. Thank you, therefore, to all the friends I have met online and the many who take time out of their busy lives to read my posts. I have learned so much along the way, especially from reading some of *your* blogs.

Comments and suggestions from my friends and family have helped shape this book, and therefore I am grateful for the input of Andrew Cottingham, Andrew Fountain, Andrew Warnock, Anna Averkiou, Arnold Bell, Ben Virgo, Bobby Jamieson, Charis Warnock, Dave Pask, Dave Bish, Elliot Grudem, Frank Turk, Greg Haslam, Hannah Sandu, Henry Warnock, Joanne Soda, Joe Rigney, Lex Loizides, Liam Goligher, Marjorie Warnock, Matthew Hosier, Mike Lawson, Michael Reeves, Nathan Fellingham, Phil Butcher, Phil Moore, Scott Lamb, Stuart Emsley, and Ted Hans. I hope I haven't forgotten anyone. Thanks also to Annette Harrison who has for a number of years tirelessly worked to help me edit my blog, and has spent countless hours pouring over even very early drafts of this book.

Tope Koleoso, as well as commenting on the drafts, was the first person to suggest to me I should think about writing a book. I hope you realize what you started. Thank you for being my pastor. I thank God that I can follow you as you follow the resurrected Christ. I also want to thank all those, beginning with my parents, who have taught me our shared faith.

My children, Tamasin, Henry, Charis, Joel, and George, have been very understanding about Dad's need to spend so much time in front of his computer on top of his day job. You know that the times I love most are the ones we spend together as a family. You guys rock!

On earth no one is more precious to me than Andrée, my darling wife, mother of five, and an extraordinary helper well suited for me. You didn't just help so wonderfully with this book, you also lived the whole process with me. I look forward to growing old with you at my side. Thanks are not enough. I dedicate this book to you, my love, and to the God who covers all our weaknesses.

I have received much undeserved grace.

CHAPTER ONE

CHRIST HAS DIED!
CHRIST IS RISEN!
CHRIST WILL COME AGAIN!

"WHAT! DID JESUS COME BACK to life again?" This was the surprised reaction when a young Englishwoman heard about the resurrection of Jesus. She was drinking coffee with other mothers, including my wife. It seems almost impossible to believe that she had never heard that Christians believe Jesus rose from the dead. She hadn't *rejected* the gospel. No one had ever told her about it!

How many other people do we know who would have a similar reaction? It is much more comfortable for us to assume that our relatives, friends, neighbors, and coworkers have already dismissed the gospel than to think they have never heard it.

Without Jesus' resurrection there is no good news at all. John Stott[1] said, "Christianity is in its very essence a resurrection religion. The concept of resurrection lies at its heart. If you remove it, Christianity is destroyed."[2]

Some today would be surprised by Stott's comment. The church sometimes attempts to tell the gospel story without any reference to the resurrection of Jesus. In a relatively recent development, some in the liberal movement of the last century or so have even denied the resurrection, making them the first significant group in history to claim to be Christians without believing Jesus rose from the dead.

---

[1]A leading evangelical Anglican minister who many credit alongside Martyn Lloyd-Jones with personally reinvigorating British evangelicalism in the twentieth century. See http://johnstott.org.
[2]John Stott, cited in Mark Driscoll and Gerry Breshears, *Vintage Jesus* (Wheaton, IL: Crossway Books, 2007), 131.

Reflecting on this has led me to suggest the following definition of a Christian, with which almost any member of any church denomination throughout history would identify: *A Christian is someone who believes in the physical resurrection of Jesus Christ and lives in light of the implications of that event.*

Historically everyone would have understood that you cannot be a Christian without believing in the resurrection of Jesus. Of course, there are other things necessary to be a Christian. But I would argue that they all arise as necessary deductions from the historicity of this miraculous event. The challenge is that we tend to disagree with each other on precisely what those implications are. The definition above will sound vague unless they are carefully identified. It is critical, therefore, that we discover precisely why the resurrection is so important, in what ways we can be changed by it, and what are its consequences in our thinking and behavior. That is the theme of this book.

The definition I suggested is supported by Paul's description of the gospel response: "If you confess with your mouth that Jesus is Lord and believe in your heart that God raised him from the dead, you will be saved" (Romans 10:9). One of the implications of the resurrection of Jesus is his lordship and hence divinity. Since before his death he claimed to be God, we cannot consistently believe he is risen without also concluding we must worship and follow him.

Our belief in the resurrection also changes our understanding about the meaning of the death of Jesus and what it accomplished. Since Jesus was raised from the dead, and we understand that all death is a punishment, we can deduce that he didn't deserve to die on the cross and ask, why then did he die? His resurrection helps us understand that he died in place of us. To say Jesus rose again so he could share his life with us eternally would make little sense unless he had died on our behalf so we will not die eternally. The cross and resurrection are, in one sense, two sides of the same coin.

We may disagree with Christians from other denominations about the implications of the resurrection, but all genuine Christians agree that this event, together with the cross of Christ, defines our lives.

HOW THIS BOOK CAME TO BE WRITTEN

I was asked to preach on Easter Sunday in 2007. Usually I enjoy preaching, but I was busy, weary, and to be honest, on this occasion I was not initially thrilled at the prospect. I politely made my excuses but promised to pray about it.

Preachers don't often talk about how they decide what to speak about. Sometimes, however, they do experience a strange compulsion to preach on a certain subject. Martyn Lloyd-Jones[3] described his own experience in this way: "One morning while dressing, quite suddenly and in an overwhelming manner, it seemed to me that the Spirit of God was urging me to preach a series of sermons on 'spiritual depression.'"[4]

Something remarkably similar happened to me that night. Having prayed halfheartedly before bed, I woke suddenly in the night. A simple phrase was burning in my mind: *"Adrian, preach about the resurrection."* I could not ignore this thought. I agreed to preach after all and began to study Jesus' resurrection.

I soon realized that resurrection is not often discussed in detail today. I found, however, that all of the sermons recorded in Acts focus on the resurrection of Jesus. It might initially seem like there is one exception in Acts 7, but in fact that sermon was interrupted when the risen Jesus himself opened heaven and appeared to Stephen while he was preaching! I was deeply struck by this, and realized that I had not given Jesus' resurrection the attention it deserved.

Later I discovered how Charles Spurgeon,[5] early in his outstanding preaching ministry, was also struck by his own neglect of the resurrection:

> Reflecting the other day upon the sad state of the churches at the present moment, I was led to look back to apostolic times, and to consider wherein the preaching of the present day differed from the preaching of the apostles. . . .
>
> I was surprised to find that I had not been copying the apostolic fashion half as nearly as I might have done. The apostles when they

---

[3]Previous minister of Westminster Chapel, London, and one of the most respected preachers and authors of the twentieth century. See http://www.mlj-usa.com.

[4]D. Martyn Lloyd-Jones, *Preaching & Preachers* (Grand Rapids: Zondervan, 1972), 188–190.

[5]He led the first modern "megachurch" in Victorian London with some five thousand members. His published sermons number more than three thousand five hundred and remain popular today—you could read one a day for almost ten years! See http://www.spurgeon.org.

preached always testified concerning the resurrection of Jesus, and the consequent resurrection of the dead. . . .

[This] is a doctrine which we believe, but which we too seldom preach or care to read about. Though I have inquired of several booksellers for a book specially upon the subject of the resurrection, I have not yet been able to purchase one of any sort whatever. . . . It has been set down as a well-known truth, and therefore has never been discussed. Heresies have not risen up respecting it; it would almost have been a mercy if there had been, for whenever a truth is contested by heretics, the orthodox fight strongly for it, and the pulpit resounds with it every day. I am persuaded, however, that there is much power in this doctrine . . . which is capable of moving the hearts of men and bringing them into subjection to the gospel of our Lord and Savior Jesus Christ.[6]

I too have scoured the Christian bookshops, and although there are now several helpful books on the resurrection, there are fewer in comparison to other subjects. Why has this vital doctrine been so neglected? Are we therefore missing something doctrinally, experientially, and evangelistically? Personally, I have found that the study of the resurrection has deeply impacted me.

THE STATE OF THE CHURCH

The story I told earlier of one woman's ignorance of the Easter story is a reflection of the condition of the church in the West. Could our neglect of the resurrection be both cause and effect of the alarming state we are in? Certainly the success of liberal theology in taking hold of many churches after the First World War led to an increase in the number of those who denied the resurrection of Jesus and was also associated with the beginning of the decline in church attendance recorded since then. As a direct result of this, Christians have become marginalized by society and feel uncertain about how to share their beliefs with others in a hostile world.

The vigor of our faith has waned, and church attendance is believed by many to be in a terminal decline. The general level of biblical knowledge among Christians is appalling. In a world where more study mate-

---

[6]C. H. Spurgeon, *Sermon No. 66*, "The Resurrection of the Dead," delivered on February 17, 1856, at New Park Street Chapel, Southwark; http://www.spurgeon.org/scrmons/0066.htm.

rial is available in books, software, and online than previous generations could ever have dreamed, the Bible has never been less understood by members of the church, and even by our preachers. Presumably as a direct result for many who attend church today, there seems to be little observable difference from the world in terms of personal lifestyles, values, and beliefs. The old accusation that the Western church is a mile wide and an inch deep has never been more true.

Faced with this overall situation and compared to some periods in church history and the remarkable church growth seen today in other parts of the world, many of us yearn for something more. Terry Virgo[7] explains:

> On the whole we . . . have grown up in a generation that has not seen the mighty acts of God as our forefathers did. We have not seen revivals during which thousands flock into the churches to get right with God. Unlike our fathers, we have not known whole towns change, with demonstrations of power and incredible manifestations of the glory of God. The majority of our generation knows nothing of these things.[8]

There is still a silent majority in the general population who claim to believe in God. At the same time, there is widespread ignorance about the Christian message. For example, a supermarket chain issued the following erroneous press release to promote their seasonal chocolate and embarrassed itself: "Brits will on average be enjoying over 3.5 eggs each over the Easter weekend alone. But over a quarter don't know why handing them out symbolizes the *birth* of Jesus."[9]

The company corrected and reissued the statement, but only after consulting the Church of England's press office. We may be indignant about such ignorance, but it has always been the church's job to share the good news, so this is largely *our* fault.

Many are proposing solutions for the challenges that the Western church faces today. Some lack confidence in the message of the gospel, arguing that we should speak less about our beliefs in the hope that the

---

[7]Founder of Newfrontiers, a group of over six hundred Reformed charismatic churches in more than fifty nations; see http://www.terryvirgo.org/ and http://www.newfrontiers.xtn.org/.
[8]Terry Virgo, *The Tide Is Turning* (Chichester, UK: New Wine Press, 2006), 70.
[9]*The Times*, April 4, 2007, emphasis added; http://www.timesonline.co.uk/tol/comment/faith/article 1610495.ece?pgnum=4.

world will be less offended. Others go further and quietly deny core Christian values. Some look to marketing techniques, changes in worship style, or modern management strategies. An industry has arisen offering solutions to struggling pastors in the form of leadership books and programs. We should learn everything we can without compromising the Bible, but no single solution will cure the multiple ailments of the church.

In spite of this general decline, there are many encouraging signs. This book is written in the hope that if we will faithfully proclaim the death *and* resurrection of Jesus and work out the implications of that message in vibrant, grace-filled churches, the tide will turn.

Many churches do hold firmly to the truths delivered to them. Some of those churches are growing, and a few of them are growing dramatically. It is encouraging that in at least some growing churches a gospel is preached that would have been instantly recognizable to our Christian forefathers.

One example of a church that has adapted some of its methods to better fit the modern culture but has not adjusted its message is Mars Hill Church in Seattle, led by Mark Driscoll. They have seen thousands of unchurched people turn to Jesus. Their boldness can seem almost brash at times, and some observers are quick to criticize when they believe mistakes have been made. However, such churches invade unoccupied territory to win souls for Christ in a way impossible to the more genteel churches in which some Christians feel more comfortable. Driscoll's preaching does emphasize the resurrection, and he describes being sustained and motivated by the leadership of the risen Jesus in his church today:

> The only thing that gets me out of bed on Monday is the picture in Revelation of King Jesus on his throne ruling over all of creation, which is his kingdom. I've never seen what John saw, so I am forced to take his word for it. But because Jesus is in charge of everything, there is hope, even for my city.[10]

THE FUTURE OF THE CHURCH

It sounds clichéd to say that we need to look at our young people when we consider what the future holds for the church, but it is, of

---

[10]Mark Driscoll, *The Radical Reformission* (Grand Rapids: Zondervan, 2004), 183–184.

course, true. A group of younger people is emerging who are restless. Their upbringing has been in a culture overtly hostile to Christianity. They recognize the ineffectiveness of the church on a broad level. They acknowledge that many churches today are in serious danger of quietly sleepwalking into extinction. An aging population of Christian baby boomers is presiding over a time bomb, since their children have now largely abandoned their congregations. In some cases, once thriving local churches have no members at all under the age of fifty. In the next few years, unless something dramatic happens, whole denominations and groups of churches will cease to exist.

Faced with this challenging situation, many of the young people who have not deserted church want to rise up and do something. Statistics and surveys often seem to suggest that they have one chance to get it right or face the annihilation of the Western church within a generation. Unsurprisingly, they are eager to reexamine the message and methods they have been taught. A belief that Jesus *will* continue to build his church does not translate into confidence that the right strategies are currently being pursued.

Two distinct groups have surfaced as a result. Both agree that changes in methods are essential. One group, calling itself the "emerging church," is willing to change everything about church to better fit in with postmodern, informal, twenty-first-century culture. By some, even the message is adapted for an increased appeal.[11]

The second group, the "young, restless, and reformed,"[12] is also willing to change many aspects of church organization, worship meetings, and the style of music. However, they seek, if anything, a *more* traditional message than their parents, passionately reviving a robust biblical theology of the past. Dr. Albert Mohler[13] elaborates:

> This generation of young Christians is more committed, more theologically intense, more theologically curious, more self-aware and self-conscious as believers because they were not raised in an environment

---

[11]See Kevin Young and Ted Kluck, *Why We're Not Emergent: By Two Guys Who Should Be* (Chicago: Moody Publishers, 2008).
[12]See Collin Hansen, "Young, Restless, Reformed," *Christianity Today*, September 2006; http://www.christianitytoday.com/ct/2006/september/42.32.html. Also see Collin Hansen, *Young, Restless, Reformed: A Journalist's Journey with the New Calvinists* (Wheaton, IL: Crossway Books, 2008).
[13]President of the Southern Baptist Theological Seminary and a leading conference speaker, author, and radio show host. See http://almohler.com.

of cultural Christianity. Or if they were, as soon as they arrived on a university campus, they found themselves in a hostile environment.[14]

These young Christians, whether they went to university or not, really care about understanding the true message of the Bible. They want their Christianity to be more than an inch deep. They care about authenticity and truth. They are also reacting to the modern culture of apathy and permissiveness. This results in a firm conviction about biblical truths that will not change and are non-negotiable.

On both sides of the Atlantic, conferences are mushrooming that promote a robust commitment to studying the Bible. Events like Together for the Gospel,[15] The Gospel Coalition,[16] Desiring God,[17] Together On a Mission,[18] and New Word Alive[19] are frequently oversubscribed, often with the majority of attendees in their twenties and thirties. Many of these young people are deeply committed to studying Scripture, applying it to their lives, and sharing it with an increasingly godless society.

At the time of writing, I still have a couple of years left before I turn forty, so I can just claim to be part of that second group! This book is about my own attempts to be sure that I am not missing or underemphasizing any vital element of the gospel's message. It is about a journey that, for me, began more than thirty years ago as a child but came to a head just before Easter 2007 when I felt compelled to begin studying the resurrection afresh.

AN OVERVIEW OF THIS BOOK

This book is not exclusively for pastors or theologians. You will not find a new program or method here. Instead we will take a fresh look at some old ideas from the Bible. In examining how the resurrection can change us today, we will discover some real answers to the church's predicament.

Our journey together will begin by asking the question, was the

---

[14]Cited by Hansen, "Young, Restless, Reformed."
[15]See http://togetherforthegospel.org.
[16]See http://www.thegospelcoalition.org.
[17]See http://desiringgod.org.
[18]See http://newfrontiers.xtn.org.
[19]See http://newwordalive.org.

tomb indeed empty? What exactly happened in the time between Easter Sunday and the Day of Pentecost? We will see why it is crucial for us to believe in a literal, bodily resurrection of Jesus. As Tim Keller[20] said:

> If Jesus rose from the dead you have to accept all he said, if he didn't rise from the dead then why worry about anything he said. . . . If Jesus rose from the dead, it changes everything.[21]

We will explore some of the reasons why Jesus' resurrection has been neglected and review the teaching about resurrection throughout the Bible. We will consider the implications of Jesus' resurrection for our salvation, how it changes us to be more like Jesus and is a model for our own resurrection. We will discover how to become more connected with the same power that raised Christ from the dead and therefore increase our confidence that we are indeed Christians. We will conclude by considering the mission the risen Jesus gave us and how the resurrection will affect the entire universe.

I pray that we will benefit from studying the resurrection together. May an increased confidence in this wonderful truth fill us, may our eyes be opened, our hearts thrilled, and may we experience the transforming power of Christ's resurrection at work in our lives. May God cause our faith in Christ and his message to grow. May we gain the courage we need to share this message with our friends.

I wonder how many people we know have never heard anyone share with them that they believe Jesus rose from the dead. Please join me in praying that God will raise up an army of Christians who will announce boldly the message of the gospel:

Christ has died!
Christ is risen!
Christ will come again!

---

[20]Minister of one of America's most influential megachurches, Redeemer Presbyterian Church in New York City; see http://redeemer.com.
[21]Tim Keller, *The Reason for God* (London: Hodder and Stoughton, 2008), 202.

CHAPTER TWO

THE EMPTY CROSS, THE EMPTY TOMB

He is not here, for he has risen.

MATTHEW 28:6

WE LIVE IN AN AGE OF global brands. In almost any city in the world, the golden "M" of McDonald's beckons consumers to a predictable source of American food. There are many other such global companies today, which also have a simple memorable image or logo.

Probably the most universally recognized logo in the world today is also the most ancient still in use—the cross. Almost everyone would recognize it instantly, because it remains powerfully embedded in our consciousness.

Although in some church buildings crosses have a statue of Jesus on them, since the Reformation many Christians prefer an empty cross. This underlines that the work of Jesus is complete. Christianity hinges not only on the empty cross but also on an empty tomb. Surprisingly little classical art, however, has focused on the resurrection of Jesus, as compared to the cross. Despite this, only the resurrection transforms the cross from a symbol of despair to a symbol of hope. These two evocative images are both vital to our salvation. As Paul said:

> For I delivered to you as of first importance what I also received: that Christ died for our sins in accordance with the Scriptures, that he was buried, that he was raised on the third day in accordance with the Scriptures. (1 Corinthians 15:3–4)

Some today argue that it does not really matter whether Jesus was physically resurrected. As Francis Schaeffer[1] explained, they couldn't be more wrong:

> The Bible says that Christ rose physically from the dead, that if you had been there that day you would have seen Christ stand up and walk away in a space-time, observable situation of true history. The materialist says, "No, I don't believe it. Christ was not raised from the dead." That is unbelief. Liberal theology is also unbelief because it says either that Jesus was not raised from the dead in history, or that maybe he was and maybe he wasn't because who knows what's going to happen in this world in which you can't be sure of anything. The historic resurrection of Christ doesn't really matter, says this theology; what matters is that the church got a big push from thinking he was raised in history. . . . Now I would say that the old liberalism, the new liberalism, and materialism are basically the same. To all of them finally the same word applies: *unbelief*.[2]

Jesus towers over human history. How we respond to him is foundational to how we see the world. Historians are very clear about two things concerning Jesus—he existed and he was crucified. No serious thinkers doubt those two facts. There are few events of ancient history with better evidence than this. If we cannot be sure Jesus lived and died, then we cannot be sure of almost any event in history before the modern era.

That a man lived and was crucified two thousand years ago is not unusual. Even being a great teacher, working miracles, and founding a religion does not make him unique. It is the claim of an empty tomb that marks Jesus as totally different from every other major historical figure. From an historical perspective, can we be sure that the tomb was indeed empty? What exactly happened those many years ago? Can any other explanation account for the explosive growth of Christ's church and its persistence throughout history?

Many Christian leaders have emphasized the importance of our view of the resurrection. We will share just two examples here:

---

[1]One of the best-known Christian apologists of the twentieth century; see http://francisschaeffer foundation.com.
[2]Francis A. Schaeffer, "The Universe and Two Chairs," *Death in the City*, Chapter 9, in Book IV of *The Complete Works of Francis A. Schaeffer* (Wheaton, IL: Crossway Books, 1996).

C. S. Lewis:[3] "The Christian story is precisely the story of one grand miracle, the Christian assertion being that what is beyond all space and time, what is uncreated, eternal, came into nature, into human nature, descended into His own universe, and rose again, bringing nature up with Him. It is precisely one great miracle. If you take that away there is nothing specifically Christian left."[4]

Sam Storms:[5] "I can honestly say that I've staked my life on an empty tomb. Everything I am, everything I own, everything I've done or hope to do hangs suspended on whether or not Jesus of Nazareth rose from the dead. The decision I made decades ago to put my trust in Jesus Christ as Lord and Savior is only as good as the tomb is empty. If Jesus didn't rise from the dead, my life is a sham. I've invested everything in, staked everything on, entrusted everything to the historical fact of the empty tomb of Jesus. If his body and bones are still buried somewhere in Palestine, or have long since disintegrated under the force of time and the laws of physics, nothing has meaning for me, nor do I have meaning for anything or anyone else."[6]

As we study the resurrection of Jesus, we are standing on holy ground. We are facing the most important question any human being will ever answer in his or her lifetime—did Jesus rise from the dead? Everything hinges on our response to that single question.

Human reason alone cannot prove to anyone that Jesus rose from the dead. We "know" that people simply do not stay dead for three days and then return to life. Since we have not seen such an event, our reason tells us it cannot have happened. To persuade our intellect to believe in the resurrection requires not only rational arguments but a gift of faith from God. Christianity is, however, a reasonable faith. So we need to study the evidence for the resurrection and be "prepared to make a defense to anyone who asks you for a reason for the hope that is in you" (1 Peter 3:15). We need both a softened heart and an alert mind. Our powers of reasoning can strengthen our faith, and we have nothing to be ashamed of intellectually. As George Eldon Ladd[7] concluded:

---

[3]Author of The Chronicles of Narnia and many other books; an English professor and theological writer from Oxford, England.
[4]C. S. Lewis, *God in the Dock* (Grand Rapids: Eerdmans, 1994), 80.
[5]Pastor of Bridgeway Church, Oklahoma City and conference speaker; see http://enjoyinggodministries.com.
[6]Sam Storms, "What If Christ Is Not Risen?—Part 1"; http://enjoyinggodministries.com/article/35-what-if-christ-is-not-risen-part-1.
[7]Previously Professor of New Testament Exegesis and Theology at Fuller Seminary.

The historical evidences which prove the resurrection are obvious for all to see. The reason that all men do not see them is the sinful blindness of the human heart. Only the man of faith can see the facts of history. . . . Faith is not a blind leap in the dark without any historical evidences. Neither will historical evidences *demand* faith, for the man of unbelief will always come up with different historical explanations. However, faith is supported and reinforced by historical evidences.[8]

We will therefore use our minds to consider the evidence for the resurrection. Even many non-Christian historians and scholars now accept that the Gospels were written down within at most a few decades of Jesus' life and convey eyewitness testimony of what Christians claim happened on the first Easter Sunday. Thus, the best place for us to begin our quest to discover whether Jesus rose from the dead is by examining what the Bible claims to have occurred.

THE BIBLICAL EVIDENCES FOR THE RESURRECTION

In the following section, I will attempt to harmonize the various resurrection stories in the Bible.[9] These accounts show a remarkable degree of agreement despite some apparent discrepancies (e.g., the number of women attending the tomb). We will see that small details that seem unclear within an individual Gospel account make perfect sense in the context of the other Gospels. A remarkably clear picture emerges from the stories taken as a whole.

We should not, however, put too much importance on exactly how these independent eyewitness accounts fit together. The Gospel writers deliberately did not attempt anything like the task I have perhaps foolishly set for myself here. The separate Gospel reports come across as eyewitness testimony of the same events, with the typical minor inconsistencies and differing perspectives that any lawyer recognizes would be humanly expected. These kinds of dis-

---

[8]George Eldon Ladd, *I Believe in the Resurrection of Jesus* (London: Hodder and Stoughton, 1975), 10–12.
[9]I acknowledge the influence of others on the following account including Ladd, *I Believe in the Resurrection of Jesus*, 91ff.; Gary Gromacki, "The Historicity of the Resurrection of Jesus Christ," *Journal of Ministry and Theology*, 6:1, 63–88 (Baptist Bible College and Seminary, 2002); John Walvoord, "The Person of Christ—Part IV: The Earthly Life of the Incarnate Christ," *Bibliotheca Sacra*, 117:291–300 (Dallas Theological Seminary, 1960); M. S. Mills, *The Life of Christ: A Study Guide to the Gospel Record* (Dallas: 3E Ministries, 1999).

crepancies are accepted as far more common in genuine testimony than would be seen in a manufactured story where every detail is agreed upon together.

It could be argued that any attempt to harmonize these stories is neither historically viable nor helpful for interpreting the Gospels. I am proceeding with a potentially fruitless endeavor to demonstrate that it is possible to weave these different reports into one consistent story. If the four Gospel accounts of the resurrection can be logically pieced together, like a jigsaw puzzle, in at least one way then, even if we are incorrect in some of our conclusions, we can be more confident that there must be a correct way of doing so. It is important to appreciate that some of the rest of this chapter is speculative. We have to trust God that he did not think it was necessary for us to know the answers to some of the questions we have about these events.

Before we continue, I encourage you to first read through Matthew 28, Mark 16, Luke 24, John 20–21, Acts 1, and 1 Corinthians 15.

Matthew tells us that Jesus died more quickly than many victims of crucifixion, and his death was associated with some miraculous signs. "Jesus cried out again with a loud voice and yielded up his spirit. And behold, the curtain of the temple was torn in two, from top to bottom. And the earth shook, and the rocks were split. The tombs also were opened. And many bodies of the saints who had fallen asleep were raised, and coming out of the tombs after his resurrection they went into the holy city and appeared to many" (Matthew 27:50–53). These remarkable events demonstrate that even as he died, Jesus remained in control of nature. The Lord of all was continuing to sustain the universe "by the word of his power" (Hebrews 1:3). Even as he died, he still had life-giving power that could empty tombs.[10]

Although his divine nature shared in the experience of the agony of death and separation from the Father, only his body was placed in the tomb. His spirit returned to God, and he promised the repentant thief, "Truly, I say to you, today you will be with me in Paradise."[11] Jesus effectively experienced hell on the cross, since hell means being separated from God. Despite some translations of an ancient creed, which

---

[10]These events do leave us with unanswerable questions. For example, why did those who had been raised not return to the city until Jesus' resurrection and what did they do in the meantime?
[11]Luke 23:43.

suggest that Jesus later "descended into hell,"[12] there is no biblical evidence to suggest that he actually did so.

Watching that day were some women who later played an extraordinary role in the events of the resurrection. We must spend a few moments understanding why this is so surprising. For Jesus to have a group of women traveling with him as disciples was very unusual in those days and revealed that he was no mere conservative follower of the culture of his day.[13] Jesus gave great dignity to women. He treated them as friends and was willing to sit with them and teach them, defying all traditions of the day.

As an example of his amazing attitude toward women, we see the way he gently showed a Samaritan woman the way of salvation.[14] Here was a teacher who did not despise women. He did not see them merely as servants to wait on the men. On one occasion he honored Mary, Lazarus' sister, for choosing to sit with him and learn like the men rather than bustling about preparing the food.[15] As a result of Jesus' radical acceptance, many women followed him as part of his group.[16] Unlike the male disciples who all "fell away"[17] and deserted Jesus, the women remained faithful, even when Jesus was being crucified.

It was in the events of the resurrection that Jesus gave the highest honor to women. In the world of first-century Israel, the testimony of women did not count for much, and they could not testify in court.[18] It is astonishing that Jesus made his first post-resurrection appearance to women including Mary Magdalene, who had been demonized[19] and is believed by many to have had a dubious moral past. To then appoint them as the first messengers of the good news that he was risen from the dead shows the total absence of prejudice in Jesus. This astonishing

---

[12]The Apostles' Creed. See the excellent discussion in Wayne A. Grudem, *Systematic Theology* (Leicester, UK: Inter-Varsity Press, 1994), 587. Grudem argues, "Until A.D. 650 no version of the Creed included this phrase with the intention of saying that Christ descended into hell" and then reviews other explanations Christians have put forward to understand the phrase in a non-literal manner.

[13] For a review of the role of women in the first century and the Bible, see Joel B. Green, Scot McKnight, and I. Howard Marshall, *Dictionary of Jesus and the Gospels* (Downers Grove, IL: InterVarsity Press, 1992), 884.

[14]John 4.

[15]Luke 10:38–42.

[16]Luke 8:1–3.

[17]Matthew 26:31.

[18]"But let not the testimony of women be admitted, on account of the levity and boldness of their sex." Flavius Josephus, *The Works of Josephus: Complete and Unabridged* (Peabody, MA: Hendrickson, 1996), *Antiquities*, 4.219.

[19]Luke 8:2.

aspect of the resurrection story is very strong evidence for the genuineness of the account. No one would have invented an account so dependent on women as witnesses.

As the disciples scattered and were apparently nowhere to be seen, the women followed Joseph of Arimathea to see where Jesus would be buried. Their love for him was such that they wanted to care for his body. Only the arrival of the Sabbath could delay their tender care. As soon as it was practical, just before sunrise[20] on Sunday morning, they rushed to the tomb. Approaching the tomb together were Mary Magdalene,[21] another Mary,[22] Salome,[23] Joanna,[24] and probably several other women.[25] Their discussions on the way about how to move the stone were interrupted by an earthquake and an angel who appeared and dragged the stone away from the tomb.[26] The soldiers who were guarding the tomb fainted, then fled back to the city.[27] The women looked down, turning their heads from the frightening sight.[28] It is possible that all of this occurred simultaneously with the actual resurrection of Jesus, although it is just as likely that his body had already vanished from the tomb, passing through the graveclothes and the rocks with equal ease.

The frightened women looked up[29] and saw that the stone was removed. When Mary Magdalene saw this and two men standing there, she did not realize they were angels. She must have then run away to get Peter, leaving the other women behind. This context makes sense of what she said to Peter and John, which is not clarified in the context of John's Gospel alone: "*They* have taken the Lord out of the tomb, and *we* do not know where they have laid him."[30] Meanwhile, one of the angels appears to have led some of the other women into the tomb, saying:

---

[20]Although some translations render Mark 16:2 as meaning after sunrise, others argue this can mean they had left before dark (as per John 20:1) and had arrived at the tomb "at the rising of the sun" (KJV).
[21]Matthew 28:1; Mark 16:1; Luke 24:10.
[22]Matthew 28:1; Mark 16:1; Luke 24:10.
[23]Mark 16:1.
[24]Luke 24:10.
[25]Luke 23:55–24:1.
[26]All the Gospels except Matthew reported that the earthquake happened before the women arrived at the tomb. In the Matthew account, it is possible to translate 28:2 as "a severe earthquake had occurred" (NASB).
[27]Matthew 28:2–4.
[28]Luke 24:5.
[29]Mark 16:4. Mark's comment about looking up is difficult to understand without Luke's about them looking down (24:5). With a large group of people involved, there is little surprise that some seem to have seen one or both of the angels before the stone, and some, but not all, appear to have entered the tomb itself before they heard the angel's words.
[30]John 20:2 (emphasis added).

Why do you seek the living among the dead?[31] Do not be afraid, for I know that you seek Jesus who was crucified. He is not here, for he has risen.[32] Remember how he told you, while he was still in Galilee, that the Son of Man must be delivered into the hands of sinful men and be crucified and on the third day rise.[33] Come, see the place where he lay. Then go quickly and tell his disciples that he has risen from the dead, and behold, he is going before you to Galilee; there you will see him. See, I have told you.[34]

The remaining women, too fearful to tell anyone else along the way, then ran off to find the other disciples. Peter and "the other disciple" (widely understood to be John), together with Mary Magdalene, hurried to the tomb. The angels would not have long to wait before their next assignment.

John ran ahead and was the first man to reach the tomb, seeing from the entrance that the graveclothes were lying there. However, unsurprisingly given his more impulsive nature, it was Peter who entered the tomb first.

John confessed in his Gospel that he and Peter had not at the time understood the message of the Old Testament Scriptures predicting that Christ would rise from the dead.[35] From this side of the empty tomb, resurrection teaching does emerge from the Old Testament. It is, however, easy to see why the disciples probably believed in a future resurrection of the dead but apparently did not really believe that Jesus would rise from death during their lifetime.

No doubt Peter and John were stunned and not able to fully comprehend what had happened and left. Meanwhile, the distraught Mary returned once again to the tomb. She stood alone, crying. Then Mary looked into the tomb and noticed the two angels. They asked her, "Woman, why are you weeping?"[36] Mary almost exactly repeated what

---

[31]Luke 24:5.
[32]Matthew 28:5–6. Matthew immediately adds "as he said," which is expanded in Luke's account.
[33]Luke 24:6–7.
[34]Matthew 28:6–7. Mark 16:6–7 is an abbreviation of the words Matthew uses with minimal changes. Mark reports that the angel specifically mentions Peter and with the alteration of one letter in the Greek ends by saying, "as he told you" rather than "as I told you," presumably referring to prophecies of Jesus reported in both Matthew 26:32 and Mark 14:28. This difference can be explained by the writer shortening or "telescoping" the words. The angel also refers to Jesus having predicted the resurrection elsewhere in his speech. In the above reconstruction of the angel's words, words from Luke have been inserted where they appear to make the most sense in Matthew's account.
[35]John 20:9.
[36]John 20:13.

she had said to Peter and John. Then, turning around, she saw Jesus but did not immediately recognize him.[37] Mary, in her confusion, asked him if he had taken Jesus away, thinking he was the gardener, and a Gospel full of long speeches reaches its climax in two simple but emotionally rich words that introduce the resurrected Jesus for whom creation has been waiting: "*Mary*," Jesus said. "*Master*," Mary replied.

The risen Lord of glory made his first appearance not on television or on YouTube, not before kings, not even before the future leaders of his church. Rather, he tenderly greeted a woman who, no doubt, felt that the meaning he had given to her life had been snatched away when he died. Jesus appointed her as a messenger to his disciples and then told her that he would soon ascend to be with God. We can only imagine what awe, wonder, joy, and yet fear flooded Mary at that moment.

Jesus told Mary not to cling to him because he had yet to ascend to God. There is some debate about whether he was referring to the ascension of Acts 1. Or did Jesus make his first return to heaven shortly after this meeting with Mary? Perhaps not delaying him was the reason that he asked her not to hold onto him? This would be consistent with the fact that later on Jesus *did* encourage his disciples to touch him. It would also be consistent with the way in which Jesus seemed to keep appearing and disappearing, as one source has suggested:

> When Jesus arose on that first Easter he did so in a glorified, spiritual body that immediately ascended into the presence of God. All of his post-resurrection appearances were appearances from heaven, and the visible ascension forty days later was his final but not his first departure from earth and entry into God's presence.[38]

If this view is correct, then this appearance to Mary marks the beginning of a forty-day period during which Jesus makes frequent journeys between heaven and earth[39] so that he could fleetingly, but repeatedly, visit his followers.

---

[37]We are not told why this was but can speculate that it might be because he was standing in the full light of the tomb entrance, because she was not expecting him, because his appearance was slightly different, perhaps looking older or younger than he had before the cross, or because she was in some way kept from recognizing him.

[38]Ralph P. Martin and Peter H. Davids, *Dictionary of the Later New Testament and Its Developments*, electronic edition (Downers Grove, IL: InterVarsity Press, 2000).

[39]Acts 1:3.

All of Jesus' appearances had a physicality about them. He could be held, he could eat, he could be recognized, and yet he was different somehow. He could pass through walls, his identity could be hidden, and eventually he would ascend into the sky permanently.

News of Jesus' appearance to Mary and the strange events of the morning spread rapidly to his followers, who had scattered and therefore heard different parts of the story at different times during that day. Most did not believe.[40]

Two of them had already left for Emmaus[41] before they had heard the complete story. On the way they met a man, and "their eyes were kept from recognizing him."[42] These words indicate the real reason why sometimes people were not able to recognize Jesus—they were miraculously prevented from doing so. When the apparent stranger asked them about what had been happening, they were incredulous that he had been in Jerusalem and not known about the death of Jesus. They told him about the empty tomb and appearances of angels and that no one had seen Jesus. They were perplexed and unsure about the stories they had heard.[43]

Jesus' response is remarkable. Instead of giving them some kind of glorious revelation of himself or performing a miracle, he began a Bible study, saying, "O foolish ones, and slow of heart to believe all that the prophets have spoken! Was it not necessary that the Christ should suffer these things and enter into his glory?"[44] He explained to them the Old Testament's references to himself. Later, as he broke bread for dinner, their eyes were opened. The two men suddenly recognized that they had been talking to Jesus, and then he disappeared. Immediately they ran back to Jerusalem to tell the others what had happened.

During that same day, Jesus appeared to a group of women. He urged them in a similar way as the angel had done earlier. He said, "Do not be afraid; go and tell my brothers to go to Galilee, and there they will see me."[45] Also at some point during the day, Jesus appeared to Peter. This must surely have been particularly emotional for Peter who

---

[40]Luke 24:10–11.
[41]Luke 24:13–35.
[42]Luke 24:16.
[43]Luke 24:11.
[44]Luke 24:25–26.
[45]Matthew 28:10. It is possible that this was the same appearance to Mary earlier, which would require that some of the women had either gone with Mary to fetch Peter and John or met her again in the vicinity of the garden.

had recently denied knowing Jesus three times. Perhaps as a result, we are never given details of this private moment.[46]

By the evening of that same day, almost the entire group of Jesus' followers had gathered, including ten of the eleven remaining apostles.[47] They were exchanging accounts of the day's dramatic events and told the two returning travelers, "The Lord has risen indeed, and has appeared to Simon!"[48]

These followers had locked themselves in a room for fear of the Jews.[49] Suddenly Jesus appeared. Since he had passed through a locked door, it is understandable that they feared he was a ghost. Jesus said:

> Peace to you! . . . Why are you troubled, and why do doubts arise in your hearts? See my hands and my feet, that it is I myself. Touch me, and see. For a spirit does not have flesh and bones as you see that I have. . . . These are my words that I spoke to you while I was still with you, that everything written about me in the Law of Moses and the Prophets and the Psalms must be fulfilled.[50]

Jesus also ate some food, demonstrating that his physical body was real. John tells us that during this meeting Jesus said to his disciples, "As the Father has sent me, even so I am sending you."[51] Then "he breathed on them and said to them, 'Receive the Holy Spirit. If you forgive the sins of any, they are forgiven them; if you withhold forgiveness from any, it is withheld.'"[52]

Luke's final chapter might leave you with the impression that Jesus immediately led the disciples out to Bethany and that his final ascension into heaven happened on that very same day. Since Jesus tells the disciples to stay in Jerusalem (just like in Acts 1 and unlike his commands of that first resurrection Sunday to go to Galilee), it seems likely that Luke 24 summarizes two different appearances of Jesus, and the first word of verse 50 represents a jump to a later occasion.[53]

---

[46]Luke 24:34; 1 Corinthians 15:5. Cephas and Peter are the same individual and different forms of the same name.
[47]Luke 24:36–43; John 20:19–23.
[48]Luke 24:34. Simon here refers to Simon Peter
[49]John 20:19.
[50]Luke 24:36–44.
[51]John 20:21.
[52]John 20:22.
[53]This concise method of writing is consistent with the author's style. Luke himself tells us that his Gospel "dealt with all that Jesus began to do and teach, until the day when he was taken up" (Acts 1:1–2) and then continues to explain that between the resurrection and ascension there was a forty-day period during which Jesus appeared to and taught his disciples.

It was not until eight days later that Jesus returned to his disciples as a group a second time. This time the so-called "doubting Thomas" believed, having been invited to put his hands in Jesus' wounds. He worshipped Jesus as God, to which Jesus said, "Have you believed because you have seen me? Blessed are those who have not seen and yet have believed."[54] Peter later echoed this: "Though you have not seen him, you love him. Though you do not now see him, you believe in him and rejoice with joy that is inexpressible and filled with glory."[55]

A clear theme emerges from each of these reports—the need to believe even when Jesus is hidden from sight. The disciples, having seen the risen Jesus, would be entrusted with the task of sharing the good news with others who would never have had the advantage of seeing him in the flesh as they had. We are not told why Jesus then continued to make further intermittent appearances for forty days, but perhaps as well as teaching them it was to prepare them for the time when he would not physically be with them.

Eventually the disciples obeyed Jesus' original command to travel to Galilee, where he would again meet them. The journey from Jerusalem to Galilee was not short, so several more days would have elapsed before Jesus' third appearance to his disciples as a group. John paints an informal, more relaxed scene, in contrast to the hustle and bustle of Jerusalem. Jesus met with seven disciples who were fishing, performed a miracle, and then served them a breakfast he had been cooking. He also specifically recommissioned Peter.[56]

During the days that followed, Jesus appeared to a crowd of five hundred. He made a private appearance to his brother, James, which presumably led to James' conversion and subsequent leadership role in the church.[57] Jesus also appeared on a mountain in Galilee and gave the disciples the Great Commission.[58]

Later the disciples returned to Jerusalem, and the ascension into heaven occurred (see Acts 1). Jesus promised they would receive the Spirit and become his witnesses. Then, after Jesus ascended, angels said to the disciples, "Men of Galilee, why do you stand looking into

---

[54]John 20:29.
[55]1 Peter 1:8.
[56]John 21:1–23.
[57]1 Corinthians 15:5–7.
[58]Matthew 28:16–20.

heaven? This Jesus, who was taken up from you into heaven, will come in the same way as you saw him go into heaven."[59]

There has been much discussion about the ascension. Was Jesus then further glorified? Or, was he glorified at the moment of the resurrection but veiled it for the sake of his disciples? We simply cannot answer this question with the biblical literature, so we will leave it unaddressed, except to say that the resurrection, ascension, and glorification are part of one great movement: Jesus was "raised" from the grave back into the glory of heaven.

CONCLUSION

We have now considered all the resurrection appearances as described in the four Gospels. Although the picture can seem rather disjointed until put together, there is much commonality between these accounts. Jesus met with people when they were alone, with a small handful of people, in a group of twelve or more, and in an assembly of hundreds. He met them in a formal gathering, over a meal, in a home, in secluded countryside, at work, and in the middle of a busy city.

Jesus can still meet people today in all these situations. Although he no longer meets us face-to-face, the reality of his presence remains through his Spirit and the Bible (see John 14–16). Jesus can meet us in every situation we face, just like the disciples. Throughout the rest of church history he has continued to meet with his people, sometimes by surprise, but always to keep his promises: "For where two or three are gathered in my name, there am I among them,"[60] and "Behold, I am with you always, to the end of the age."[61]

We now face two essential questions that will occupy us throughout the rest of the book: Can we believe in the physical resurrection of Jesus Christ? And, what does it mean to live in light of the implications of that event?

---

[59]Acts 1:11.
[60]Matthew 18:20.
[61]Matthew 28:20.

CHAPTER THREE

DID JESUS REALLY RISE FROM THE DEAD?

If Christ has not been raised, your faith is futile and you are still in your sins.

1 CORINTHIANS 15:17

HAVING EXAMINED THE resurrection accounts, we must address the most important question we can ever ask: Did Jesus really rise from the dead and ascend to heaven to rule over the universe? As John MacArthur said:

> Neutrality is not an option. Either Jesus rose and rightly demands your attention, repentance, trust and obedience, or he stayed dead. If he only became a rotting corpse why should you follow him?[1]

Jesus predicted his resurrection repeatedly. Was he a liar, misleading his followers deliberately to think that he was divine? Could he have been that evil? Could the man whose teaching has never been surpassed also be a con man on such a massive scale? How likely is it that instead he was a deluded fool who falsely believed death could not hold him? Jesus' credibility is destroyed if he did not rise from the dead. You cannot believe in him as a savior or a good teacher if he deceived us or was himself deceived so completely about something so fundamental. Either he rose and is therefore divine, or he did not, in which case he is no savior, and certainly not God. God is immortal and is not rotting in a tomb somewhere in Judea.

---

[1]John MacArthur's Preface, in Gerard Chrispin, *The Resurrection: The Unopened Gift* (Epsom, UK: Day One, 2002), 16.

Gary Habermas[2] reports that there is now a remarkable degree of agreement among ancient historians irrespective of their beliefs about Jesus' resurrection:

> At least twelve separate facts are considered to be knowable history. (1) Jesus died by crucifixion and (2) was buried. (3) Jesus' death caused the disciples to despair and lose hope, believing that his life was ended. (4) Although not as widely accepted, many scholars hold that the tomb in which Jesus was buried was discovered to be empty just a few days later. Critical scholars further agree that (5) the disciples had experiences which they believed were literal appearances of the risen Jesus. Because of these experiences, (6) the disciples were transformed from doubters who were afraid to identify themselves with Jesus to bold proclaimers of his death and resurrection. (7) This message was the center of preaching in the early church and (8) was especially proclaimed in Jerusalem, where Jesus died and was buried shortly before. As a result of this preaching, (9) the church was born and grew, (10) with Sunday as the primary day of worship. (11) James, who had been a skeptic, was converted to the faith when he also believed that he saw the resurrected Jesus. (12) A few years later, Paul was converted by an experience which he, likewise, believed to be an appearance of the risen Jesus.[3]

Some of these events may seem implausible, but the very early reports of them are historically accepted facts. Seemingly improbable things do happen, even if they are above our human comprehension. Sir Arthur Conan Doyle suggested the following approach to investigation: "When you have eliminated the impossible, whatever remains, however improbable, must be the truth."[4] One by one we will consider what explanations could make sense of these documented historical facts.[5]

---

[2]Professor of Apologetics and Philosophy at Liberty University and one of the world's foremost scholars of the resurrection.

[3]Gary Habermas, *The Historical Jesus* (Joplin, MO: College Press: 1996), 158.

[4]Arthur Conan Doyle, *Sign of Four* (London: Penguin Classics, 2001), 42.

[5]This is, of course, a well-worn path by apologists, and I acknowledge the influence of George Eldon Ladd, *I Believe in the Resurrection of Jesus* (London: Hodder and Stoughton, 1975); Gary Gromacki, "The Historicity of the Resurrection of Jesus Christ," *Journal of Ministry and Theology*, 6:1, 63–88 and 6:2, 45–58 (Baptist Bible College and Seminary, 2002); the various works of Josh McDowell; Wilbur M. Smith, "The Need for a Vigorous Apologetic in the Present Battle for the Christian Faith: Part 2," *Bibliotheca Sacra*, 100:532–545 (Dallas Theological Seminary, 1943); Dan Story, *Defending Your Faith* (Grand Rapids: Kregel, 1997), 87–98; and David MacLeod, "The Resurrection of Jesus Christ: Myth, Hoax, or History?," *Emmaus Journal*, 157–199 (Emmaus Bible College, 1998), among others.

IS THE RESURRECTION JUST A MYTH OR A LEGEND?

It was once popular to argue that the stories of an empty tomb arose long after the life of Jesus, prompted by a supposedly fertile ground of other ancient mythology about resurrection. We now know that resurrection was not commonly believed possible, even in the realm of mythology. Some people outside of Judaism did believe in the survival of the soul after death, but not in a bodily resurrection. The news of Jesus' resurrection had to conquer this skepticism. The Jews did not believe that the prophecies concerning the suffering servant referred to the same person as the Messiah. It is only in the light of Jesus' death and victorious resurrection that we see these two figures as the same person.[6]

N. T. Wright[7] has carefully studied all the historical evidence and concludes, "Christianity was born into a world where its central claim was known to be false. Many believed that the dead were non-existent; outside Judaism, nobody believed in resurrection."[8]

Wright also demonstrates that it is only *after* the events of Jesus' life, death, and resurrection had been taught throughout the Roman Empire that other stories of resurrection began to arise in popular culture. Far from being involved in producing the New Testament stories, these myths may well have instead been prompted by accounts of Jesus' resurrection.

It is hard to imagine any group creating a resurrection story within a few years of the death of their founder. Scholars today agree that the Gospels were written within the lifespan of people who had met Jesus. If these stories had been made up within decades after the death of Jesus, others would have been able to immediately disprove them and stop them from spreading.

If the accounts of the resurrection were a late addition to Christianity, then an early form, which did not believe in the resurrection of Jesus, would have left traces in the historical record. There are no such traces of early Christians who denied the resurrection. Only in 1 Corinthians 15 does Paul defend against the charge that Jesus did not rise. Even

---

[6]See Ladd, *I Believe in the Resurrection of Jesus*, 36.
[7]Bishop of Durham and New Testament scholar whose book on the resurrection is widely recognized to be the definitive work on the subject.
[8]N. T. Wright, *The Resurrection of the Son of God* (London: SPCK, 2003), 35.

there Paul does not attempt to prove the resurrection of Jesus; he instead assumes his readers all believe it and uses that to prove our resurrection (see 1 Corinthians 15:12–17).

The early Christians, according to the historical records available to us, all believed in the resurrection of Jesus. Such a belief, for it to be so widespread, must have arisen very early. In all the arguments about doctrine that arose over the next few hundred years, doubts about the bodily resurrection of Jesus did not feature. True Christianity does not exist without a belief in Jesus' resurrection.

Throughout the New Testament the resurrection of Jesus is assumed. Paul repeatedly prays for grace and peace "from God our Father and the Lord Jesus Christ."[9] For Jesus to be able to grant anything, he must still be alive. Similarly Paul frequently refers to himself as "an apostle of Christ Jesus."[10] An apostle is a messenger or representative and is not sent by a dead man. Certainly Paul was not appointed before Christ's death! The opening chapter of each of Paul's letters therefore has at least one mention of Jesus in a way that requires he is still alive.

Throughout these letters, Paul often mentions that God raised Jesus from the dead.[11] Jesus is referred to constantly as a living and active presence without Paul needing to elaborate on or argue for the resurrection. When an event is part of the very foundations of a group, it can be mentioned without explanation, knowing that the hearers will understand.

The Gospel resurrection stories do not reflect upon the events theologically. If they were late myths, we could expect them to be at least as reflective as Paul's writings in 1 Corinthians, if not more so. Why do the writers not even make the deduction that Jesus' resurrection guarantees our own? The accounts come across as basic eyewitness reports given by those who did not yet fully understand the significance of what they had seen and heard.

Christianity is a simple faith that has no worthwhile content if the resurrection is not true, as Paul argues strongly in 1 Corinthians 15. Few historians doubt that the church was founded on a belief that Jesus

---

[9]Romans 1:7; 1 Corinthians 1:3; 2 Corinthians 1:2; Galatians 1:3; Ephesians 1:2; Philippians 1:2; 2 Thessalonians 1:2; 1 Timothy 1:2; 2 Timothy 1:2; Philemon 3; see also Titus 1:4.
[10]1 Corinthians 1:1; 2 Corinthians 1:1; Ephesians 1:1; Colossians 1:1; 1 Timothy 1:1; 2 Timothy 1:1.
[11]See, for example, Romans 4:24; 6:4; 6:9; 7:4; 8:11; 10:9; 1 Corinthians 15:12; 15:20; Galatians 1:1; Ephesians 1:20; Colossians 2:12; 1 Thessalonians 1:10.

had literally risen from the dead. Any contrary theory needs to explain how a small group of Jews became passionately convinced of the truth of the resurrection and spread it rapidly across the Middle East and into Europe. Within a couple of centuries this novel faith had conquered the then known world without a sword being drawn.

The church did not create the resurrection stories; instead the resurrection stories created the church.

DID THE DISCIPLES SIMPLY LIE?

All of the problems facing the idea that the resurrection stories were late myths apply even more strongly to the suggestion that the disciples knowingly spread a lie. Almost all of the disciples are believed to have been executed because of their refusal to deny that Jesus rose again. People do die all the time for falsehoods that they themselves genuinely believe to be true. It is, however, impossible to believe that all of them would die for something they knew to be a deliberate deception. In addition, anyone who could prove that the disciples' story was untrue would have severely hampered the growth of the church. Spurgeon demolishes this idea of lying disciples with typical clarity:

> The resurrection of Jesus Christ from the dead is one of the best attested facts on record. There were so many witnesses to behold it, that if we do in the least degree receive the credibility of men's testimonies, we cannot and we dare not doubt that Jesus rose from the dead . . . these persons could not every one of them have been so positively deceived as to say that they had seen this man . . . they could not all, surely, have agreed together to help on this imposture: if they did, it is the most marvelous thing we have on record, that not one of them ever broke faith with the others. . . . They were men who had nothing to gain by it; they subjected themselves to persecution by affirming the very fact; they were ready to die for it, and did die for it. . . . How, then, dare any man say that the Christian religion is not true, when we know for a certainty that Christ died and rose again from the dead? And knowing that, who shall deny the divinity of the Savior? Who shall say that he is not mighty to save? Our faith hath a solid basis, for it hath all these witnesses on which to rest, and *the more sure witness of the Holy Spirit witnessing in our hearts.*[12]

---

[12]C. H. Spurgeon, *Sermon No. 66*, "The Resurrection of the Dead," delivered on February 17, 1856, at New Park Street Chapel, Southwark; http://www.spurgeon.org/sermons/0066.htm.

Spurgeon also reminds us that the work of the Spirit in us is more important in causing us to believe than rational arguments. Today a purely intellectual approach to faith has infiltrated the church. Spurgeon, however, does not encourage us to park our brains nor to discard our Bibles. This quote is a helpful pointer to a different way. We are urged to consider the facts *and* look to a form of persuasion directly from the Spirit himself. This might surprise some, but it is true nonetheless. As we continue to look at the logical reasons for our belief in the resurrection, let's pause for a moment and pray that God will grant us ever-increasing faith.

DID THE DISCIPLES STEAL THE BODY?

This theory at least has the benefit of an early origin. It was the primary explanation circulating during the decades after Jesus' life and is the only suggestion rebutted in the New Testament. Matthew reports that the story had its origin in a conversation held between the guards and the Jewish authorities. When the guards reported the empty tomb, they were ordered, "Tell the people, 'His disciples came by night and stole him away while we were asleep.' And if this comes to the governor's ears, we will satisfy him and keep you out of trouble" (Matthew 28:13–14).

Without the intervention of the leaders, these Roman soldiers would have faced a certain death penalty for grossly neglecting their duty. It seems impossible that an elite group of soldiers would have been this careless. Also, if they *were* asleep, how could they have known who stole the body?

Finally, what possible motive would drive the followers of a failed messiah to rob a grave and go to their own graves for propagating the lie that he was the risen Lord of Glory? This theory hasn't gained much favor. It is also implausible that anyone else would have stolen the body because the only thing of value (the graveclothes) was left behind.

DID THE AUTHORITIES HIDE THE BODY?

The Christian faith was rightly perceived as a threat by both the Jews, whose monotheism did not fit well with the idea of worshipping a dead man, and the Romans, who proclaimed that Caesar, and not Jesus, was the "son of god" and to be worshipped. As strange as it must have seemed when the empty tomb was discovered, in a remarkably short course of time Christianity would succeed in overthrowing the worship of the emperor. Nothing less than a revolution began on that first Easter Sunday.

If the authorities had possession of the body, it is obvious that they would have taken the earliest possible opportunity to display it and thereby destroy this dangerous new faith at its inception. Jesus' disciples were boldly declaring the resurrection of Jesus, and many people were now turning to this new faith. If it were possible to easily prove that Jesus was still dead, the Romans or the Jewish authorities would have immediately done so and the new religion would have been quashed. Even if the authorities had somehow disposed of the body and so could not display it, they could have easily cleared up the whole misunderstanding by informing the public. But there is no record of this happening.

DID THEY GO TO THE WRONG TOMB?

It is impossible that the disciples, the women, the guards, the authorities, and Joseph of Arimathea would all forget where Jesus' tomb was. If anyone remembered, it would have been very easy to halt the church's growth before it even started by publicizing where the tomb was and even putting on a show of the slowly decomposing body.

DID JESUS ONLY SWOON ON THE CROSS?

Surprisingly many people have argued that Jesus never actually died on the cross. Theories of a substitution by another man or a faint or a near-death experience on the cross abound, but as Mark Driscoll explains:

> The biblical record is emphatic that Jesus died. First, he underwent a sleepless night of trials and beatings that left him exhausted. Second, he was scourged—a punishment so horrendous that many men died from it before even making it to their crucifixion. Third, Jesus was crucified, and a professional executioner declared him dead. Fourth, to ensure Jesus was dead, a spear was thrust through his side and a mixture of blood and water poured out of his side because the spear burst his heart sac. Fifth, he was wrapped in roughly one hundred pounds of linens and spices, which, if he was able to somehow survive beatings,

floggings, crucifixion, and a speared heart, would have killed him by asphyxiation. Sixth, even if through all of this Jesus somehow survived (which would in itself be a miracle), he could not have endured three days without food, water, or medical attention in a cold tomb carved out of rock. In short, Jesus died.[13]

Let's just suppose for a moment that Jesus had somehow been alive in the tomb. He would have had to summon a convenient earthquake, push back the stone, fight off the soldiers who were guarding him, and then convince his disciples he was the resurrected King. His wounds and his general state of health would have made him a source of horror, not faith! Dan Story, an apologist who has written more than fifteen books, said:

> There is not a shred of evidence to support this theory. Nowhere in Roman or Jewish history does anyone argue or even imply that Jesus did not die on the cross. It took *eighteen centuries* after Christ's death before this idea found an advocate. The fact is that the historical record refutes this theory at every turn.[14]

In order to breathe while nailed to a cross, you have to visibly move your body and undergo excruciating pain. To fake death on the cross and still breathe without this being noticed would be physically impossible.

> Adequate exhalation required lifting the body by pushing up on the feet and by flexing the elbows. . . . However, this would place the entire weight of the body on the tarsals and would produce searing pain. Furthermore, flexion of the elbows would cause rotation of the wrists about the iron nails and cause fiery pain along the damaged median nerves. . . . Muscle cramps and paresthesias of the outstretched and uplifted arms would add to the discomfort. As a result, each respiratory effort would become agonizing and tiring and lead eventually to asphyxia.[15]

Thus without this physical exertion, which would be obvious to any observer, the victim would die very quickly, thus making it impossible

---

[13]Mark Driscoll and Gerry Breshears, *Vintage Jesus* (Wheaton, IL: Crossway Books, 2007), 133.
[14]Story, *Defending Your Faith*, 93, emphasis added.
[15]William D. Edwards, Wesley J. Gabel, and Floyd E. Hosmer, "On the Physical Death of Jesus Christ," *Journal of the American Medical Association*, March 21, 1986, 255:1455–1463; http://jama.ama-assn. org/cgi/content/abstract/255/11/1455.

to fake death. Soldiers would often break people's legs to speed up their death. This swoon theory has been surprisingly popular in recent years, despite its total lack of historical plausibility.

DID THE DISCIPLES SEE HALLUCINATIONS?

George Ladd said, "The empty tomb of itself did not create faith in the resurrection."[16] It was only the appearances of Jesus that allowed the radical conclusion that Jesus had risen again to an eternal life. Many a skeptic will argue that the resurrection appearances of Jesus were simply a phenomenon of vulnerable people seeing what they wanted to see. Newly bereaved people frequently experience hallucinations of their loved ones.

Having worked as a psychiatrist and having spoken to many people with hallucinations, I can confirm that nothing about these appearances of Jesus sounds similar to either the "normal" experiences of the recently bereaved or the troubling nightmares of the mentally ill. It is extremely rare for any hallucination to be shared by two people. I have certainly never heard of any case of a larger group of twelve, let alone five hundred, sharing the same such experience. Hallucinations tend to be fleeting and of an ethereal nature. The Gospel writers took great pains to report concrete facts—for example, that Jesus had a physical body that could eat and drink and that they could touch.

Hallucinations are not usually associated with a positive and persistent life transformation. They tend to weaken someone's mental well-being. These so-called "hallucinations" drove away the fear and despondency of the disciples and gave boldness to preach their new gospel throughout the Roman Empire at great risk to their own lives. This is completely inconsistent with the results of hallucinations as described in any medical textbook.

Additionally, many post-resurrection converts to the faith had not previously believed that Jesus was the Son of God. Jesus' brothers and mother were skeptical of his claims during his life and yet became members of his church, proclaiming the resurrection. They, like the archpersecutor Saul (also known as Paul), were not prepared for such an experience. Paul's case is particularly compelling. Philippians 3 shows us

---

[16]Ladd, *I Believe in the Resurrection of Jesus*, 89.

that his persecution of Christians was motivated out of religious sincerity. He believed that they were blaspheming the one true God and that he had a commission to wipe them out. The disciples' teaching from the Scriptures did not convince him. The miracles they performed were not persuasive. He may even have heard Jesus preaching in the flesh, but if so, that did not convince him. His passionate response to the new sect has always made me think he must have met Jesus during his life. As a young, smart Pharisee being brought up in Jerusalem and trained under Gamaliel (Acts 22:3), he would very likely have been part of the groups of Pharisees sent to check out Jesus. Some of Luke's material about the Pharisees may have come from Paul himself as eyewitness reports. Paul speaks of previously regarding Christ "according to the flesh" (2 Corinthians 5:16). On the road to Damascus Paul met the risen Jesus. Only that encounter can explain his radical transformation. He realized he had been wrong and that Jesus had risen and that God was therefore on the side of the Christians. He had been opposing Christ himself!

Whatever explanations we offer for the events of the Gospels and Acts must explain *both* the empty tomb *and* the appearances of Jesus. It simply will not do to dismiss these appearances without explaining how the tomb came to be empty. No other newly departed well-known leader, no matter how much loved by his followers, has ever appeared to them for several weeks after his death and somehow convinced them that, far from being a spirit, he had risen from the dead. Jesus is undeniably unique in this regard.

OTHER HISTORICAL EVIDENCE FOR
THE RESURRECTION

We will now look at a few examples[17] of other historical evidence for the resurrection of Jesus. Roman administrator Pliny wrote around A.D. 112 about the Christians in his area whom he was persecuting as they had become very numerous:

> They [the Christians] were in the habit of meeting on a certain fixed day before it was light, when they sang in alternate verses a hymn to Christ, as to a god, and bound themselves by a solemn oath, not to any wicked deeds, but never to commit any fraud, theft or adultery, never

---

[17]For more see, for example, Habermas, *The Historical Jesus.*

to falsify their word, nor deny a trust when they should be called upon to deliver it up; after which it was their custom to separate, and then reassemble to partake of food—but food of an ordinary and innocent kind.[18]

The worship of Jesus as "a god" by people raised as Jews would only be possible if he had risen from the dead. Their early-morning meetings seemed to be timed to celebrate his resurrection.

A remarkable inscription of a direct order from the Roman emperor was uncovered in Nazareth. Dated between A.D. 40 and 50 it reads:

> Ordinance of Caesar. It is my pleasure that graves and tombs remain perpetually undisturbed for those who have made them for the cult of their ancestors or children or members of their house. If, however, anyone charges that another has either demolished them, or has in any other way extracted the buried, or has maliciously transferred them to other places in order to wrong them, or has displaced the sealing on other stones, against such a one I order that a trial be instituted, as in respect of the gods, so in regard to the cult of mortals. For it shall be much more obligatory to honor the buried. Let it be absolutely forbidden for anyone to disturb them. In case of violation I desire that the offender be sentenced to capital punishment on charge of violation of sepulcher.[19]

That this should be found in Nazareth, and with such an unusually severe penalty, suggests to many scholars that it had been prompted by news of the claim that Jesus had risen from the dead and the counter-claim that the body had been stolen. This order would then be a form of attempting to lock the stable door after the horse has bolted.

An early Christian apologist, Justin Martyr, wrote an open letter to the Roman emperor, soon after A.D. 150, claiming that at the time the emperor could find information about the birth of Jesus from the records of a census and his life, miracles, raising the dead, and the reports of his own resurrection from official reports filed by Pilate. He wrote a similar letter to the Jews, claiming that far from accepting their Messiah, they had appointed teachers to spread the lie that the disciples had stolen his body. He could never have written in such a way if the

---

[18]Cited in ibid., 199.
[19]Cited in ibid., 176.

recipients of his letter could easily disprove such claims. The fact that Pilate's reports have not survived does not discredit this letter, as opponents of Christianity did not contradict Martyr at the time. His work would never have become as popular as it was at the time if it contained blatant lies.[20]

The testimony of enemies is sometimes the most compelling. Around A.D. 175 Celsus wrote *The True Word*, the first critique of Christianity, and tried to discredit the resurrection as being witnessed by "a hysterical female,"[21] which itself demonstrates that the Gospels represent what was being widely discussed at the time.

A Jewish document written around A.D. 600 but claimed to be based on older sources has the following account for why Jesus' body had disappeared from the tomb. This does not ring true, but it does provide further evidence of a persistent rumor from the Jews that the disciples stole the body:

> The disciples came to the original tomb, found Jesus' body gone and proclaimed him risen. The Jewish leaders also proceeded to Joseph's tomb and found it empty. Juda then took them to his grave and dug up the body of Jesus. The Jewish leaders were greatly relieved and wanted to take the body. Juda replied that he would sell them the body of Jesus and did so for thirty pieces of silver. The Jewish priests then dragged Jesus' body through the streets of Jerusalem.[22]

There is simply no record of any significant group of early Christians who doubted that Jesus had risen from the dead. The early existence of a group of people who believed Christ had risen from the dead is confirmed by multiple secular sources. Many secular historians have concurred that the evidence is exceptionally good that Jesus existed, was killed, and that his followers claimed he had risen from the dead.

The evidence for the rapid expansion of the church is compelling. No other successful movement has ever claimed its founder rose from the dead. Ultimately, the persistence and growth throughout history of the largest movement the world has ever seen is the strongest evidence for the resurrection. Many millions of people have claimed that their

---

[20]See ibid., 235.
[21]Joel B. Green et al., *Dictionary of Jesus and the Gospels* (Downers Grove, IL: InterVarsity Press, 1992), 884.
[22]Habermas, *The Historical Jesus*, 205.

lives have been transformed by Jesus and that they had a relationship with Jesus. Even today, testimonies of lives that have been changed continue to flabbergast the skeptic and give more faith to the believer. According to Robert Stein:[23]

> [Another] witness to the resurrection is the existential experience of the risen Christ in the heart of the believer. As one familiar hymn states it, "You ask me how I know He lives? He lives within my heart." To those who would minimize this argument and reject it as unscientific and subjective, the evangelical would point out that millions of Christians have for nearly two thousand years made this very claim. It is a simple fact that throughout the history of the church, the single most important witness to the resurrection of Jesus has been the witness of the risen Christ within the heart of the believer![24]

Many Christians today from all backgrounds are embarrassed by such a statement and do not seek or value such an experience. I fear that all wings of the church today are weaker for this lack. William Barclay stressed our need to be aware of the personal presence of our Lord Jesus:

> Jesus is not a figure in a book but a living presence. It is not enough to study the story of Jesus like the life of any other great historical figure. We may begin that way but we must end by meeting him. Jesus is not a memory but a presence. . . . Jesus is not someone to discuss so much as someone to meet. The Christian life is not the life of a man who *knows about* Jesus, but the life of a man who *knows* Jesus. . . . The greatest scholar in the world who knows everything about Jesus is less than the humblest Christian who knows him.[25]

CONCLUSION

We have examined the Gospel accounts of the resurrection, and have considered all possible explanations, and conclude that the only realistic interpretation of the first Easter is that Jesus did rise from the dead. Habermas reports that, even by critical scholars who are not Christians, it is now largely accepted that

---

[23]Previous Professor of Divinity and Biblical Criticism at Glasgow University.

[24]Robert H. Stein, "Was the Tomb Really Empty?" *Journal of the Evangelical Theological Society*, 20:23–29 (The Evangelical Theological Society, 1977). Also reprinted in *Themelios* and available online at http://s3.amazonaws.com/tgc-documents/journal-issues/5.1_Stein.pdf.

[25]William Barclay, ed., *The Gospel of Mark*, The Daily Study Bible Series (Philadelphia: The Westminster Press, 2000), on Mark 16:9.

Alternative hypotheses that seek to explain away the resurrection in natural terms have failed to adequately account for the known historical facts. Not only is this conclusion dictated by the data themselves, but critical scholars have even admitted this failure. Few researchers have favored any of these [theories] in recent times.[26]

After a lifetime of serious scholarly study, N. T. Wright concludes, "The only possible reason why early Christianity began and took the shape that it did is that the tomb really was empty and that people really did meet Jesus, alive again."[27]

N. T. Wright counters six conclusions that liberal scholars have come to about the resurrection of Jesus. I will conclude by simply stating the reverse of these liberal statements. Thanks to the work of scholars of the resurrection we now know that:

1. In ancient times both the Jews and Greeks had a clear understanding that resurrection meant a restoration of physical life after death. Greeks believed this was impossible. Some Jews had a belief in bodily resurrection at the end of the age.

2. The earliest Christian writer, Paul, clearly believed in a physical, bodily resurrection both of Jesus and in the future for believers.

3. From the earliest times, Christians believed in an empty tomb and a bodily resurrection of a Jesus who could be seen and touched rather than in some kind of "spiritual" glorification.

4. The resurrection stories of the Gospels are early, credible, consistent, eyewitness-based accounts that are clearly intended to describe literal historical events.

5. The accounts of the appearances of the risen Jesus cannot be explained as some kind of fantasy, hallucination, or "spiritual experience" without any external reality.

6. Jesus' body was really dead, not comatose; it was truly buried, and it actually left behind an empty tomb that had been guarded by soldiers. His tomb really is now as empty as the cross is.[28]

Wright concluded that the empty tomb and the reports of appearances of the risen Jesus are "in the same sort of category, of historical

---

[26]Habermas, *The Historical Jesus*, 170.
[27]Wright, *The Resurrection of the Son of God*, 8.
[28]Adapted from ibid., 7.

probability so high as to be virtually certain, as the death of Augustus in AD 14 or the fall of Jerusalem in AD 70."[29]

As amazing as a belief in the resurrection is, and as terrifying as its implications are, this has always been the most reliable identifying mark of movements that call themselves Christian. It is the fundamental basis of Christianity. Astonishingly, as we will see in the next chapter, the resurrection is so familiar to us it can often be simply assumed and even neglected. Yet Paul makes accepting this glorious truth the touchstone of true Christian faith:

> If you confess with your mouth that Jesus is Lord and believe in your heart that God raised him from the dead, you will be saved. (Romans 10:9)

---

[29]Ibid., 710.

CHAPTER FOUR

RESURRECTION NEGLECTED?

In this the love of God was made manifest among us,
that God sent his only Son into the world,
so that we might live through him.

1 JOHN 4:9

AS A YOUNG CHILD I asked my father a series of questions one evening as he put me to bed. This is the conversation as I remember it:

"Why is Good Friday called 'good'?"

"Because Jesus died for us."

"But why was it called good when someone died?"

"Because he came back to life."

"But why is it not Bad Friday and Good Sunday then?"

I somehow instinctively knew that the cross could not be good news without the resurrection.

My dad then explained that sin led to punishment—something I understood as a child growing up in the seventies. Jesus, unlike us, did not deserve to be punished by death or hell. I could be forgiven only if I accepted the grace of God. The offer seemed almost too good to be true. In that moment, a rather one-sided deal was struck between me and God. I offered him my sinful heart and surrendered to him, and he gave me the gift of his righteousness. Because of his sustaining grace, I have never really looked back.

Many times when I heard the gospel explained in later years, the resurrection was either omitted altogether or briefly discussed in passing. When I began to share the Christian message with others individually and while preaching, to my shame I often did so without mentioning that Jesus is alive. The resurrection had become an afterthought to the message that Jesus died for our sins.

This lack of emphasis on the resurrection is not a new phenomenon. We have already seen that the young Spurgeon became concerned about this curious neglect of the resurrection. He became convinced that preaching the resurrection would lead to salvation.[1] Every time he preached he expected such results, and his words challenge us even today:

> You must also believe in the power of that message to save people. You may have heard the story of one of our first students, who came to me, and said, "I have been preaching now for some months, and I do not think I have had a single conversion." I said to him, "And do you expect that the Lord is going to bless you and save souls every time you open your mouth?" "No, sir," he replied. "Well, then," I said, "that is why you do not get souls saved. If you had believed, the Lord would have given the blessing." I had caught him very nicely; but many others would have answered me in just the same way as he did. They tremblingly believe that it is possible, by some strange mysterious method, that once in a hundred sermons God might win a quarter of a soul. They have hardly enough faith to keep them standing upright in their boots; how can they expect God to bless them? I like to go to the pulpit feeling, "This is God's Word that I am going to deliver in his name; it cannot return to him void; I have asked his blessing upon it, and he is bound to give it, and his purposes will be answered."[2]

Were so many saved through Spurgeon's preaching partly because Spurgeon emphasized the resurrection? In his published sermons, he mentioned resurrection a staggering 7,620 times, which averages more than twice per sermon.[3]

Billy Graham has spoken to live meetings attended by more people and has been associated with more public professions of faith than any other evangelist in previous history. He seems to have come to a similar conclusion about the importance of the resurrection. The Billy Graham

---

[1]See chapter 1, pages 21–22.
[2]C. H. Spurgeon, "Qualifications for Soul-Winning: Godward," *The Soul Winner*; http://www.spurgeon.org/misc/sw02.htm.
[3]There are 3,563 published sermons by Spurgeon. A Logos Bible Software search of the electronic editions was performed for the following search term: "resurrection OR (raised NEAR dead). OR (risen NEAR dead). OR (Christ NEAR raised). OR (Christ NEAR risen). OR (Jesus NEAR raised). OR (Jesus NEAR risen)." For comparison purposes the search "crucifixion OR (Jesus NEAR death). OR (Jesus NEAR died). OR (Christ NEAR death). OR (Christ NEAR died)" returned 12,157 hits, i.e., an average of just over three per sermon.

Center, located on the campus of Wheaton College, plays clips from his preaching. A paraphrased summary of what you hear is: *Jesus died for you, but not just that—he was raised! He's a living Jesus, and he's here today, wanting to have a relationship with you.* Could this emphasis help explain the power with which he preached and the millions of conversions that resulted?

In contrast, in many gospel messages I have heard, this strong emphasis on the resurrection has been absent, while the emphasis on the death of Jesus has remained. What is the reason for this difference?

WHY MIGHT THE RESURRECTION BE NEGLECTED?

1. The Resurrection Could Be Eclipsed by the Prominence of the Cross

The cross is the basis by which we can be forgiven. Our penalty was placed on Jesus; there our debt was discharged. Because the cross is literally crucial, it sometimes overshadows the resurrection. Richard Gaffin[4] explains:

> As a generalization . . . Christ's resurrection has been relatively eclipsed. In Eastern Orthodoxy . . . the accent has been on his incarnation. . . . In Western Christianity (both Roman Catholic and Protestant) . . . attention has been focused heavily and at times almost exclusively on Christ's death and its significance. The overriding concern, especially since the Reformation, has been to keep clear that the Cross is not simply an ennobling and challenging example but a real atonement. . . . In short, the salvation accomplished by Christ and the atonement have been virtually synonymous.
>
> My point is not to challenge the validity or even the necessity of this development, far less the conclusions reached. But in this dominating preoccupation with the death of Christ, the doctrinal . . . significance of his resurrection has been largely overlooked. Not that the Resurrection has been deemed unimportant, but all too frequently it has been considered exclusively as a stimulus and support for Christian faith (which it undoubtedly is) and in terms of its apologetic value, as the crowning evidence for Christ's deity and the truth of Christianity in general.[5]

---

[4]Emeritus Professor of Systematics at Westminster Theological Seminary, Philadelphia.
[5]Richard B. Gaffin, "Redemption and Resurrection," *Themelios*, Vol. 27.2, Spring 2002, 16–31; see www.beginningwithmoses.org/articles/redemptionresurrection.htm.

Books like *The Cross Centered Life* by C. J. Mahaney, *The Jesus Gospel by* Liam Goligher, and *Pierced for Our Transgressions* by Steve Jeffery, Mike Ovey, and Andrew Sach all help us greatly. I am not concerned that there is *too much* emphasis on the cross. I am, however, anxious that as we "survey the wondrous cross" we also study the resurrection. We must remember that the cross is just as empty as the tomb, and Christ is now glorified, having completed his work. The truth is, we cannot be truly cross-centered without also being empty-grave-centered! Jesus was not just our prophet and priest—he is our reigning King.

At the cross we learn true humility, our hopeless sinfulness, and our need of God. At the empty tomb we fully appreciate what Christ has achieved for us and receive power to live for him. A deeper, fuller insight into the truth of Jesus' resurrection will cause our lives to be radically transformed.

2. The Resurrection Has Missed out on the Beneficial Effects of Controversy and Heresy

The cross has prompted vociferous debate and hence much study. Most books about the cross of Jesus were written as a direct response to disagreements over the meaning of Jesus' death. Recent controversy has centered on whether Jesus died in our place to take the punishment for our sin (penal substitution) and experience the full force of the wrath of God. This concept is taken from Romans, Isaiah 53, and elsewhere in Scripture. It can easily be explained to a child, yet its depths continue to puzzle the professor. A divine exchange occurred. He took our sin; we gained his righteousness. As a result, God's attitude toward us changed, and now we are forgiven, and the guilt of our sin is washed away. God now sees us covered in the righteousness of his Son. With our debt paid, we come freely and boldly into the presence of a holy God. Paul explains this transaction as follows:

> For the love of Christ controls us, because we have concluded this: that one has died for all, therefore all have died; and he died for all, that those who live might no longer live for themselves but for him who for their sake died and was raised. . . . Therefore, if anyone is in Christ, he is a new creation. The old has passed away; behold, the new has come. All this is from God, who through Christ reconciled us to himself. . . .

> For our sake he made him to be sin who knew no sin, so that in him
> we might become the righteousness of God. (2 Corinthians 5:14–21)

This idea has recently been attacked by some leaders in the evangelical movement. Two key books popularized this. Steve Chalke and Alan Mann rejected this teaching as "cosmic child abuse."[6] Chalke, who remains one of the most influential figures in the UK's evangelical movement, has since reaffirmed that he rejects the whole notion of penal substitution.[7] In addition, from the other side of the Atlantic, Joel B. Green and Mark D. Baker argue that this teaching is a form of sadomasochism.[8] Incensed by such inflammatory language, some evangelicals responded robustly, arguing that such thinking is misguided and contrary to Scripture.

This argument has led directly to some positive results, including books being written and, in the UK, a significant new Christian conference, New Word Alive.[9] This caused many Christians to come together with one accord, from a variety of denominational backgrounds, and has strengthened many churches.

Therefore, because persistent and ongoing doctrinal arguments are difficult to ignore, controversy tends to heighten our awareness of certain doctrines, while noncontroversial ones become neglected. Biblical truths seem, at least in the long term, to actually *benefit* from being attacked. Truth appears to be most visible when viewed against a backdrop of error. Many have rightly stressed that when we define true doctrine, we simultaneously define false teaching. As J. Gresham Machen said:

> Every really great Christian utterance, it may almost be said, is born in controversy. It is when men have felt compelled to take a stand against error that they have risen to the really great heights in the celebration of truth.[10]

The average preacher does not directly explain heresy in his preaching; he is, however, well aware of it during his own preparation. He may deliberately engage the latest popular errors by preaching biblical truth

---

[6]Steve Chalke and Alan Mann, *The Lost Message of Jesus* (Grand Rapids: Zondervan, 2003), 182.
[7]Steve Chalke, in Derek Tidball et al., *The Atonement Debate* (Grand Rapids: Zondervan, 2008), 34–48.
[8]Joel B. Green and Mark D. Baker, *Recovering the Scandal of the Cross* (Downers Grove, IL: InterVarsity Press, 2000), 30.
[9]See http://newwordalive.org.
[10]J. Gresham Machen, "Christian Scholarship and the Defense of the Faith," in *J. Gresham Machen: Selected Shorter Writings*, ed. D. G. Hart (Phillipsburg, NJ: P&R, 2004), 148–149.

as a specific antidote. Tim Challies[11] compared discernment to identifying fake money:

> In discerning what is true from what is false it is best to focus more attention on what is genuine than what is counterfeit. It would be tempting to train people to identify what is fraudulent by focusing a great amount of time on what is false. However, because falsehood is always changing, it is more beneficial to focus on what is unchanging. Knowing and identifying what is false can be done best by knowing and understanding what is true. A person who studies and understands what is true is necessarily equipping himself to discern what is false.[12]

This same approach is also seen in the New Testament, where most of the epistles are written in response to error in the churches. Surprisingly, Paul never elaborates in any real detail on precisely what false teaching he is addressing. Instead he explains the truth in a way that contradicts the specific errors, while not providing them a platform for further attention. This reads a bit like a transcript of one side of a telephone conversation. We could strain our brains in the fruitless task of trying to infer what is being said on the other end, or we can focus instead on understanding what the apostle is communicating.

At no point in church history has there been widespread debate among Christian theologians about the resurrection of Jesus. Certainly all major groups that say they are part of the Christian church today, including Roman Catholics, Orthodox, and all the Protestant denominations, believe that Jesus was raised bodily for us and that we too will be raised. Of course, some liberals deny the physical resurrection of Jesus, but there is broad agreement that by abandoning this view they lose their right to call themselves Christians at all. Because of this relative lack of controversy, we might incorrectly assume that all churchgoers believe in Jesus' resurrection and fully understand its significance. Unfortunately, this doctrine is rarely discussed in great detail, and hence understanding about its full ramifications is often vague.

We can be passionate about the glorious truths of God's Word, even when they are not directly under assault. The relative absence of controversy or heresy concerning the resurrection is not a sufficient excuse for

---

[11]Author of one of the most widely read Christian blogs, www.challies.com.
[12]Tim Challies, *The Discipline of Spiritual Discernment* (Wheaton, IL: Crossway, 2007), 142.

us to fail to fully explore the impact of this doctrine. *All* of our doctrinal walls must be firmly built, not just those that currently are under attack. We cannot afford to allow any important doctrine to fall into neglect simply because no one seems to be publicly contradicting it. Too many Protestants are so busy protesting about what they are against that they forget to declare as loudly what they are in favor of.

3. Our Neglect of the Resurrection Could Be Part of a Satanic Strategy

Without becoming obsessed with the Devil, we must recognize that "we do not wrestle against flesh and blood" (Ephesians 6:12). It is quite likely that Satan has at least two different strategies that he utilizes to undermine truths that are essential to our faith. The first approach is to assault a biblical truth directly by encouraging us to doubt it or to form wrong conclusions about it. However, we have seen that attacks of this kind can often backfire and inadvertently benefit the church. Athanasius, Augustine, Luther, Calvin, Spurgeon, and countless others taught glorious truth in direct reaction to the erroneous teaching of their day.

Satan's other strategy might well be to encourage us to neglect a doctrine by merely assuming it. Everyone, in principle, accepts it, even though few may really understand it. Perhaps this is precisely how Satan has assaulted the doctrine of Jesus' resurrection, as well as our own future resurrection.

We could even speculate that this doctrine is so distasteful to him that he cannot bear to think about the resurrection or even formulate false teaching on it. Given that it was such a glorious victory for Jesus, I am sure that Satan does not wish to be reminded of it, though he daily feels its effects. Satan might hope, therefore, that if he does not try to promote controversy and/or false teaching concerning the resurrection, perhaps the full implications of this important doctrine will remain relatively undiscovered. Since it is the power of the resurrection that enables us to live as Christians, it is no surprise if Satan is indeed trying to stop us from applying this power to our lives.

Satan sometimes also entices Christians to believe that they are defending a righteous cause even though they are profaning God's name by the manner in which they are doing it. This is not dissimilar to the way many of the Pharisees of Jesus' day behaved. For example, some bloggers seem to exist purely to root out the many and varied errors that are out there. They do so in a nasty manner and are nicknamed "watch bloggers." We must not allow our enemy to define our agenda. We have a positive body of truth to proclaim irrespective of the latest popular theological heresy.

4. The Bible Appears to Rarely Mention Resurrection

If we measured significance by merely comparing a count of those verses in the Bible where subjects are mentioned, we could assume that very little emphasis is placed on resurrection. However, there is little sense in this approach, since hell would then be more important than heaven, and money more important than forgiveness. The virgin birth of Jesus is mentioned only rarely in Scripture, but does that make it any less central?

HAS THE RESURRECTION BEEN COMPLETELY NEGLECTED?

Absolutely not! Christians have *not* totally ignored the resurrection. The resurrection is, after all, precious to us and is acknowledged as a vital factor in our salvation. "No tenet of Christianity is more central. . . . Resurrection is at once the foundation of Christian faith and the focus of Christian hope."[13] We must not use either the cross or the resurrection to reduce the value of the other.[14] Many evangelicals *do* value this doctrine, but we must look more closely at "the most important doctrine of the New Testament."[15]

John Piper also declared, "The gospel has at its center the events of the cross and the resurrection."[16] He included these words even though the purpose of that book was to discuss how the cross is involved in saving us. Elsewhere in the same book he quotes[17] 1 Corinthians 15:3: "For I delivered to you as of first importance what I also received: that Christ died for our sins in accordance with the Scriptures."

In the context of his defense of the importance of the cross, we can understand why Piper ends the quote where he does, thereby emphasizing his point. It is troubling, however, how frequently people omit the

---

[13]Donald K. McKim and David F. Wright, *Encyclopedia of the Reformed Faith* (Louisville: John Knox Press, 1992), 319.
[14]See G. C. Berkouwer, *The Work of Christ* (Grand Rapids: Eerdmans, 1965), 192.
[15]George Eldon Ladd, *I Believe in the Resurrection of Jesus* (London: Hodder and Stoughton, 1975), 10.
[16]John Piper, *The Future of Justification* (Wheaton, IL: Crossway, 2007), 82.
[17]Ibid., 89.

second half. If we do make a habit of doing this, we would appear to underemphasize "that he was buried, that he was raised on the third day in accordance with the Scriptures" (1 Corinthians 15:4).

This is a good example of how our focus on the cross can make us appear to assume the resurrection. Leading evangelical theologian Don Carson warns that "When we assume the gospel we are one generation away from denying it."[18] We could apply this specifically to talking about the resurrection, without which there is no gospel.

Most of us are not intentionally neglecting the resurrection. We do appreciate its importance and value it highly. But the resurrection has not been explored as fully as many of the other doctrines and has not been given the attention it deserves.

Paul states emphatically that without the resurrection we would still be in our sins. Without the resurrection we are lost and there is *no hope!* There is no salvation without a *living* Jesus. We need the resurrection to have its power-generating effect inside of us if we are to be born again. We really are "saved by his life" (Romans 5:10). We need a change within us that only the resurrection can produce. We must make sure that in our thinking and our speaking we give the resurrection the prominence it deserves. We must not neglect either the resurrection or the cross in order to focus on the other. We need *both*, as Mark Driscoll explains:

> Sadly, there are those who err in emphasizing either the crucifixion or the resurrection of Jesus at the expense of the other. Some preach only the cross and its result of forgiveness of sin and justification. Without preaching the resurrection of Jesus as well, Christians are prone to overlook the mission of Jesus and the new life he has for them on the earth. They tend to see Christian life as little more than going to church to soak in teaching until they get to heaven. This is the perennial error of Christian fundamentalism.
>
> Conversely, there are others who preach only the new kingdom life that Jesus offers through his resurrection. These Christians excel at helping the poor and handing out hugs and muffins, but fail at repenting of personal sin and calling others to repent of personal sin so that they might be forgiven and reconciled to God through Jesus. This is the perennial error of Christian liberalism.[19]

---

[18]Don Carson, "The Primacy of Expository Preaching, Part 1"; www.desiringgod.org/ResourceLibrary/ConferenceMessages/ByConference/23/2085_The_Primacy_of_Expository_Preaching_Part_1/.
[19]Mark Driscoll and Gerry Breshears, *Vintage Jesus* (Wheaton, IL: Crossway, 2007), 125.

The degree to which we neglect the resurrection is also the degree to which we neglect to think about Jesus as he really is, now. Jesus is enthroned in heaven and is reigning inside every believer. His powers are limitless, and he is at liberty to do as he wishes. While on earth he did not fully reveal his glory and divine power. To only think of Jesus as a long-haired, gentle man in a robe and wearing sandals has devastating effects on the church. This perception has permeated the attitudes of many who perceive Jesus as a weak character but a good teacher. The world seems blind to the Bible's description of the resurrected Jesus, full of power and authority. This description is highly offensive to the world. But to worship Jesus as the artists have portrayed him, instead of as the Son of Man in all his glory, is nothing short of idolatry.

To meditate on the reality of the risen Jesus promises to be of great benefit to us. Hope, optimism, enthusiasm, and certainty are likely to result. Angst, uncertainty, and complexity, as well as attempts to deny ourselves legitimate pleasures in an attempt to carry our own cross, might be the result if we neglect to meditate on Christ's glorious victory over death. This kind of condemnation and legalism is widespread in the church today. In the modern world, many accuse the church of being dead. This impression will merely be confirmed if they only hear us preaching about a Jesus who was crucified for them, speaking about him and acting as though he is still dead. Colossians 2:6–4:1 contrasts the legalism of religion with the resurrection life that is ours in Christ Jesus. Without setting our minds on our living Master in heaven we will never be able to live as God intended.

Jesus is glorious and very much alive. He is the one in control of his church and his world, as uncomfortable as that might make us. As a good friend said to me in an email:

> If we leave him in the tomb we can systematize his teaching and sanitize his actions. We can manage the church and keep things in order. If we leave him in the tomb, then Christianity belongs to us to make of it what we will, to reform it in our image and sell it to the highest bidder. If the tomb is empty, the implications for the church are explosive to say the least. If he is truly with us in a way not so dissimilar to how he was with his disciples, then nothing will ever be the same again.[20]

---

[20] Andrew Cottingham, who blogs at http://andycottingham.com.

CHAPTER FIVE

THE IMPORTANCE OF RESURRECTION IN THE BIBLE

For I delivered to you as of first importance what I also received: that Christ died for our sins in accordance with the Scriptures, that he was buried, that he was raised on the third day in accordance with the Scriptures.

1 CORINTHIANS 15:3-4

HAVE YOU EVER MET a wise person who seems to say very few words? Some people use many words, of which we remember very few. Others will remain silent, perhaps even while watching a debate, saying nothing at all. Then, when everyone else is finished, they may finally add a sentence that dramatically cuts through everything that has been said. The theme of resurrection in the Bible is a bit like that wise person. We read patiently through many other subjects, and then suddenly a single phrase interjects, illuminating everything and bringing a hope that goes beyond death itself.

Despite first appearances, the concept of resurrection is stressed throughout Scripture from Genesis to Revelation. The emphasis is placed on the subject, not by repetition, but by the way in which we are made to anticipate it.

The Bible is, in many ways, a book about death. It begins in Genesis, when Adam and Eve sinned and death entered the world. It ends in Revelation with the judgment of sin and the celebration of the end of death for all believers. The Bible constantly reminds us of the human predicament and of the inevitability of our mortality. So, whenever resurrection is mentioned, it is a shaft of light penetrating our helplessness and hopelessness. Because of the repeated discussion of death, the subject of resurrection assumes a dramatic prominence whenever it appears.

As we remind ourselves that resurrection is the only answer to the problem of death, we will appreciate its important place in the biblical message of hope to a helpless world. Jesus' resurrection shouts out that this hope is real, that we can fully trust God to resurrect us.

Let's consider a few illustrations to underline this point. In art, contrast is often used to highlight the focal point of a painting or photograph. Sometimes that feature will not be the largest one. In a dark scene, the illuminated object stands out more than if it had been surrounded by other bright objects. In the Bible, resurrection benefits from a similar type of contrast.

Suppose a doctor spends a long time telling you about your life-threatening cancer. If toward the end of the conversation he says, "But all you need is an operation and you will be fine," this hope would be the most important thing he said. The detailed explanation of the problem only increases the impact and appreciation of the solution.

Again, in a compelling film or book, the plot builds, leading to a critical point. There seems to be no way out. Things are on the edge of disaster. Then, at the last minute, a solution is found, a happy ending. The Bible is like that, showing first man's total inability to save himself. The turning point is Jesus' life, death, and resurrection. This good news of salvation provides the treatment for the illness that the rest of the Bible has been diagnosing. Thus, resurrection is at the very core of the Christian message. It is only because of Jesus' resurrection that Paul was able to say, "'O death, where is your victory? O death, where is your sting?'" (1 Corinthians 15:55).

WE MAY MISS HOW THE BIBLE SUBTLY IMPLIES RESURRECTION

The Bible often hints at or implies resurrection rather than referring to it directly, much like the foundation of a house. To demonstrate how easily resurrection can be missed, let's look at the first chapter or so of 1 Corinthians. On a quick read, it appears that these verses center all their attention on the cross of Christ. If we only focused on the following phrases, we might easily miss the theme of resurrection:

Was Paul *crucified* for you? (1:13)

The word of *the cross* is folly to those who are perishing. (1:18)

We preach Christ *crucified*. (1:23)

I decided to know nothing among you except Jesus Christ and him *crucified*. (2:2)

This strong emphasis has led to these verses being widely and correctly used to uphold the centrality of the cross. But if we look more closely at this passage as a whole, we will see that the resurrection underpins and authenticates everything that Paul teaches. It is precisely because of the resurrection that the following things are possible:

We can be "sanctified in Christ Jesus" (1 Corinthians 1:2). To be sanctified in Jesus requires being in union with one who is able to sanctify. If Jesus had not risen from the dead, there would be no holiness or any other benefit to be gained from union with him.

We can "call upon the name of our Lord Jesus Christ" (1 Corinthians 1:2). Our prayers can be directed to the risen Christ who still acts on our behalf, receives worship, and directs us as Lord. The first disciples had been taught to worship one God but began calling Jesus "Lord"—the name used for God. It is impossible to imagine them doing this if the resurrection had not confirmed for them beyond all doubt that Jesus was indeed divine.

We can receive "grace . . . and peace from God our Father and the Lord Jesus Christ" (1 Corinthians 1:3). Christians are to be marked by both receiving and giving inexplicable grace and peace, which is a direct gift from both God and the living Christ.

We can be "in every way . . . enriched in him in all speech and all knowledge" (1 Corinthians 1:5). It is the risen Jesus himself who is the source of all knowledge and wisdom.

The apostles' *"testimony about Christ was confirmed among you"* (1 Corinthians 1:6). This risen Jesus dwells within believers. He transforms us, and without this confirming work of his Spirit, we cannot be saved.

We are to "wait for the revealing of our Lord Jesus Christ" (1 Corinthians 1:7). Christians are to be a people of anticipation, looking forward to the return of the resurrected Lord Jesus in all his glory. The Christian lives within an interlude between Jesus' glorious resurrection and his triumphant return. We will fully enjoy some aspects of what he has achieved for us only when we meet him in glory. We live with such a hope for the future that it changes us, but we also begin to experience some of the benefits here and now.

We are "called into the fellowship of his Son" (1 Corinthians 1:9). Christians are offered a true relationship with the resurrected Jesus.

Like Paul, we are called by the living Jesus to a mission. He writes, "Christ did not send me to baptize but to preach the gospel" (1 Corinthians 1:17). It was the living Jesus who intervened in Paul's life on the road to Damascus, changing him from murderous persecutor to preacher. Every Christian is called to this mission of sharing the good news.

Paul summarizes his work as *"we preach Christ crucified"* (1 Corinthians 1:23). This initially seems to suggest that the entire focus of his preaching is on the cross of Jesus. However, he then immediately says that the message of the cross is "Christ *the power of God*" to believers (1 Corinthians 1:24). The message of the crucifixion must include the resurrection, for it is impossible to conceive that Christ is revealed as the power of God unless it is proclaimed that he has defeated death.

Just in case we missed the point, Paul then becomes even more explicit when he says, "And because of him you are in Christ Jesus, who became to us wisdom from God, righteousness and sanctification and redemption" (1 Corinthians 1:30). A dead man cannot be a source of wisdom, righteousness, or sanctification! From the context, therefore, there is no doubt that Paul preaches Christ and him crucified; yet in these words he implies a death that was not permanent and over which Christ triumphed.

While these references in 1 Corinthians 1 are subtle, it's clear that both the death *and* resurrection of Jesus are central to Paul. His gospel hinges on the fact that Jesus was raised from the dead. This is also consistent with Paul's emphasis in 1 Corinthians 15.

There is obviously a direct link between death and resurrection. Without Jesus' death, there could not have been a resurrection, but equally, without the resurrection even the death of Jesus would have been a meaningless tragedy. In order for Jesus' death to be of any benefit to us, he had to emerge from the grave alive, and as we have seen, Paul repeatedly confirms that fact for us.

THE BIBLE SEES JESUS' DEATH AND RESURRECTION AS ONE SAVING EVENT

I argued earlier that when Paul said "Christ and him crucified," he meant us to understand "Christ and him both crucified and raised." For Paul, the death and resurrection of Jesus were inseparable. I would go so far as to suggest that when he referred to either the death or resurrection of Jesus individually, he usually intended to refer to both events, as a form of shorthand.

Driscoll and Breshears argue similarly: "We consider both the death and resurrection of Jesus as intimately related truths that are a singular event. Thus when we speak of Jesus' death or cross, do assume that we are including Jesus' resurrection and empty tomb, because apart from his ongoing life the cross is without any power."[1]

This notion also becomes apparent when we examine some verses in 1 Peter, where at first glance Peter seems to say that it is the resurrection rather than the death of Jesus that saves us:

> Blessed be the God and Father of our Lord Jesus Christ! According to his great mercy, he has caused us to be born again to a living hope through the resurrection of Jesus Christ from the dead. (1:3)

We are to have a *living* hope that can only be given to us because of the resurrection of Jesus. It is God himself who works in us to give us this hope. This power that works actively in the Christian's life is the same power God used when he raised Jesus from the dead (see Ephesians 1:19–20).

It is the resurrection itself to which salvation is attributed. The emphasis in this passage is on the saving nature of Jesus' resurrection. Have you ever stopped to consider how Jesus' resurrection *saved* you?

---

[1] Mark Driscoll and Gary Breshears, *Death by Love* (Wheaton, IL: Crossway, 2008), 13–14.

Or do you think only of Jesus' death in that way? In another chapter, Peter attributes salvation to "an appeal to God for a good conscience, through the resurrection of Jesus Christ" (1 Peter 3:21). There is no mention at all in this verse of the cross.

All this cannot mean that Peter attributes our salvation solely to the resurrection of Jesus, since he would then be contradicting himself elsewhere in the same letter. In 1 Peter 1:2 he says it is "sprinkling with his blood" that saves us, and in 1 Peter 1:19 it is "with the precious blood of Christ" that we are ransomed. In these two verses there is no mention that the resurrection makes our salvation possible; instead the focus is on Jesus' death.

So which is it, Peter? Is it Jesus' death or his resurrection that saves us? The only way we can understand this apparent contradiction is if, when Peter refers to the cross, he also implies that Christ rose from the dead, and when he refers to Jesus' resurrection he also implies his death. Without this understanding we could get very confused, attributing our salvation first to the death, then to the resurrection of Jesus. Could our failure to understand this point have led to our tendency to attribute salvation solely to Jesus' death? The truth is that we are saved by *both* the death *and* resurrection of Jesus working together.

Peter does connect these two events explicitly himself. When he describes the prophecies concerning the work of Jesus, he speaks of "the sufferings of Christ and the subsequent glories" (1 Peter 1:11).

In view of all these verses, we can argue that when Peter speaks of either the death or resurrection of Jesus, the two are so entwined in his mind that when he refers to one he means to include the other. The same thing seems true of other New Testament writers. I am essentially arguing that they so presuppose that the death and resurrection of Jesus are entwined that they refer to either one of them and intend for us to understand that they mean both of them. If this is the case, straightforward sentences that tell us "Jesus died to save us" or "Jesus was raised to save us" actually mean exactly the same thing.

This might sound like a radical new idea to some. If it actually was novel, you would be quite correct to be wary of it. After two thousand years of Bible study by many godly people, what makes us think we have the ability to construct a new, correct interpretation? Few of us will do this even once in our lives, and none of us can expect to do so on a regular basis. But this idea is far from new, and others of you are probably dumbfounded that I only recently stumbled upon it! Centuries ago John Calvin identified the same phenomenon:

> Let us remember, therefore, that when [in Scripture] death only is mentioned, everything peculiar to the resurrection is at the same time included, and that there is a like synecdoche in the term resurrection, as often as it is used apart from death, everything peculiar to death being included.[2]

Calvin is implying that Jesus' death and resurrection are so closely interrelated and connected to each other, they constitute one saving event, and when the Bible mentions one of them, the other one is usually also intended to be inferred.

If, like me, you enjoy collecting unusual words (much as some might collect rare stamps or coins), the word *synecdoche* may be an interesting addition to your vocabulary. Not very commonly used today, this word basically means what I have been describing. It is a figure of speech in which a word usually used to refer to a part of something is used to refer to the whole.

For example, we might say, "I need to rest my weary head" when what we really mean is "I need to rest my entire body." In 2 Corinthians 7:5 Paul says, "For even when we came into Macedonia, our bodies had no rest." Vine argues that it is obvious that he is referring to their whole beings rather than just their physical bodies.[3]

Paul actually explains another biblical synecdoche in Ephesians 4:8. In speaking about gifts apportioned by the risen and ascended Jesus, he quotes Psalm 68:18: "When he ascended on high he led a host of captives, and he gave gifts to men." He continues, "In saying, 'He ascended,' what does it mean but that he had also descended into the lower regions, the earth?" (Ephesians 4:9). Paul explains that in the one word "ascension," the descent from heaven is also implied.

Another good example of synecdoche is found in Romans 5:18.

---

[2]John Calvin, *Institutes of the Christian Religion* (Bellingham, WA: Logos Research Systems, 1997), II, xvi, 13.
[3]W. E. Vine et al., *Vine's Complete Expository Dictionary of Old and New Testament Words* (Nashville: Thomas Nelson, 1996), 2:242.

Here Paul says, "one act of righteousness leads to justification and life for all men." It appears from the context that he is speaking about Jesus' death. Since so many verses refer to the resurrection as the event that gives us life, it seems very likely that he had both death and resurrection in mind at this point. Just a few verses later he says, "We were buried therefore with him by baptism into death, in order that, just as Christ was raised from the dead by the glory of the Father, we too might walk in newness of life" (Romans 6:4).

The clearest example of all is 2 Corinthians 5:15, "And he died for all, that those who live might no longer live for themselves but for him who for their sake died and was raised." Here the first "died" functions as shorthand for the more complete phrase "died and was raised." Paul expands his own synecdoche. Since he used the word "died" here and intended us to infer the crucifixion and resurrection, then we can conclude that he may well have done the same thing elsewhere.

In 1 Corinthians 2:2 Paul summarizes his message by saying that he preaches "Jesus Christ and him crucified." This would seem to contradict the description of Paul's message in Acts 17:18, where Luke says that Paul preached "Jesus and the resurrection." Either Luke and Paul disagreed about what was at the heart of Paul's preaching, or the cross and resurrection of Jesus were considered so intermingled that they meant essentially the same thing and one could be used while inferring the other, making it almost impossible to talk about one without implying the other. Calvin argues that such phrases are synecdoches.[4] Therefore, both descriptions of Paul's preaching mean essentially the same thing. Without the resurrection, the cross was just another senseless death perpetrated by the Romans, and without the cross there would be no need for a resurrection. Both must be preached, and they must be preached together.

The biblical language surrounding the death and resurrection of Jesus is, therefore, easily misunderstood by today's reductionistic approach to understanding language. We can agree that when the biblical writers spoke of either Jesus' death or his resurrection, they were often using one of these events as shorthand for both of them. An inad-

---

[4]John Calvin, *Commentary on Acts*, 1, 107, in *Calvin's Commentaries*, electronic ed., Logos Library System (Albany, OR: Ages Software, 1998).

equate understanding of this point may very well have contributed to our neglect of the resurrection.

The perfect life, obedient death, and life-giving resurrection of Jesus should be thought of as one saving work—a combined and inseparable act of God. It is only through the life, death, *and* resurrection of Jesus that salvation is possible. There is a single complete arc of movement down through incarnation, death, and burial and then up through resurrection, ascension, and enthronement. Christ Jesus himself is our salvation. Paul says of his own ministry:

> According to the grace of God given to me, like a skilled master builder I laid a foundation. . . . For no one can lay a foundation other than that which is laid, *which is Jesus Christ*. (1 Corinthians 3:10–11)

It is indeed Jesus himself and *all* that he has done that provides the only sure foundation for our lives. He himself is the only way of salvation. The saving effects of his death and resurrection are combined. As Ridderbos[5] said:

> It is, moreover, of the greatest importance to see the significance of Christ's death and resurrection, which are the center of Paul's proclamation, as an inseparable unity; and particularly to keep in view how the significance of Christ's resurrection is determined by that of his death and vice versa.[6]

All this is not to say that it is never appropriate to talk of either the death or the resurrection of Jesus independently. Nor is it to deny that the cross and resurrection contribute to our salvation in distinct ways. Sometimes, even with a very well-known synecdoche, the constituent part may actually be what someone is speaking about. For example, I might say, "I have a new set of wheels," and most people would immediately understand that I meant I had bought a complete car. If I added more information to that statement and instead said, "I went to the tire shop after driving over glass and got a new set of wheels," you would immediately understand that what I actually meant was that I had purchased new tires, not a new car. We therefore need to be

---

[5]Former Professor of New Testament at the Theological School of the Reformed Churches of the Netherlands.
[6]Herman Ridderbos, *Paul, an Outline of his Theology* (Grand Rapids: Eerdmans, 1975), 54.

especially careful as we seek to understand the use of synecdoche in the New Testament.

CONCLUSION

We tend to pay little attention to the reality of our own future death. We have somehow learned to ignore the fact that someday we will die, thinking of it as a long way off, far away from the overriding concerns of our day-to-day lives. The truth, however, is that the only difference between those of us who are healthy and those who know they are dying is that we act as if we are immortal, thinking of our death as a remote and almost unreal occurrence. One of the tragedies of life is that in this we are sometimes mistaken. Statistically speaking, it is highly likely that some of the readers of this book will one day be surprised that their own death came much earlier than they expected, and with little or no warning. Since death seems so distant to us, is it any wonder that we speak so little of resurrection?

By its emphasis on both death and resurrection, the Bible urges us to answer these crucial questions: Are you ready for your own death? Do you have a hope that goes beyond the grave? As we consider our own mortality, the truth of the resurrection of Jesus prepares us to face death and assures us that we have a secure place in heaven that is being prepared for us by Jesus (see John 14:2). Christians approach death very differently than others because we have already begun to truly live. We have a foretaste of that heavenly life already, and God gives us life to the full that will never cease (John 10:10).

A disembodied heavenly state is not our final resting place. One day we too will be like Jesus, living in God's presence, but with a new, glorious resurrection body. For anyone with the diagnosis of a terminal illness, the message of the resurrection will provide more comfort and reassurance than any other doctrine. Life is itself a terminal condition, so we might be forgiven for arguing that resurrection is *the* most important theme in the Bible—at least practically for us.

GLIMPSES OF RESURRECTION

If a man dies, shall he live again?

J O B   1 4 : 1 4

ONE EVENING, as I began writing this chapter, my mind was rather distracted by some news I had received that afternoon. A bus had hit a child on her way home from the school our children attend. Everyone assumed the worst. A rumor began to spread that she had died.

Coincidentally, that was also the first day we allowed our eldest daughter to walk home from school alone. Our thoughts were filled with the one subject we prefer to ignore—death. In Western society we are relatively well insulated from our mortality, so such news is all the more shocking. No parents ever expect to bury their own child.

The Bible knows no such reticence. Indeed, a cursory look at the historical books might lead us to conclude that the Bible is a book about death. The Bible describes death without any attempts to tone it down for the purposes of decency. This is unlike many children's Bible storybooks, which change the stories in order to avoid the full impact of death for young readers. For example, in the story of Noah's Ark, there is often no mention of the huge catastrophe that occurred in the drowning of the world's population.

God, in his wisdom, is not directing the biblical authors to talk relentlessly about death in order to depress us, but to emphasize the seriousness of our condition and our need for him to save us. By reminding us so forcefully of the problem of death, the Bible prepares us to fully appreciate the importance of the solution that resurrection offers. Only

Jesus' death and life-giving resurrection can give us hope. There is no mention of the word *resurrection* until the New Testament, although in some of the most faith-inspiring verses in the Bible, we do see that death is not the end.

I did not make much progress writing on the day this child was injured. Hearing about the potential death of someone you know has a way of dominating your thoughts, making any other task seem trivial. I suspect that the life of every parent who heard about that accident was also forcefully interrupted that night. Death reminds us of the temporary nature of our lives. The uncomfortable truth is, none of us knows exactly when we will die. As Peter put it, "All flesh is like grass and all its glory like the flower of grass. The grass withers, and the flower falls" (1 Peter 1:24).

Later I gave up attempting to write and instead tried to sleep. I did not fare much better at that activity. The next morning, however, on taking our children to school the whole neighborhood was relieved to learn that the girl was not dead after all but rather was expected to make a full recovery. It was almost as though she had been raised from the dead. Indeed, she did recover and returned to school a few weeks later.

The net result of that event for our family was not only to remind us of the need for caution in crossing the road, but also to make us more fully appreciate the value of life and to understand its fleeting nature. Without a belief in the resurrection, our lives seem short in the extreme. Talking and thinking about death is good for us. This prepares our hearts to fully appreciate the resurrection. For Christians, it also helps us to be thankful for what Jesus has done and motivates us to make the most of the life on earth we still have in serving him. Jonathan Edwards famously declared that he had "resolved to think much on all occasions of my own dying, and of the common circumstances which attend death."[1]

Let's examine what the Bible says about resurrection in the Old Testament. There is a substantial body of teaching on life after death from which a consistent doctrinal framework emerges. Jesus told two

---

[1]Jonathan Edwards, *Letters and Personal Writings*, WJE Online, Vol. 16, 753; http://edwards.yale.edu/archive?path=aHR0cDovL2Vkd2FyZHMueWFsZS5lZHUvY2dpLWJpbi9uZXdwaGlsby9nZXRvYmplY3QucGw/Yy44xNTo3NDoxLndqZW8=.

of his disciples that his own resurrection (here described as entering into his glory) was predicted in the Old Testament:

> "O foolish ones, and slow of heart to believe all that the prophets have spoken! Was it not necessary that the Christ should suffer these things and enter into his glory?" And beginning with Moses and all the Prophets, he interpreted to them in all the Scriptures the things concerning himself. (Luke 24:25–27)

Paul also tells us Jesus "was raised on the third day *in accordance with the Scriptures*" (1 Corinthians 15:4), obviously referring to the Jewish Bible, which we know as the Old Testament. As we embark on our exploration of all that the Old Testament says about resurrection in general, we will also highlight where Jesus' own resurrection was predicted.

It is worth acknowledging at the outset that I am deliberately writing from the perspective of a New Testament Christian, looking back at these accounts with the benefit of hindsight. It is not clear how many Old Testament believers truly had a full-orbed view of the resurrection. In many of the verses we will examine, a different interpretation is possible. We will not address these debates here. Although some commentaries do discuss them, many others pay surprisingly little attention to how appropriate it is for us to read these texts as referring to resurrection. Consider this therefore to be an exploratory chapter.

RESURRECTION IN THE BOOKS OF MOSES

Adam and Eve

In the Garden of Eden, two significant trees were identified, but only one was prohibited before the Fall. Adam and Eve were able to eat freely from the tree of life. The tree of the knowledge of good and evil led to death. Paul says before sin there was no death: "Sin came into the world through one man, and death through sin, and so death spread to all men because all sinned" (Romans 5:12).

Medical experts are not completely sure why we all eventually die. It would seem that since cells divide and replace themselves they could, in theory, go on doing so forever. However, because of Adam's sin we will all die. The whole creation was also put into "bondage to corruption" (Romans 8:21).

God, by his grace, delayed the full effects of his judgment—Adam and Eve did not physically die immediately. Death is the only thing they deserved from God, and the sacrifice of animals to cover their guilt and shame demonstrates that mercy requires a death. The animals died so that Adam and Eve were spared from immediate death.

From then on, every day Adam and Eve came closer to the moment of their final breath. Their bodies became subject to sickness and decay. Biblically, death is a separation from loved ones and from God, and this is what happened to Adam and Eve. Cast out from the presence of God, mankind was now spiritually dead (see Ephesians 2:1).

These events also implied that since God can be merciful in delaying death, a way of permanent salvation would become available. The tree of life was not destroyed, and it appears in Revelation—every Christian will enjoy it forever. The tree of knowledge of good and evil does not make any return appearance.

The defeat of Satan by the "offspring" of Eve is predicted in Genesis 3:15. This word was translated "seed" in the King James, and as Paul points out it is singular and refers to Christ (Galatians 3:16). Although the Messiah will be wounded on the cross, the Devil will be killed. "Beware, Lucifer," says God, for "Jesus Christ shall bruise your head, and you shall bruise his heel" (see Genesis 3:15). In light of later prophecies predicting the death of the Messiah, this description of a minor injury implies that Jesus will be resurrected. Here the fact that God speaks to Adam and Eve about events far in the future suggests that they will somehow survive the grave. If this were not the case, why would he tell them?

Genesis is understood to be a book about beginnings. It is also, however, a book about endings. We are told repeatedly that people died. Like a relentless drum beating out a rhythm we hear again and again, "and he died." One day it will be our turn. I wonder, when was the last time each of us seriously considered the day of our own death?

Enoch

"Enoch walked with God, and he was not, for God took him" (Genesis 5:24).

Unlike the other men and women in Genesis who are described as flawed and sinful, here was a man who walked with God. The writer to the Hebrews says, "By faith Enoch was taken up so that he should not see death, and he was not found, because God had taken him. Now before he was taken he was commended as having pleased God" (11:5).

Enoch's story tells us that it is possible to permanently escape death altogether. There is another realm into which human beings can enter. While his experience was not the norm, God shows us that he is able to ensure that a person can escape death. Enoch never actually died, so he was not really resurrected, although he did require a spiritual resurrection since he was born dead toward God. He did not depart into some kind of celestial spiritual home to float around. Enoch took his body with him, renewed, free from all effects of sickness and decay and fit for an eternity in God's presence. That transformation is analogous in some way to what will happen to all Christians. God shows here that he has a purpose for the physical body in eternity.

The God of Abraham, Isaac, and Jacob

We see this in Exodus 3:6. God is regularly described as being the God of people who have died. Jesus does this to make an incisive point in an argument with the Sadducees over whether there is such a thing as resurrection. He says, "That the dead are raised, even Moses showed, in the passage about the bush, where he calls the Lord the God of Abraham and the God of Isaac and the God of Jacob. Now he is not God of the dead, but of the living, for all live to him" (Luke 20:37–38).

Jesus explains that God does indeed continue to be the God of people after they die. If that is so, then this means that one day they will not be dead. Jesus is not speaking about a merely spiritual resurrection here, but a physical one that is yet to come. It is unclear how many of the original readers of Genesis would have understood the glimpse of resurrection in this phrase, but it is there.

The Sacrifice of Isaac

One of the key moments in the story of salvation is when Abraham's faith was tested to the limit. Isaac was a child born after a strong test. Paul said Abraham trusted in "the God in whom he believed, who gives life to the dead and calls into existence the things that do not exist" (Romans 4:17). Thus, because of the deadness of Sarah's womb and Abraham's loins, the very birth of Isaac paralleled resurrection according to Paul. Few other events are as dramatically miraculous in the experience of the patriarchs. If God can create life, why should he not also be able to re-create life from death?

After Isaac's birth, Abraham may well have felt his faith had been tested sufficiently. He would have been wrong. Later God directed him to sacrifice the son he had been promised would succeed him. The writer to the Hebrews explains that Abraham "considered that God was able even to raise him from the dead, from which, figuratively speaking, he did receive him back" (Hebrews 11:17–19).

We see in Genesis that Abraham believed that he would be able to obey this shocking command, but that somehow his son would survive. He said that he and the boy would return (Genesis 22:5). At the last moment a substitute was found caught in the thicket, and God stopped Abraham from sacrificing his son.

Many Christians today see this story of Abraham and Isaac as a kind of precursor to the death and resurrection of Jesus, the difference being that for Jesus there could be no last-minute reprieve as he himself was our substitute. Jesus died at the hand of his own Father but was resurrected from the dead.

The God Who Makes Alive

God says, "See now that I, even I, am he, and there is no god beside me; I kill and I make alive; I wound and I heal; and there is none that can deliver out of my hand" (Deuteronomy 32:39). "Make alive" may refer to birth or recovery from an almost fatal sickness or accident. However, since God is the creator of all life, surely this could infer that he gives life back to the dead. Later repetitions of this phrase more strongly suggest resurrection.

Moses

Moses died, but his body was never found. He was buried by God (Deuteronomy 34:5–6) but appeared alongside Elijah on the Mount of Transfiguration in bodily form (Mark 9:4). It seems likely that, like

Enoch and Elijah, at some point his body was transported to heaven. Moses did experience physical death, unlike Enoch and Elijah. If indeed his body was at some point resurrected and taken up into heaven, then this would be the first physical resurrection of the Bible. We should be a little careful, however, as this is a mystery, and it is just possible that Moses' appearance on the Mount of Transfiguration was only a manifestation of his spirit. The Bible does not tell us precisely what happened.

We can, however, firmly conclude that throughout the books of Moses, the hope of resurrection, although not named, is implied, and we are led to understand that a resurrection does include the physical body.

RESURRECTION IN THE BOOKS OF HISTORY

Hannah

When Hannah thanked God for the gift of her son Samuel, she said, "The Lord kills and brings to life; he brings down to Sheol and raises up" (1 Samuel 2:6).

The two parts of this verse make up a parallel statement in which both halves are intended to say the same thing. The same Lord who kills and brings down to Sheol (the grave) is the one who raises up and brings to life. Long before the complete message of salvation was proclaimed, God inspired this statement, declaring that he is able to resurrect. The Hebrew word translated here "brings to life" is the same word used when the resurrections associated with Elijah and Elisha are described. This strengthens the argument that Hannah here refers to bodily resurrection.

King David

David expressed a hope in life after death. Following his sin of adultery with Bathsheba and the murder of her husband to cover up her resultant pregnancy, he was found out. Although forgiven, one of the consequences of his sin was that his baby, the product of adultery, became sick and was at the point of death. David was in a terrible emotional state and was praying and fasting. When the baby died, his servants were afraid to tell him, for fear he would harm himself. When David realized this, he got up from his mourning, worshipped, and ate, saying, "I shall go to him, but he will not return to me" (2 Samuel 12:23).

David's unusual response to the death of his son revealed a clear hope for the salvation, resurrection, and reunion of himself and his baby. If David had only meant that, like his child, he too would die, he would not have experienced comfort. David had a hope that went beyond the grave because he knew he had received forgiveness from God for sins that should have led to execution according to the Mosaic Law. These words of David have given hope to bereaved parents for thousands of years.

Elijah and Elisha

A few generations later, when Elijah and then Elisha prayed for resurrections (1 Kings 17; 2 Kings 4:32–37), we again see that death need not be the end of human existence. Elijah also escaped physical death in a similar manner to Enoch before him. He ascended to heaven with his body intact. Again we see that the biblical hope is not just some kind of spiritual existence but rather an eternal life complete with a physical body (2 Kings 2).

In the aftermath of the news of these resurrections, a leper was sent to the ruler of Israel to request a cure. The king exclaimed, "Am I God, to kill and make alive, that this man sends word to me to cure a man of his leprosy?" (2 Kings 5:7).

During their lives, Elijah and Elisha only performed one resurrection each. These resurrections or, as some call them, resuscitations (since those involved did not experience an eternal transformation of their bodies but died again later) foreshadow the hope that is to come. In addition, even death itself did not remove the Spirit's anointing on Elisha's physical body, with a dramatic result:

> As a man was being buried, behold, a marauding band was seen and the man was thrown into the grave of Elisha, and as soon as the man touched the bones of Elisha, he revived and stood on his feet. (2 Kings 13:20–21)

Sleeping with the Fathers

Throughout the historical books the death of kings is described by using sleep as a metaphor. Sleep is a temporary state. This perhaps leaves open the possibility of a future awakening.

RESURRECTION IN THE PSALMS

The psalmists had a well-developed doctrine of the afterlife. They frequently refer to "Sheol." Sheol is a form of separation from God and the land of the living. It is a form of sleep. In Sheol people do not worship God. Sheol is not hell, but it is not heaven either. At times a descent into Sheol is described as though it is a permanent and final resting place—for example, "For in death there is no remembrance of you; in Sheol who will give you praise?" (Psalm 6:5).

Sometimes, however, psalmists paint a clear hope that some may escape Sheol:

> The wicked shall return to Sheol, all the nations that forget God. For the needy shall not always be forgotten, and the hope of the poor shall not perish forever. (Psalm 9:17–18)

> O LORD, you have brought my soul from Sheol; you restored me to life from among those who go down to the pit. (Psalm 30:3)

> Our God is a God of salvation, and to GOD, the Lord, belong deliverances from death. (Psalm 68:20)

Some of these verses may refer to a delivery from almost dying. But if God can deliver from the point of death, he can also deliver even after death. It is just such a permanent rescue from death that David envisages in a crucial psalm that includes the following remarkable paragraph:

> For you will not abandon my soul to Sheol, or let your holy one see corruption. You make known to me the path of life; in your presence there is fullness of joy; at your right hand are pleasures forevermore. (Psalm 16:10–11)

This verse appears to refer to the writer himself not dying, and hence his body not decomposing in a tomb. However, David did die. His body did see corruption. Both Peter (Acts 2:31) and Paul (Acts 13:35–37) apply these words as a prophecy concerning Jesus, whose body would never decompose.

The wonderful truth is that because of Jesus' death and resurrection, the corruption seen by David's body will one day be reversed, and, like us, he will enjoy pleasures at the right hand of God for all eternity. When the first billion years of eternity have passed, David will still sing these words, secure in the knowledge that God will continue to sustain his life forevermore.

David declared elsewhere that he would "dwell in the house of the LORD forever" (Psalm 23:6). He must have known that he would die, and yet he was confident that he would be with God forever. Another of the messianic psalms (Psalm 22) contains a similar sentiment. The early part of this psalm prophesies Jesus' painful death by putting a detailed description of the crucifixion into his mouth. Having spoken about the death of Jesus, the psalm goes on to suggest that the suffering of Christ will not be permanent: "Deliver my soul from the sword, my precious life from the power of the dog!" (vv. 19–21). David also foreshadows New Testament language about a ransom being paid to save us:

> Truly no man can ransom another, or give to God the price of his life, for the ransom of their life is costly and can never suffice, that he should live on forever and never see the pit. . . . Their graves are their homes forever, their dwelling places to all generations. . . . Their form shall be consumed in Sheol, with no place to dwell. But God will ransom my soul from the power of Sheol, for he will receive me. (Psalm 49:7–15)

David also says elsewhere that it is the Lord himself "who redeems your life from the pit" (Psalm 103:4). This reminds us of Anselm's words: "This debt was so great that, although no one ought to have paid it except man, no one could except God."[2]

David was certain that he would experience salvation from Sheol. The Savior to come had to be God himself. When Christ was born, he was given the name Jesus, which means "God saves," and the angel said this was because "*he* will save his people from their sins" (Matthew 1:21). This is a clear declaration that the man Jesus is also God and that this uniquely qualified him for the task that was set before him.

So God would die to pay a ransom and rescue David from the pow-

---

[2]Anselm, *Cur Deus Homo—Why God Was Made Man* (Oxford: John Henry and James Proctor, 1865), 104–105.

ers of Sheol after his death. The one paying the ransom is also the one who would receive David, and thus Jesus must be resurrected. Jesus paid the ransom and then was raised from the dead to enable resurrection from death for David and for all believers.

In Psalm 21 "the king" is described, and it is said of him, "He asked life of you; you gave it to him, length of days forever and ever" (v. 4) The context suggests this is again speaking of the future Messiah. We now know that because we share in his life, those words can also be said of us.

Another psalmist, Asaph, also spoke of future glory into which he would be received:

> Nevertheless, I am continually with you; you hold my right hand. You guide me with your counsel, and afterward you will receive me to glory. Whom have I in heaven but you? And there is nothing on earth that I desire besides you. My flesh and my heart may fail, but God is the strength of my heart and my portion forever. (Psalm 73:23–26)

Another psalm declares that we will escape the fate of the rest of mankind and experience eternal life: "The dead do not praise the LORD, nor do any who go down into silence. But we will bless the LORD from this time forth and forevermore" (Psalm 115:17–18).

In another great psalm of hope, we read a promise of protection for our lives:

> The LORD will keep you from all evil; he will keep your life. The LORD will keep your going out and your coming in from this time forth and forevermore. (Psalm 121:7–8)

This psalm uses such physical words as "going out" and "coming in" and "forevermore," and this represents a promise of eternal life. Thus, given that we do die, the verse hints at a future resurrection.

RESURRECTION IN THE WISDOM LITERATURE

Job

Amidst the death of his family, the loss of his goods, and his own terrible sickness, we are given a close-up view of the distress of Job. God accepts this man even though he struggles with pain and expresses his questions to the Almighty. Job's hope in God, although tested to the extreme, never leaves him.

In Job 14, we find a passage that begins by speaking of the hopelessness of death. It seems to argue that there is nothing after death for mankind. Suddenly, toward the end, Job hints that there is life beyond the grave, that on a certain day men will be raised from death:

> Till the heavens are no more he will not awake or be roused out of his sleep. Oh that you would hide me in Sheol, that you would conceal me until your wrath be past, that you would appoint me a set time, and remember me! If a man dies, shall he live again? (vv. 12–14)

The answer to this question is, "Yes, when the heavens and earth are renewed!" There is an even clearer demonstration of hope for a future resurrection later on in the book of Job. It is precisely because this whole book is so full of death, destruction, and misery that the following words are so dramatic. Job introduces the subject with great emphasis: "Oh that my words were written! Oh that they were inscribed in a book! Oh that with an iron pen and lead they were engraved in the rock forever!" (Job 19:23–24). Hopefully, that got your attention! He goes on to say:

> For I know that my Redeemer lives, and at the last he will stand upon the earth. And after my skin has been thus destroyed, yet in my flesh I shall see God, whom I shall see for myself, and my eyes shall behold, and not another. (vv. 25–27)

The New Testament agrees with Job's remarkable description, and so we today can also rejoice that standing on the earth someday, in our same body, we will worship our Savior.

The Book of Proverbs

In Proverbs we see a number of promises that are not literally fulfilled in this world. Here is an example: "In the path of righteousness is life, and in its pathway there is no death" (12:28).

On first glance, this proverb seems to be simply not true! Ultimately, though, death for Christians is not permanent, and our lives will be transformed into eternal life. Death has no significance in the context of eternity for the Christian.

The Book of Ecclesiastes

Ecclesiastes speaks repeatedly of the meaninglessness of life and the inevitability of death. It does, however, say that at death the body and spirit are separated, as we now know, to be reunited at a future date: "Remember also your Creator in the days of your youth, before . . . the dust returns to the earth as it was, and *the spirit returns to God who gave it*" (12:1, 7).

Though this is not a prediction of true bodily resurrection, this verse at least implies that man's spirit survives in some way.

RESURRECTION IN THE PROPHETS

The Book of Isaiah

Isaiah contains several references to what happens to us after death. The first tells us of the inevitability and the equalizing nature of death:

> Sheol beneath is stirred up to meet you when you come. . . . Your pomp is brought down . . . maggots are laid as a bed beneath you, and worms are your covers. (Isaiah 14:9–11)

This is not the end, however:

> And he will swallow up on this mountain the covering that is cast over all peoples, the veil that is spread over all nations. He will swallow up death forever; and the LORD God will wipe away tears from all faces, and the reproach of his people he will take away from all the earth, for the LORD has spoken. It will be said on that day, "Behold, this is our God; we have waited for him, that he might save us. This is the LORD; we have waited for him; let us be glad and rejoice in his salvation." (Isaiah 25:7–9)

Jesus' death later occurred on a mountain, and by his resurrection he swallowed up death forever. Death is the single greatest dilemma or veil clouding people. Isaiah prophesied that death will one day be taken away and its effects reversed, and all tears will be wiped from people's eyes. God's "salvation" here is the reversal of all the effects of death.

In another passage Isaiah makes a glorious promise. There is a clear expectation of a return from the very dust that our bodies will one day become. Once a feast for worms, we will be resurrected to life:

> Your dead shall live; their bodies shall rise. You who dwell in the dust, awake and sing for joy! For your dew is a dew of light, and the earth will give birth to the dead. (Isaiah 26:19)

Take a look at your hand. One day that hand will no longer be able to move, and it will, with the rest of your body, be buried. But your hand will be renewed and perfected and will form part of your renewed body. Dust to dust is not the end of the story!

Isaiah 53 made a very tangible prediction of the judicial suffering of Jesus many years before it occurred. What we can easily miss is the clear statement in the middle of this famous chapter that, for Jesus, death would not be the end:

> When his soul makes an offering for guilt, he shall see his offspring; he shall prolong his days; the will of the LORD shall prosper in his hand. Out of the anguish of his soul he shall see and be satisfied; by his knowledge shall the righteous one, my servant, make many to be accounted righteous, and he shall bear their iniquities. (vv. 10–11)

The Book of Jonah

Jesus referred to the story of Jonah as a type foreshadowing his own death and resurrection:

> For just as Jonah was three days and three nights in the belly of the great fish, so will the Son of Man be three days and three nights in the heart of the earth. (Matthew 12:40)

Jonah can therefore be seen as a picture of the death, burial, and resurrection of Jesus that would later occur. Just like Jonah, it was critical that Jesus himself rise or else he couldn't have saved anyone.

Like many such prototypes that foreshadow Jesus in the Old Testament, there are ways in which the two stories are similar and ways in which they are different. Like Jonah, Jesus was sent to a sinful world.

Unlike Jonah, Jesus obeyed willingly, immediately putting the needs of a lost world before his own. Like Jonah, Jesus found himself in a world that was in a desperate situation and experiencing the wrath of God against sin. Unlike Jonah, he did not add to the troubles of this world by fleeing the presence of God, but rather he manifested that presence. Like Jonah, Jesus willingly laid down his life as a sacrifice to save others. Unlike Jonah, it was Jesus himself who prayed that his executioners be forgiven. Like Jonah, Jesus did not remain in the depths but was raised from the dead and was given a new task to accomplish. The Savior had himself escaped from the hold of death. Unlike Jonah, Jesus rejoiced unreservedly when his message led to the repentance of many.

The Book of Daniel

Daniel contains the clearest description of a bodily resurrection in the Old Testament. The prophet also adds that there will be a bodily resurrection for unbelievers:

> And many of those who sleep in the dust of the earth shall awake, some to everlasting life, and some to shame and everlasting contempt. And those who are wise shall shine like the brightness of the sky above; and those who turn many to righteousness, like the stars forever and ever. (Daniel 12:2–3)

The Book of Hosea

In Hosea we see a passage that seems to prefigure what would happen to Jesus, which itself reflects what will happen to us:

> Come, let us return to the LORD; for he has torn us, that he may heal us; he has struck us down, and he will bind us up. After two days he will revive us; on the third day he will raise us up, that we may live before him. (Hosea 6:1–2)

The book of Hosea contains another hint of a future rescue from Sheol in the following words:

> Shall I ransom them from the power of Sheol? Shall I redeem them from Death? O Death, where are your plagues? O Sheol, where is your sting? (13:14)

The Book of Ezekiel

We see an astonishing picture in Ezekiel, when the prophet is told to prophesy to an entire dead army so that they might be physically resurrected. God gathered dry bones together with a great rattling sound as though they were a jigsaw puzzle, then clothed them with flesh, and finally breathed new life into the corpses. This whole event may have been a vision. But besides metaphorically referring to the return from exile, it gives a very clear picture of what will happen in the end-time resurrection. At the end of the passage, there is an explicit promise that the people of God will indeed experience a bodily resurrection:

> Thus says the Lord GOD: *Behold, I will open your graves and raise you from your graves, O my people.* . . . And I will put my Spirit within you, and you shall live, and I will place you in your own land. Then you shall know that I am the LORD; I have spoken, and I will do it, declares the LORD. (Ezekiel 37:12–14)

CONCLUSION

It has become fashionable in some circles to conclude that the Old Testament saints did not believe in a resurrection. I trust that this overview has shown that this is not the case. Certainly the writer to the Hebrews was very clear about what it was that the great heroes of our faith were trusting God for. He says, "Without faith it is impossible to please him, for whoever would draw near to God must believe that he exists and that he rewards those who seek him" (Hebrews 11:6). While many of them received things from God in this world, they were, however, all hoping for a future reward:

> These all died in faith, not having received the things promised, but having seen them and greeted them from afar, and having acknowledged that they were strangers and exiles on the earth. For people who speak thus make it clear that they are seeking a homeland . . . they desire a better country, that is, a heavenly one. Therefore God is not ashamed to be called their God, for he has prepared for them a city. (Hebrews 11:13–15)

Thus we can conclude that in the Old Testament people did believe in God raising the dead.

CHAPTER SEVEN

RESURRECTION
BEFORE THE CROSS

I am the resurrection and the life. Whoever believes in me,
though he die, yet shall he live, and everyone who lives
and believes in me shall never die.

JOHN 11:25-26

SOME INSECTS ARE born and die within the space of a few hours. Most of us hope we will live into our eighties or beyond, but even then we feel robbed if told we are terminally ill. When a baby lives just a few short minutes after birth, we feel outraged. We have a hunger to live forever because we were designed to live forever.

We now turn to the accounts of a person whose life was cut short in his prime. By the age of approximately thirty-three Jesus had not married, had not been a parent, and had not received a retirement lump sum or gone on a long-awaited cruise. His life had achieved only a three-year period of notoriety that would have faded quickly if his crucifixion had been the end. But Jesus' death was not the end of the story, and so we have in the Gospels the culmination of all previous resurrection hopes. Let's examine the references to resurrection throughout the Gospels prior to the cross.

THE FIRST-CENTURY JEW'S VIEW OF RESURRECTION

By the time of Jesus, Jews had a variety of opinions about resurrection. The Old Testament does teach a resurrection of the dead. However, it is easy to see why some of these passages might have seemed less than clear to many of their original readers. Indeed, even today many Jews do not believe in a physical resurrection.

One historical example of belief in resurrection was the Jewish rebel who rather than be captured cut himself open with a sword and pulled out his bowels, throwing them at the crowd and proclaiming his belief that God would give them back to him in the future age to come.[1]

The Pharisees held a firm belief in the physical resurrection of the dead, based on their interpretation of the Old Testament Scriptures. The Sadducees, on the other hand, believed death was the end. As many of us remember learning in Sunday school, this belief caused them to be "Sad, you see." Paul took advantage of this fact in his speech in Acts 23, leading to an argument between the Pharisees and the Sadducees.

Some Jews believed the Messiah would be able to raise the dead. When John the Baptist's followers asked Jesus if he was the Messiah, Jesus listed this evidence: "The blind receive their sight and the lame walk, lepers are cleansed and the deaf hear, and *the dead are raised up*, and the poor have good news preached to them" (Matthew 11:5).

King Herod showed he was aware of the possibility of resurrection when he said of Jesus, "This is John the Baptist. He has been raised from the dead; that is why these miraculous powers are at work in him" (Matthew 14:2).

MIRACULOUS RESURRECTIONS PERFORMED BY JESUS

That Jesus had raised the dead was every bit as dramatic in the first century as it would be today. It would be naive to think that the Jews of Jesus' day were any less ignorant of the "fact" that once someone has died, they simply do not rise from the dead in everyday experience. The Jews were as skeptical as we would be today if we heard such stories.

Thus, the miraculous resurrections Jesus performed were incredibly significant. Only three clear resurrections (those associated with Elijah and Elisha) had been recorded in Scripture until this point. It would have been astonishing for anyone in those days to hear of a man who raised the dead.

If you invited Jesus to a funeral, there was a real chance that he

---

[1]See 2 Maccabees 14:46 in the Apocrypha.

might disrupt the proceedings by raising the body from the dead (see Luke 7:11–17). Three of the Gospels record the story of Jairus' daughter being raised from the dead (Matthew 9:18–26; Mark 5:22–43; Luke 8:41–56). Jesus' claim that she was only asleep prompted the same mockery that it would today. He viewed death very differently than the mourners. Death is merely a rest from which we will all one day be awakened, whatever our destiny thereafter.

One of the most emotive events in the whole Bible takes place when a friend of Jesus dies. The pain of Lazarus' sister is tangible. In a sense everything the Bible has shown us about the problem of death climaxes at this moment. Suddenly we see the compassion of Jesus and the strength of his emotional response to the devastating impact of death. Jesus' heart is moved and he shares the pain we all feel at losing people to this unwelcome intruder into God's perfect universe. Jesus is about to demonstrate for all to see his mastery over death in raising his friend from the dead. But, first, he weeps. Jesus is the God who knows every pain, who understands, who weeps. He is the God who has come to us, the comforter. Simon Brading and Graham Kendrick have written a song on the Lazarus account that beautifully portrays this perspective ("God of Compassion," available on the album *Have You Heard*; see http://haveyouheard.cck.org.uk). Before Lazarus was resurrected, a revealing conversation took place between Jesus and Martha.

> Jesus said to her, "Your brother will rise again." Martha said to him, "I know that he will rise again in the resurrection on the last day." Jesus said to her, "I am the resurrection and the life. Whoever believes in me, though he die, yet shall he live, and everyone who lives and believes in me shall never die." (John 11:21–27)

There is scarcely a more dramatic statement in the whole of Scripture.

JESUS' TEACHING ABOUT RESURRECTION

N. T. Wright argues that, surprisingly, in Jesus' teaching, "resurrection was obviously not one of his central or major themes."[2] Jesus does, however, speak about resurrection, and because of the universal fear of

---

[2]N. T. Wright, *The Resurrection of the Son of God* (London: SPCK, 2003), 403.

death, it seems clear that great importance would have been given to his teaching on that subject.

Jesus spoke about "the age to come"[3] and promised that the kingdom of God was coming.[4] Much of his teaching required a time of future blessing as a reward for present obedience. A good example of this is found in Luke 12, when, as N. T. Wright indicates, "The only point in telling people not to be afraid of those who can kill the body is if there is a life to look forward to beyond bodily death."[5] This future reward is elsewhere described as "entering life."[6] Jesus also promised that if we obey him, we "will be repaid at the resurrection of the just" (Luke 14:14).

Jesus taught that our earthly bodies will rise to face an eternal future of life or judgment: "An hour is coming when all who are in the tombs will hear his voice and come out, those who have done good to the resurrection of life, and those who have done evil to the resurrection of judgment" (John 5:28–29). Elsewhere he says, "No one can come to me unless the Father who sent me draws him. And I will raise him up on the last day" (John 6:44).

Jesus assures us, "Because I live, you also will live" (John 14:19) and promises, "My sheep hear my voice, and I know them, and they follow me. I give them eternal life, and they will never perish, and no one will snatch them out of my hand. My Father, who has given them to me, is greater than all, and no one is able to snatch them out of the Father's hand" (John 10:27–29). Jesus announces that he himself is the answer to all the concerns people have about the brevity and frailty of life, effectively saying, "Come to me, and I will give you a life that lasts forever—life in all its fullness" (see John 10:10).

In fact, this language suggests that a new life is required here and now. It reminds us of the words found in John 1 and 3 that speak of our need to be born again. The implication is that without Christ, people are already in a sense dead. Jesus also hints at this idea in the parable of the prodigal. When the son returns, the father reprimands the ungracious older brother: "It was fitting to celebrate and be glad, for this

---

[3]Matthew 12:32; Mark 10:30; Luke 18:30.
[4]Luke 17:20; 22:18.
[5]Wright, *The Resurrection of the Son of God*, 431.
[6]Mark 9:43–48.

your brother was dead, and is alive; he was lost, and is found" (Luke 15:32). While these words are almost certainly meant metaphorically in that the deadness of the prodigal reflects his separation from the father, our spiritual deadness is caused precisely by such a separation from our heavenly Father through sin. A reunion with our own Father will result in a spiritual resurrection inside us. As Jesus prayed shortly before his death, "And this is eternal life, that they know you the only true God, and Jesus Christ whom you have sent" (John 17:3).

A number of Jesus' parables talk about the coming kingdom of God, resurrection, and/or the afterlife. The most well-known is the story of the rich man and Lazarus found in Luke 16:19–31. We are told there of a divide between the righteous and the unrighteous in the afterlife. The message is that even if someone were to be resurrected and returned to the earth, people would not believe his warnings. This is poignant in light of the namesake of this parable, Lazarus, who was indeed resurrected and whom the Jewish rulers promptly wanted to murder (John 12:10).

JESUS PREDICTS HIS OWN RESURRECTION

Jesus repeatedly told his disciples that "he must go to Jerusalem and suffer many things from the elders and chief priests and scribes, and be killed, and on the third day be raised" (Matthew 16:21).[7]

Jesus warned that following him requires short-term sacrifice, possibly even death, for long-term gain: "The hour has come for the Son of Man to be glorified. Truly, truly, I say to you, unless a grain of wheat falls into the earth and dies, it remains alone; but if it dies, it bears much fruit. Whoever loves his life loses it, and whoever hates his life in this world will keep it for eternal life" (John 12:23–25).

By allowing his three closest disciples to see him in his transfigured and glorified state, Jesus demonstrated the importance of resurrection. If they had any doubts about his deity, this experience might be expected to remove them. However, it seems that they simply did not understand what was happening. On the mountain he was transfigured into a similar state to his risen and ascended glorification. Also, the presence of Elijah and Moses underlined the reality of eternal life for the believer.

---

[7]See also Matthew 17:23; 20:19; Mark 8:31; 9:31; 14:28.

In case they hadn't understood from their reading of the Old Testament, they saw that not only had Elijah escaped death (2 Kings 2:11), but Moses was also now alive and well. In case the disciples had missed the faith-stimulating implications of this moment and its demonstration of resurrection power, Jesus ordered them, "Tell no one the vision, until the Son of Man is raised from the dead" (Matthew 17:9).

Jesus did not want reports of his transfiguration to be immediately proclaimed to others. This was a revelation of God's power, but it was not yet the time for it to be made known. Jesus' resurrection would be the ultimate sign to everyone that he was the Son of God. It would be the act that would make forgiveness and eternal life for all believers possible.

The disciples were somewhat bemused by Jesus' words about him rising from the dead. What seems like very clear words to us were not understood by them. On the return from the mountain they were "questioning what this rising from the dead might mean" (Mark 9:10). We can only speculate whether they were kept from understanding by their own beliefs about how the Messiah would come as a conquering military figure or whether they were suffering spiritual blindness, which can make otherwise intelligent people not understand the simple truth of the gospel.[8]

Jesus also promised that he would send his Spirit to them and that this would not be possible unless he went away. He even said that this would be better for them and that the Spirit would lead them into all truth. This enabled some of them to write the New Testament for us so we would have an objective source of truth to live by (see John 14–16).

On the night that he would be betrayed, Jesus promised that he would rise again and that his followers would also share in his future glory. Jesus looked through the agony of the cross and saw it as enabling his glorification, which obviously presupposed his resurrection:

> Father, the hour has come; glorify your Son that the Son may glorify you, since you have given him authority over all flesh, to give eternal life to all whom you have given him. And this is eternal life, that they know you the only true God, and Jesus Christ whom you have sent. I glorified you on earth, having accomplished the work that you gave

---

[8]See 2 Corinthians 4:3–5.

me to do. And now, Father, glorify me in your own presence with the glory that I had with you before the world existed. . . .

Father, I desire that they also, whom you have given me, may be with me where I am, to see my glory that you have given me because you loved me before the foundation of the world. (John 17:1–5, 24)

These wonderful words promise us an eternal future of joy with our Savior united with God. However, for this to be accomplished Jesus knew he must first experience the agony of the cross. His words later that night in the Garden of Gethsemane should be seen in the context of his faith in a glorious future resurrection. He is, however, painfully aware of the cup of God's wrath that must first be drained by him for his people to enjoy this wonderful future. It really was for the joy that was set before him that he endured the cross (see Hebrews 12:2). It was essential that the punishment was to be borne in this way so that we could experience new life. The words of Jesus' prayer are all the more poignant if we understand just what was at stake and what he was suffering for:

My Father, if it be possible, let this cup pass from me; nevertheless, not as I will, but as you will. . . . My Father, if this cannot pass unless I drink it, your will be done. (Matthew 26:39–42)

The resurrection of Jesus is the key event in human history that makes sense of all the Old Testament references to resurrection, and the rest of the New Testament's teaching flows from this event.

CHAPTER EIGHT

WHAT DID THE RESURRECTION EVER DO FOR US?

God raised him up, loosing the pangs of death,
because it was not possible for him to be held by it.

ACTS 2:24

IN A FAMOUS BRITISH comedy sketch from *Monty Python's Flying Circus*, a group of first-century Jews repeatedly ask, "What have the Romans ever done for us?" Each time another positive result of the Roman occupation is mentioned, such as roads or aqueducts, the reply is always, "Well, apart from *that*, what have they done for us?"

This humorous scene illustrates how easily we can assume things without ever realizing their full impact on our lives. We could similarly ask ourselves, what has the resurrection of Jesus done for us? All Christians believe in Jesus' resurrection, but how does it affect us on a daily basis? The significance of the resurrection may actually be much greater than we fully appreciate.

As I studied the apostles' preaching in Acts, I discovered something of a parallel with this piece of comedy. Each sermon makes Jesus' resurrection its focus, but it also highlights a particular aspect of what the resurrection accomplished. Sermon by sermon, line by line, I found myself saying something like, "Well, yes, I suppose I *did* realize that Christ's resurrection did do that for me." But prior to that study I had definitely spent more time thinking about what Jesus' *death* had achieved. While his resurrection was in the back of my mind, I was inclined to simply feel glad that Jesus was no longer dead, rather than giving much thought to how the resurrection might impact me personally.

You may find yourself in a similar position. Like the Monty Python characters, you may already be aware of the things accomplished by the resurrection of Jesus. But like me, perhaps you haven't firmly grasped how crucial the resurrection is to your salvation. Paul tells us, "If Christ has not been raised, your faith is futile and you are still in your sins" (1 Corinthians 15:17). Without the resurrection there is no salvation. The cross functioning alone, apart from the resurrection, would have no power to be of any benefit to us.

We will now examine each occasion in Acts when the apostles addressed the crowds to discover how these resurrection-focused sermons answer this question: What are the implications of the resurrection for us? We could rephrase the question like this: What is the resurrected Jesus *doing for us now*? Before the crucifixion, Jesus promised, "*I will build my church*" (Matthew 16:18). Although hidden from public view, Jesus is alive, and his work is far from over. The sermons in Acts, taken together, are recorded to help us understand just how active he is.

Luke could easily have titled his second book, "The Ongoing Acts of Jesus." We see this from the opening verses, which refer to the Gospel of Luke: "In the first book, O Theophilus, I have dealt with all that Jesus *began* to do and teach, until the day when he was taken up" (Acts 1:1–2). The implication is that in this, his second book, he will deal with all that Jesus *continued* to do during the early years of church history.

It is impossible to overstate the importance of the bodily resurrection of Jesus to the apostles and the early church. The church was birthed through the resurrection of Jesus. Before the resurrection they were ashamed, terrified, and disorganized and had deserted Jesus. The resurrection and subsequent empowering with the Spirit transformed them forever.

Remember that Jesus' disciples had been brought up as Jews. Without the reality of the resurrection it is unthinkable that they would change so much about the faith they had inherited. They began to worship a man as God, ate forbidden foods, and even changed their main day of worship. Only the resurrection could have led them to change their meeting day from the Jewish Sabbath (Saturday) to a weekly celebration of the resurrection of Jesus on Sunday.

The early believers reportedly met before dawn on Sunday mornings. As they watched the sunrise, it would mirror to them the glorious rebirth of creation begun by Christ's victory over death. But more important than all those changes is the fact that the disciples had a very simple message for their early listeners, one that focused almost entirely on the announcement that Jesus had risen from the dead. It's not surprising then that the apostles' job description at the beginning of Acts is simply, *witnesses to his resurrection* (Acts 1:22).

Although we may not be eyewitnesses of the resurrection in the way the apostles were, our task is to proclaim this same message: *Christ is risen!* Yet today we often don't seem to emphasize this aspect of the gospel. We can learn much, therefore, from the style and content of the sermons in Acts.

The apostles were preoccupied by the resurrection and emphasized it much more than the cross. We need to be careful here, as Luke does not record complete accounts of everything that was said, and the apostles were aware that their listeners had already heard of the death of the man from Galilee. Luke summarizes their preaching style: "with great power the apostles were giving their testimony to the resurrection of the Lord Jesus" (Acts 4:33). In these messages the resurrection is stressed and the cross is assumed. Much of the preaching of the gospel today would reverse that emphasis, stressing the cross while assuming the resurrection.

As we examine each of these sermons, both to confirm their emphasis on the resurrection and to identify specifically what the resurrection accomplished for us, we will discover just how Christ's victory over death can impact our lives today.

PETER'S MESSAGE ON THE DAY OF PENTECOST

On the Day of Pentecost, Peter addressed a crowd of people gathered in Jerusalem who were bewildered by the coming of the Holy Spirit. He began by explaining this and then turned to speak of the death of Jesus. Nowhere in this address did he assert that it is the *death* of Jesus that brings us salvation. Instead, a significant part of his sermon focused on the resurrection, beginning with, "God raised him up, loosing the pangs of death, because it was not possible for him to be held by it"

(Acts 2:24). Peter referred to two of the psalms of David that predicted the resurrection of Jesus.

But perhaps the most surprising aspect of Peter's sermon was when he said, "Being therefore exalted at the right hand of God, and having received from the Father the promise of the Holy Spirit, he has poured out this that you yourselves are seeing and hearing" (v. 33).

This set the pattern for the remaining sermons preached in Acts. Peter was not content to merely tell his listeners that Jesus was raised. Rather, he told them about the implications of that resurrection for them. The risen Christ had done something wonderful for them—he had poured out the Holy Spirit! That act was explicitly connected with Jesus having been raised from the dead and exalted to the right hand of God, where he then received the Spirit from the Father and poured him out (v. 33).

Peter stated that the resurrection was the necessary precursor that enabled believers to receive the Holy Spirit. He went on to state that this promise is available to all believers. This has enormous implications for Christians today. We have seen, then, in this first sermon in Acts that the sending of the Holy Spirit was a direct result of the resurrection of Jesus Christ.

PETER'S MESSAGES AFTER THE HEALING OF THE LAME MAN

Here Peter once again used the resurrection as the climax of his sermon and linked it directly to a healing: "And you killed the Author of life, whom God raised from the dead. To this we are witnesses. And his name—by faith in his name—has made this man strong whom you see and know, and the faith that is through Jesus has given the man this perfect health in the presence of you all" (Acts 3:15–16). The power of Jesus' resurrection was revealed through a miraculous healing.

Jesus was described here as "the Author of life," which raises the question, how could he then have died at all? Peter didn't answer that question but instead declared boldly that this source of all life could not be restrained by any tomb and was raised to life by God. Having experienced death, Jesus is now alive and has defeated death and sickness. Jesus is not a departed dead hero. He is still with us, victoriously alive and fully active. When Peter used terms like "faith in his name" and healing being given "through Jesus," he was effectively saying, "We are not the ones who have done this; rather it was Jesus whom you killed and who has now been raised. It is he who has done this!"

Peter claimed that this healing was a direct result of faith in Jesus, who would be powerless to perform miracles if he was still rotting in a tomb somewhere in Palestine. Later, when challenged by the Jewish leaders regarding the healing, Peter emphasized that it was through the crucified and now resurrected Jesus that this man had been healed: "By the name of Jesus Christ of Nazareth, whom you crucified, whom God raised from the dead—by him this man is standing before you well" (Acts 4:10). Healing is repeatedly described as a direct result of faith in the resurrected Jesus. Because of the resurrection, Peter was saying, the man Jesus, who was crucified, was still able to heal as he did during his earthly ministry.

Peter's emphasis was also on the direct link between salvation and the resurrection. When Peter first responded to accusations about this healing of the lame man, he said, "God, having raised up his servant, sent him to you first, to bless you by turning every one of you from your wickedness" (Acts 3:26). Peter stressed the fact that Jesus was raised and still had work to do. Conversion is not described as an act of man in response to hearing about the death of Jesus but rather as an act of the resurrected Jesus himself. God raised him from the dead so that Jesus could save us.

Peter's second speech to the council regarding the healing of the lame man had a similar emphasis: "This Jesus is the stone that was rejected by you, the builders, which has become the cornerstone. And *there is salvation in no one else*, for there is no other name under heaven given among men by which we must be saved" (Acts 4:11–12).

Despite his death, Jesus is now the most important being in the universe, "the cornerstone." Not only that, by saying our salvation is "in" Jesus, Peter was referring to a recurring New Testament theme—we are saved by being united with or hidden in Christ. Peter pointed out that our salvation is possible only in union with the *risen* Christ. Jesus, crucified, was like a rejected stone, and having been raised to life he is now the bedrock of our salvation. Peter again showed that Jesus is still active in saving us by stating that it is in the "name" of Jesus that we are saved. He could have said, "Thanks to the death of Jesus, it is now possible for us to be saved." Instead, however, he said something like, "Because Jesus has been raised from the dead, he now has the power and authority to save us."

ANOTHER DEFENSE BEFORE THE COUNCIL

Peter later found himself again in front of the Jewish leaders following an arrest and an angelic release. Peter referred to conversion as being a direct act of the resurrected Jesus when he said, "The God of our fathers raised Jesus, whom you killed by hanging him on a tree. God exalted him at his right hand as Leader and Savior, *to give repentance* to Israel and forgiveness of sins" (Acts 5:30–31). It is the risen and exalted Jesus himself who grants us repentance and proclaims our forgiveness. He is the Leader and Head of his church. The risen Christ is building his church. We are under his authority. When things do not seem to be going according to plan, remembering that Jesus is in control gives us the faith we need. We do not serve the memory of a dead teacher; rather we serve at the pleasure of a risen Master.

STEPHEN'S MARTYRDOM

In Acts 7 the resurrected and ascended Jesus appeared to Stephen who had been arrested and called to give an account of his actions to his captors before being stoned to death. Stephen preached a sermon that confronted the people with their role in the death of Jesus. They were enraged at what he had said and ground their teeth at him. It does not appear that he had finished his speech, but Jesus interrupted the proceedings, and as Luke tells us, "He [Stephen], full of the Holy Spirit, gazed into heaven and saw the glory of God, and Jesus standing at the right hand of God. And he said, 'Behold, I see the heavens opened, and the Son of Man standing at the right hand of God'" (Acts 7:55–56).

The risen Jesus supplied Stephen with an extraordinary confidence that he would be welcomed into heaven by his Lord. Jesus empowered Stephen to pray both for his persecutors and for himself and then to cry out, "Lord Jesus, receive my spirit" (Acts 7:59). Jesus often provides such glimpses, even if on a less dramatic scale, to believers before death.

The remarkable assurance of many martyrs at the time of their execution is legendary, and many of them spoke with absolute certainty that Jesus would receive them into heaven. The resurrection of Jesus brings comfort and boldness and confidence, even when facing death.

THE CALL OF THE APOSTLE PAUL

The resurrection of Jesus also led to the commissioning of great messengers of the gospel, not least the apostle Paul (also called Saul). Having appeared to Stephen, the risen Jesus now specifically answered his dying prayer—that his persecutors would be forgiven. The glorified Jesus personally confronted one of these tormenters, a young man who had stood watching while Stephen was being stoned. On the road to Damascus, Jesus appeared to Saul, saying, "Saul, Saul, why are you persecuting me?" He then identified himself, saying, "I am Jesus, whom you are persecuting. But rise and enter the city, and you will be told what you are to do" (Acts 9:4–6).

Saul, the persecutor, was arrested by the persecuted. The Lord Jesus told Saul that by oppressing his church, he was opposing Christ himself. This is a stunning confirmation of the union between believers and their risen Lord. The relationship between Jesus and his people is so intimate that they are often described in the Bible as his body. When Saul persecuted and killed members of Jesus' body on earth, their Head in heaven felt the pain.

It is not possible to understand Saul's transformation from persecuting Pharisee to passionate preacher without this encounter with the resurrected Jesus. This simple statement about Jesus summarizes Saul's first proclamation: "He is the Son of God" (Acts 9:20). The use of the present tense here is a claim for the resurrection. Paul did not say, as the centurion who witnessed Jesus' death did, that he "*was* the son of God" (Mark 15:39), which would imply that Jesus was still dead.

In this whole event we see the risen and glorified Jesus implementing his authority as Head of the church, putting an end to a period of suffering, and calling the church's greatest human enemy to become one of his greatest ever servants. Jesus commissioned Paul as a messenger of the good news of his resurrection.

PETER'S MESSAGE AT JOPPA

Peter was sent to Cornelius' house by a divine command and subsequently began to preach to the Gentiles. He described another effect of the resurrection of Jesus: "They put him to death by hanging him on a tree, but God raised him on the third day and made him to appear, not to all the people, but to us who had been chosen by God as witnesses, who ate and drank with him after he rose from the dead. And *he commanded us to preach* to the people and to testify that he is the one appointed by God to be judge of the living and the dead" (Acts 10:39–42).

Again, as a direct result of the resurrection, Jesus commissioned and still sends messengers into the world to declare the good news. Before his ascension he promised that he would be with us always to ensure that the gospel would be preached and his mission fulfilled (Matthew 28:18–20). Throughout church history Jesus himself has been sending messengers to preach the good news of salvation. They may not have seen the risen Jesus with their own eyes or had a call as dramatic as Peter's or Paul's, but they were, nonetheless, certain that Jesus had appointed them too. Lives are dramatically changed today because Jesus himself still calls, commissions, and sends his messengers into the world to share the good news. Without a call, there would be no preachers. Without people who are willing to share the message with both individuals and multitudes, there would be no church (see Romans 10:14–15).

PAUL'S MESSAGE AT ANTIOCH IN PISIDIA

Paul's first recorded public address occurred during the second stop of his first missionary journey. He built further on the idea that salvation comes through the inherent power of Jesus' resurrection. We have already seen that forgiveness is through and by Jesus. We now also see that the believer can be made free: "He whom God raised up did not see corruption. Let it be known to you therefore, brothers, that through this man forgiveness of sins is proclaimed to you, and by him everyone who believes is freed from everything from which you could not be freed by the law of Moses" (Acts 13:37–39).

The word "freed" here is often translated as "justified," and it is only because of the sentence structure that translators conclude that here it means freed.[1] This helps us to see that for Paul, salvation is not just about being declared righteous, it is also about being set free.

This echoes Paul's letter to the Romans, where he says:

> There is therefore now no condemnation for those who are in Christ Jesus. For the law of the Spirit of life has set you free in Christ Jesus from the law of sin and death. For God has done what the law, weakened by the flesh, could not do. By sending his own Son in the likeness of sinful flesh and for sin, he condemned sin in the flesh, in order that the righteous requirement of the law might be fulfilled in us, who walk not according to the flesh but according to the Spirit. (8:1–4)

There are two specific things from which we are freed—the *power* and the *consequences* of sin. There seems little doubt, therefore, that when Paul spoke of our being "freed" in Acts 13, he had in mind not a theoretical freedom, but one that enables us to live godly lives. In other words, in addition to justification, he is referring to the progressive freedom from the drive to sin. Theologians call this *sanctification*. We are actively freed from our bondage to sin by what Christ has done for us, and thus righteous living becomes possible. The same Jesus who died to bear the punishment for our sin lives to ensure that we are transformed daily into ever-increasing holiness.

PAUL'S MESSAGE IN THESSALONICA

Luke records a useful summary of Paul's entire preaching ministry: "He reasoned with them from the Scriptures, explaining and proving that it was necessary for the Christ to suffer and to rise from the dead, and saying, 'This Jesus, whom I proclaim to you, is the Christ'" (Acts 17:2–3).

In this summary the death and the resurrection of Jesus are mentioned together. It is one of the rare occasions in Acts where Jesus' death is given equal prominence with the resurrection. We also see that the Old Testament Scriptures were used. The aim is again to announce an event or tell a story. Although the apostles did preach about what this story has done for us, the overriding emphasis in all of these messages has been to announce the news and to introduce listeners to a living person who can save them.

---

[1]See Spiros Zodhiates, *The Complete Word Study Dictionary: New Testament*, electronic edition (Chattanooga: AMG Publishers, 1992, 1993, 2000), G1344. The same structure is used in Romans 6:18.

PAUL IN ATHENS

An intriguing misunderstanding in Athens provided a fascinating glimpse into the centrality of the resurrection to Paul. Mistakenly, some who heard him concluded, "'He seems to be a preacher of foreign divinities'—because he was preaching *Jesus* and *the resurrection*" (Acts 17:18). Many have argued that the Athenians believed he had preached about two gods, "Jesus" and "Resurrection." This confused notion is amusing and demonstrates the prevalence of the word *resurrection* in Paul's preaching.

Later in the same chapter we have the famous address by Paul to the Athenians, which took place at the Areopagus or Mars Hill. Much attention is given to Paul's ingenious attempts to engage his audience by speaking in a way relevant to his culture. The whole missional approach to cultural engagement is in large part based on this event. We must, however, also pay attention to the conclusion of this message:

> [God] commands all people everywhere to repent, because he has fixed a day on which he will judge the world in righteousness by a man whom he has appointed; and of this he has given assurance to all by raising him from the dead. (Acts 17:30–31)

Jesus has been given a role that he obviously could not have performed had he remained dead. It will be Jesus himself—the one who can sympathize with all our weaknesses, having lived as a perfect man—who will be judge of the world. We can know this for sure, argued Paul, because Jesus has indeed been raised from the dead. How thoroughly we are convinced of the truth of the resurrection is directly related to how confident we are about our salvation. Our belief in the reality of the resurrection gives us confidence in the truth of the gospel.

A DEADLY SERMON AND RESURRECTIONS OCCURRING IN ACTS

Many preachers love to refer to Acts 20:7–12. Paul, knowing he was leaving the church he had fathered, gave them the greatest gift he could. He was passionate about declaring and explaining God's Word and therefore spent a long evening preaching to them. As a result, his teaching stretched on until midnight, and a young man sitting in a third-floor window fell asleep; he tumbled out of the window and was killed. After raising the young man back to life, Paul returned to his preaching and continued until morning.

This story has offered encouragement to preachers who like to give long sermons, and it has been heartening to know that even Paul could talk in such a way that one of his listeners dozed off. But as someone responded when I cited this story as a potential excuse for longer sermons, "By all means, preach long sermons, provided you can raise the dead!"

Dorcas, a much loved believer, was also raised from the dead in Acts 9:36–42. In both of the cases in Acts, news of these resurrections had a similar effect to hearing the news of Jesus' resurrection. In the Acts 20 story, people "were not a little comforted," while in Acts 9 "many believed" as a direct result of this news.

Christian preachers and all of us who want to share the good news with others individually should emulate the sermons of Acts, stressing more often than we do the fact that Jesus was raised from the dead and is alive today. There is a great potential for an increase in faith when this news is proclaimed.

PAUL'S DEFENSES BEFORE ROMAN JUDGES

The importance of resurrection to Paul was also shown by his shrewd but accurate declaration during his trial in Jerusalem: "It is with respect to the hope and the resurrection of the dead that I am on trial" (Acts 23:6). This was shrewd because it caused an argument between his accusers.

Later, when Paul was before a Roman judge in Acts 24, he similarly said, "But this I confess to you, that according to the Way, which they call a sect, I worship the God of our fathers, believing everything laid down by the Law and written in the Prophets, having a hope in God, which these men themselves accept, that there will be a resurrection of both the just and the unjust" (vv. 14–15). This statement implies that there will be a future judgment of all people by God.

After listening to his defenses, Paul's Roman judge had a clear understanding of the difference between Paul and his Jewish accusers. That distinction remains the crucial factor which distinguishes the Christian from the unbeliever:

> They had certain points of dispute with him about their own religion and about a certain Jesus, who was dead, but whom Paul asserted to be alive. (Acts 25:19)

A Christian is someone who asserts that Jesus was dead but is now alive and that as a result of this fact we can be saved. The question asked at the opening of this chapter was, *what, in light of all these sermons, has the resurrection of Jesus made possible for us?* We have seen that if Jesus had not been raised, none of the following things, listed in order of their appearance in Acts, would have been possible:

- The sending of the Spirit (Acts 2:33)
- Physical healings (Acts 3:15–16)
- The conversion of sinners (Acts 3:26)
- Salvation by union with Jesus (Acts 4:11–12)
- Jesus' role as the leader of his church (Acts 5:30–31; 9)
- Forgiveness of sins (Acts 5:30–31)
- Comfort for the dying (Acts 7)
- The commissioning of gospel messengers (Acts 9; 10:42)
- Freedom from the penalty and power of sin (Acts 13:37–39)
- Assurance that the gospel is true (Acts 17:31)
- Our own resurrection (Acts 17:31)
- Jesus' future judgment of this world (Acts 17:31)

CONCLUSION

In summary, because of his life, death, and resurrection, Jesus has brought God close to us. He remains active and is very much at work in the world through his Spirit. A heavy emphasis is placed on Jesus' resurrection throughout the book of Acts. We find the apostles proclaiming that because of the resurrection we can be saved. This is in strong contrast to much preaching today that stresses that Jesus saves us through his death. Of course, the apostles faced a different environment where people would have known of Jesus' death. It was only the resurrection that was shocking news, and we do only have summaries of these messages.

It is not too much of a stretch, however, to agree with Ladd who says, "The whole gospel is encapsulated in the proclamation of the resurrection of Jesus."[2] We should never neglect to stress how Jesus died and bore the punishment for our sins. But without any declaration that Jesus Christ has risen from the dead and is now reigning, the biblical gospel has not been preached at all.

In Acts, the emphasis on Jesus' resurrection as the source or foundation of salvation is so strong that we might wrongly conclude that the death of Jesus was almost incidental to our salvation. But Acts is not ignorant of the importance of the cross for our salvation. For example, when Paul speaks to the Ephesian elders he speaks of Jesus' church "which he obtained with his own blood" (Acts 20:28).

Conversely, we would be wrong to contrast the theology of Acts negatively with that of the epistles, which some have used to argue that it is the cross of Jesus, rather than his resurrection, that saves us. As we saw previously, when the New Testament writers refer to either the death or resurrection of Jesus they usually mean to infer both.[3] In the next chapter we will explore how *both* the cross *and* the resurrection are intertwined in producing our salvation.

---

[2]George Eldon Ladd, *I Believe in the Resurrection of Jesus* (London: Hodder and Stoughton, 1975), 41.
[3]See Chapter 5, pages 74–76.

CHAPTER NINE

RAISED FOR OUR JUSTIFICATION

*Jesus our Lord . . . was delivered up for our trespasses
and raised for our justification.*

ROMANS 4:24-25

JESUS' RESURRECTION IS NOT merely an event that simultaneously poses a challenge to us in our evangelism and a comfort to us in our faith. It also plays a vital role in saving us. This chapter will examine what Paul meant when he linked Jesus' resurrection and our justification. Christians are usually more comfortable with the idea that it is the cross that justifies. However, it is our union with Christ's obedient life, sacrificial death, *and* victorious resurrection that saves us. A developed doctrine of the resurrection need not downplay the central importance of the cross. As N. T. Wright said:

> For Paul, the resurrection of Jesus of Nazareth is the heart of the gospel (not to the exclusion of the cross, of course, but not least as the event which gives the cross its meaning). It is the object of faith, the ground of justification, the basis for obedient Christian living, the motivation for unity, and, not least, the challenge to the principalities and powers. It is the event that declares that there is "another king," and summons human beings to allegiance, and thereby to a different way of life, in fulfillment of the Jewish Scriptures and in expectation of the final new world which began at Easter and which will be completed when the night is finally gone and the day has fully dawned.[1]

Many commentaries do not discuss Romans 4:25 extensively.

---

[1]N. T. Wright, *The Resurrection of the Son of God* (London: SPCK, 2003), 266.

However, it seems to mark an important transition point in Paul's argument, as a conclusion and summary of the whole of chapters 1–4. Paul has been discussing how God can remain just while declaring us righteous. He then moves on to the implications of this doctrine in the rest of Romans. Some have argued that Romans is all about the implications of the resurrection of Jesus.[2] These few words are so essential to our correct understanding of Christian doctrine that some believe that Romans 4:25 was actually an early creed.[3]

Paul appears to make a distinction between the role of Jesus' death and of his resurrection in our salvation. Neither the cross nor the resurrection achieves anything without the other. However, perhaps the best description of the distinction we can make comes from Calvin:

> By his death sin was taken away, by his resurrection righteousness was renewed and restored. For how could he by dying have freed us from death, if he had yielded to its power? How could he have obtained the victory for us, if he had fallen in the contest? Our salvation may be thus divided between the death and the resurrection of Christ: by the former sin was abolished and death annihilated; by the latter righteousness was restored and life revived, the power and efficacy of the former being still bestowed upon us by means of the latter.[4]

Preacher Bill Johnson is said to have argued that the cross was for our old life and the resurrection for our new life. The cross deals with our guilt, and the resurrection gives us victory. In the cross we see Jesus the Son of God in apparent weakness. In Jesus' resurrection we see him revealed as the Son of God in power.

The resurrection forever explodes any ideas we might have of nature as a closed system where miracles can't happen. God is no clockmaker who has wound up the universe and left it running according to invisible laws. Seeing the power of God at work in the resurrection should make us wonder how we too can connect with this power. We will return to that question in a later chapter. For now we will examine Romans 4:25, and we will begin by asking what Paul means by justification.

---

[2] Ibid., 241: "Squeeze this letter at any point and resurrection spills out."
[3] See Michael Bird, "Raised for Our Justification: A Fresh Look at Romans 4:25," *Colloquium*, 35(1), 2003, 31–46.
[4] John Calvin, *Institutes of the Christian Religion*, II, xvi, 13.

WHAT IS JUSTIFICATION?

1. A Declaration of Righteousness

Justification is simply "the act of God declaring men free from guilt and acceptable to him."[5] It is not that God instantaneously changes us and makes us completely holy and sinless, but it is rather a declaration that God has changed our status because he credits Jesus' perfect righteousness to our account. This is not to say that at the moment of conversion we remain entirely the same, nor is it to deny that Christians have within them a divine impulse compelling them to change and become more holy. We are justified because we are incorporated into the people of God and have been made pure because of our connection with our Head, Jesus.

2. A Gift Purchased by Christ

Much in the Bible leads us to think quite correctly of justification as being accomplished by the cross. For example:

> [We are] justified by his grace as a gift, through the redemption that is in Christ Jesus, whom God put forward as a propitiation by his blood, to be received by faith. This was to show God's righteousness . . . so that he might be just and the justifier of the one who has faith in Jesus. (Romans 3:24–26)

Our justification was purchased by the punishment that Jesus received on the cross. As Isaiah says, "He was wounded for our transgressions; he was crushed for our iniquities; upon him was the chastisement that brought us peace . . . the LORD has laid on him the iniquity of us all. . . . Yet it was the will of the LORD to crush him; he has put him to grief . . . his soul makes an offering for guilt" (Isaiah 53:5–10).

Romans 4:25 tells us it is because of our sins that Jesus was killed. Death is not merely a natural phenomenon but a punishment for sin, since "the wages of sin is death" (Romans 6:23). Thus, we understand Jesus was taking our punishment since the sinless one did not deserve to die. Our gospel presentations must explain our predicament and the solution offered.

---

[5] James Strong, *The Exhaustive Concordance of the Bible*, electronic edition (Ontario: Woodside Bible Fellowship, 1996), G1347.

The most famous verse in the Bible says, "For God so loved the world, that he gave his only Son, that whoever believes in him should not perish but have eternal life" (John 3:16). Many assume this verse refers solely to Jesus' death. But it is the Son himself who is given to us. His perfect life was for us, his death and his resurrection were also for us, and even now in heaven he is still giving himself to us. He now lives inside us, and he intercedes for us. We receive Jesus and are saved by him by the complete work he has done and the applying of that work that he is still doing.

3. Justification Received through Faith

Our salvation depends not on good works or on any merit that God sees in us but rather on his free, undeserved mercy and grace. We do not contribute anything to our salvation but come to God with empty hands and a humble heart, asking for forgiveness. We are saved through the means of our faith.

> We know that a person is not justified by works of the law but through faith in Jesus Christ, so we also have believed in Christ Jesus, in order to be justified by faith in Christ and not by works of the law, because by works of the law no one will be justified. (Galatians 2:16)

Some believe justification is a final end-time event before the judgment seat of Christ when we will be declared to be righteous. However, for the true Christian any final justification is merely the implementation of a declaration made by God the moment that faith is born in a believer's heart. We will be no more justified then than we are already now. No future act of obedience will make God more pleased with us or make us more saved than we are now. Yes, the full effects of our justification will only be ours in that glorious future, but we can also taste the reality of our salvation right now as our standing before God is entirely the same. B. B. Warfield states:

> There is nothing in us or done by us, at any stage of our earthly development, because of which we are acceptable to God. We must always be accepted for Christ's sake, or we cannot be accepted at all. This is not true of us only when we believe. It is just as true after we have believed. It will continue to be true as long as we live. Our need

of Christ does not cease with our believing, nor does the nature of our relation to him or to God through him ever alter, no matter what our attainments in Christian graces or our achievements in behavior may be. It is always on His blood and righteousness alone that we can rest.[6]

WHAT DOES "RAISED *FOR* OUR JUSTIFICATION" MEAN?

In Romans 4:25 the Greek behind our English word "for" could mean either "because of" or "in order to produce." The ESV here, as it often does, deliberately maintains the ambiguity of the original. Some have argued that both "fors" must mean the same thing. However, Jesus' death did not produce sin in us, and surely Jesus' resurrection was not as a result of our justification. It is almost certainly the case that Paul intended to say that Jesus died to deal with our sin and was raised to produce our justification. In the rest of this chapter I will explore several aspects of that link between Jesus' resurrection and our justification, which seems to have many facets.

1. Raised to Give Us a Future Resurrection

Some believe that "justification" here includes the future result of our justification, our resurrection. Because of Jesus' resurrection, one day our physical bodies will also return to life. There are more straightforward ways of saying this, however, which means that it is unlikely that this first suggestion is what Paul intended here.

2. Raised to Prompt Faith in Us

The resurrection of Jesus has faith-giving power. It is the good news of Jesus' resurrection, following his sin-defeating death, that will inspire us to believe in, trust, obey, and worship this man who lived two thousand years ago in a small country in the Middle East. Thus, hearing about the resurrection of Jesus has power to save. Like the cross, it challenges the mind and is mocked by the skeptic. Yet, even the skeptics have little to say to counter this message. They would much rather speak with us

---

[6]B. B. Warfield, *The Works of Benjamin B. Warfield* (Grand Rapids: Baker, 1931, reprint 1991), 7:113.

about any other subject than the key question, did Jesus rise from the dead?

Justification is "by grace . . . through faith" (Ephesians 2:8), and our faith itself requires the resurrection of Jesus. Unless Jesus had defeated death, we could never have the faith in him that is necessary for our justification. It seems impossible to imagine having faith in a dead Savior. How could we convince ourselves that Jesus' death achieved anything for us if he was not alive? One scholar explained that "the resurrection was needed to actualize [justification], since faith is kindled only by the resurrection, a corpse being no true object of faith."[7] Calvin also understood the importance of the resurrection in creating faith:

> For seeing that in the cross, death, and burial of Christ, nothing but weakness appears, faith must go beyond all these, in order that it may be provided with full strength . . . as he, by rising again, became victorious over death, so the victory of our faith consists only in his resurrection.[8]

Because of Jesus' resurrection, we can have confidence that we too will be raised. The resurrection causes in us the faith that saves, and it is faith in the resurrection itself that saves. According to Romans, the substance of a saving response to God consists of a declaration of the lordship of Jesus, which presumably includes both his divinity and his right to rule over our lives, and faith in the fact of the resurrection. Thus Jesus' resurrection is in this sense the source of the faith that is the grounds of our justification: "If you confess with your mouth that Jesus is Lord and believe in your heart that God raised him from the dead, you will be saved" (Romans 10:9).

3. Raised for His Own Justification

It may sound strange to talk about Jesus' need for justification. But justification is a declaration, a vindication. The resurrection of Jesus has evidencing power. In one place, Edwards interprets Romans 4:25 as meaning that "his resurrection is a glorious evidence of, and therefore

---

[7]Gerhard Kittel et al., *Theological Dictionary of the New Testament* (Grand Rapids: Eerdmans, 1964-c1976), 2:224.
[8]Calvin, *Institutes of the Christian Religion*, II, xvi, 13.

is called, his justification."[9] In this sense, justification is a proof that he is who he said he was. Spurgeon explained, "Nobody witnessing our Lord's resurrection could doubt his divine character, and that his mission upon earth was from the eternal God."[10] We see this concept in Paul's letters:

> [He] was declared to be the Son of God in power according to the Spirit of holiness by his resurrection from the dead, Jesus Christ our Lord. (Romans 1:4)

> Great indeed, we confess, is the mystery of godliness: He was manifested in the flesh, vindicated by the Spirit . . . taken up in glory. (1 Timothy 3:16)

As one scholar said, "God's final verdict on his Son is not seen in the cross, but in the resurrection."[11] If Jesus wasn't who he said he was, then how could he have saved us? Jesus' vindication convinces us that he is the Messiah, the Son of God, the Prince of Life, that he had fulfilled Scripture, that God was pleased with him, that the work of the cross was now complete, and that he had no need to remain dead.

The resurrection proves Christ's divinity because not only is the event described as an act of God (see Acts 13:30) and of the Holy Spirit (see Romans 8:11), it was also an act of Jesus himself. The resurrection, as the beginning of the new creation, was an act of the whole Trinity. Jesus has the divine power to raise himself from the dead:

> I lay down my life that I may take it up again. No one takes it from me, but I lay it down of my own accord. I have authority to lay it down, and I have authority to take it up again. (John 10:17–18)

It is important that we understand Jesus' status on the cross. Two things were simultaneously true. He was still the only sinless man who had ever lived. He had not committed any wrong and had lived a life of righteousness that had warranted merit and reward from God. He,

---

[9]Jonathan Edwards, *Notes on Scripture*, WJE Online, Vol. 15, 286; http://edwards.yale.edu/archive?path=aHR0cDovL2Vkd2FyZHMueWFsZS5lZHUvY2dpLWJpbi9uZXdaGlsby9nZXRvYmplY3QucGw/Yy4xNDozLndqZW8=.

[10]C. H. Spurgeon, *Sermon No. 2080*, "The Power of His Resurrection," delivered on April 21, 1889 at the Metropolitan Tabernacle, Newington; http://www.recoverthegospel.com/Old%20Recover%20the%20Gospel%20Site/Spurgeon/Spurgeon%202001-3000/2080.pdf.

[11]D. A. Carson, *New Bible Commentary* (Leicester, UK: Inter-Varsity, 1994), on Acts 2:1.

however, also took our sin and bore our punishment. He remained at all times the holy Son of God who was unstained by sin. Yet he was voluntarily "made" sin (2 Corinthians 5:21) and so was simultaneously subject to the wrath, rejection, and punishment of God.

Yet his Father never stopped loving him. God did not permanently reject him. Jesus cried out, "My God, my God, why have you forsaken me?" because at that moment it was as though a rift had opened in the Trinity and God really did turn his back on him. However, the Trinity did not in any sense break up. Some ask, how could God be displeased with his Son on the cross? The answer is that God was displeased with the sin that Jesus was carrying but remained pleased with Jesus' infinite goodness, which was greater than that sin. Jesus bore the wrath of God against our sin, which had been imputed to him. Calvin elaborates:

> We do not, however, insinuate that God was ever hostile to him or angry with him. How could he be angry with the beloved Son, with whom his soul was well pleased? Or how could he have appeased the Father by his intercession for others if he were hostile to himself? But this we say, that he bore the weight of the divine anger, that, smitten and afflicted, he experienced all the signs of an angry and avenging God.[12]

The credit of Jesus' righteousness is much larger than the debt of our sin. His account had more positive approval than the negative disapproval that was due to all of us. The debt was paid, and as a result, as a righteous man and the beloved Son of God, the Father was entirely just to raise him. Jesus had turned away God's wrath, he had destroyed sin, our guilt could now be taken away, and we could be counted righteous. If the cross was Jesus' payment for our sins, then the resurrection marked God's acceptance of that payment.

Jesus is declared to still be righteous by his resurrection, just as he was declared to have become sin by his death. God's wrath has been satisfied. Jonathan Edwards explains:

> Great stress seems to be put upon the resurrection of Christ everywhere in the New Testament, as if it were what had great influence unto our salvation. For if Christ were not risen, it would be evidence

---

[12]Calvin, *Institutes of the Christian Religion*, II, xvi, 11.

that God was not yet satisfied for [our] sins. Now the resurrection is God declaring his satisfaction; he thereby declared that it was enough; Christ was thereby released from his work; Christ, as he was Mediator, is thereby justified.[13]

The resurrection was more than simply the evidence of Jesus' justification. It was an active demonstration and itself made it real. For example, a prisoner in the dock is only justified and vindicated when he is freed and released. Dr. Martyn Lloyd-Jones explains:

If the Lord Jesus Christ had not literally risen physically from the grave, we could never be certain that he had ever really finished the work . . . if he has died for our sins, we must not only be certain that he has died, but that he has finished dying, and that there is no longer death . . . when God raised his Son from the dead, he was proclaiming to the whole world . . . he has done everything. He has fulfilled every demand. Here he is risen—therefore I am satisfied with him. . . .

The devil cannot hold him; death and hell cannot hold him. He has mastered them all; he has emerged on the other side. He is the Son of God, and he has completed the work which the Father had sent him to do. . . . It is only in the light of the Resurrection that I finally have an assurance of my sins forgiven. It is only in the light of the Resurrection that I ultimately know that I stand in the presence of God absolved from guilt and shame and every condemnation.

If it is not a fact that Christ literally rose from the grave, then you are still guilty before God. Your punishment has not been borne, your sins have not been dealt with, you are yet in your sins. It matters that much: without the Resurrection you have no standing at all.[14]

4. Justified So We Can Be Justified

The resurrection of Jesus has justifying power. Despite our usual understanding that the cross alone is responsible for our forgiveness, Paul is elsewhere very clear. "If Christ has not been raised, your faith is futile and you are still in your sins" (1 Corinthians 15:17). We share in the justification of Jesus. Because of his right standing with God, his people are made righteous too.

---

[13]Jonathan Edwards, *The Miscellanies*, WJE Online, Vol. 13, 227; http://edwards.yale.edu/archive?path=aHR0cDovL2Vkd2FyZHMueWFsZS5lZHUvY2dpLWJpbi9uZXdwaGlsby9nZXRvYmplY3QucGw/Yy44xMjo0OjE6OTU0ud2plbw==.

[14]Martyn Lloyd-Jones, *The Assurance of Our Salvation* (Wheaton, IL: Crossway, 2000), 492.

Unless Jesus himself had been justified, it is impossible to see how we could have been. If he could not even save himself, how could he save others? The resurrection shows the positive delight of God in his Son, which is now shared by us. Many people think of salvation as the removal of our sin and its punishment. If Jesus had only wiped the slate clean, forgiven our wrongdoing, and taken the wrath God had for us, we would be left in a neutral position. We would no longer be under God's displeasure, but he would not be pleased with us either. Many Christians, even if they do not articulate their theology like that, certainly live as though it was true. Many live as though they must still work to please God.

The resurrection was necessary to allow the credit of Jesus' righteousness to be shared with us, for it demonstrated that the credit was greater than the debt. Jesus' favor still remained when sin was destroyed. God's hatred for sin was not greater than his love for his Son. Righteousness remained available to credit to our account.

Jesus was so full of merit that not only did he have enough righteousness to cancel out our sin and enough that he deserved to be raised from the dead, but he still had abundantly more credit remaining in his account. As a result, our justification consists not just of a canceling of our debt, but also of an imputing to us of the righteousness of Christ. It is not only "just as if I'd never sinned," but also "just as if I'd already completed a perfect life." Jesus doesn't merely give us a clean slate and then sit back and watch whether we will mess it up again.

If you think of sin as producing an overdraft, Jesus takes over our bank account and pays off our debt. He then gives us access to his own account which holds so much money that no matter how much sin we commit we could never exhaust the supply. But those who know they have been the recipients of such grace do not live to scorn the giver. Jesus' resurrection itself is imputed to us, declaring us eternally righteous, not merely forgiven of past sin. John Piper explains:

> In historic Reformed exegesis, (1) a person is in union with Christ by faith alone. In this union, (2) the believer is identified with Christ in his (a) wrath-absorbing death, (b) his perfect obedience to the Father, and (c) his vindication-securing resurrection. All of these are reckoned—that is, imputed—to the believer in Christ. On this basis,

(3) the "dead," "righteous," "raised" believer is accepted and assured of final vindication and eternal fellowship with God.[15]

Piper states that the resurrection, as well as the death of Jesus, has been credited to our account so that we might be justified. I wonder how often our presentations of the gospel include the concept of Jesus' resurrection being credited to our account.

The righteousness of Jesus was credited to us, not only our sin to him. God declares his positive favor toward us, and as a result we will ultimately never die. Life is the judicial reward for righteousness. Jesus was made to be sin, and so he died, but once sin was dealt with, he remained righteous. As a result he was raised. Spurgeon explains:

> As the rising of the sun removes the darkness, so the rising of Christ has removed our sin. The power of the resurrection of Christ is seen in the justifying of every believer; for the justification of the Representative is the virtual justification of all whom he represents.[16]

Jonathan Edwards says that Jesus' resurrection and glorification are part of his justification and that we too will share in that. To Edwards, justification consists of the declaration and the results of that declaration. What God proclaims becomes true in reality. When God says we are justified, by necessity he will grant us the reward of that justification. "The justification of a believer is no other than his being admitted to communion in, or participation of the justification of [Christ]."[17]

5. Raised So He Can Apply Justification to Us

We now turn to our own experience of receiving justification. It is important that we understand what saving faith looks like and what changes occur in us when we become Christians. Faith is putting our trust in the person Jesus and in the fact that he died and rose again for us. But we must understand, as Piper puts it, "what we believe in Jesus' death and resurrection *for*. It is not saving faith to believe in Jesus

[15]John Piper, *The Future of Justification* (Wheaton, IL: Crossway, 2007), 124–125.
[16]C. H. Spurgeon, *Sermon No. 2080*, "The Power of His Resurrection," delivered on April 21, 1889 at the Metropolitan Tabernacle, Newington; http://www.recoverthegospel.com/Old%20Recover%20the%20Gospel%20Site/Spurgeon/Spurgeon%202001-3000/2080.pdf.
[17]Jonathan Edwards, *Sermons and Discourses*, WJE Online, Vol. 19, 151–191; http://edwards.yale.edu/archive?path=aHR0cDovL2Vkd2FyZHMueWFsZS5lZHUvY2dpLWJpbi9uZXdwaGlssby9nZXRvYmplY3QucGw/Yy4xODo5OjE6MS53amVv.

merely for prosperity or health or a better marriage. . . .The summons, 'Believe the gospel of Jesus' death and resurrection' has no content that is yet clearly *good news*. Not until the gospel preacher tells the listener what Jesus offers him personally and freely does this proclamation have the quality of good news. . . . Of course, it is *Jesus* who saves, not the doctrine. And so our faith rests decisively on Jesus. But the doctrine tells us what sort of Jesus we are resting on and what we are resting on him for. Without this, the word *Jesus* has no content that could be good news."[18]

It is Jesus himself who saves the Christian, as these verses demonstrate:

> . . . to wait for his Son from heaven, whom he raised from the dead, Jesus who delivers us from the wrath to come. (1 Thessalonians 1:10)

> For the love of Christ controls us, because we have concluded this: that one has died for all, therefore all have died; and he died for all, that those who live might no longer live for themselves but for him who for their sake died and was raised. (2 Corinthians 5:14–15)

> Since, therefore, we have now been justified by his blood, *much more* shall we be saved by him from the wrath of God. For if while we were enemies we were reconciled to God by the death of his Son, *much more*, now that we are reconciled, shall we be saved by his life. (Romans 5:9–10)

The two phases of Jesus' saving work for us are described in complementary ways. It is the blood or death of Jesus that saves us, but we are "much more" saved by his life, since he himself continues to save us from the wrath of God. Would the teaching of the gospel in an average evangelical church today leave you with the idea that it is "much more" the resurrection that saves us than the cross?

In Isaiah 53, it is only after the resurrection of Jesus is prophesied in verse 10 that we read in verse 11, "by his knowledge shall the righteous one, my servant, make many to be accounted righteous." Thus, it is the task of Jesus, after he has risen, to justify us.[19]

Jesus himself saves us in the present. Our salvation is not some

---

[18]Piper, *The Future of Justification*, 86.
[19]*New Interpreters Bible*, Volume 10 (Nashville: Abingdon Press, 2002), 504.

automatic process that happens when we become convinced of certain intellectual truths about what Jesus did for us on the cross. Rather, we require saving by Jesus today. We need him to rescue us from God's wrath and to do something to us so that we can be saved. Spurgeon puts this with typical eloquence:

> You could not feel any confidence in a dead Christ; you would say, "He sees corruption, yet the true Christ was never to see corruption. He is dead; and what can a dead Christ do for us?" Beloved, the dying Christ has purchased for us our justification, but the risen Christ will see that we get it. The risen Christ has come to bring it to us, and herein we rest.
>
> Oh, that you would all rest in the finished work of Jesus on the cross, which is set forth to you in all its brightness by his rising again from the dead! Put the two parts of our text together, "Who was delivered for our offenses, and was raised again for our justification." You need them both, trust in them both; trust in the Savior who died upon the cross, and trust in the Christ who rose again, and is now the living Christ.[20]

Jonathan Edwards similarly said, "It was necessary in order to Christ's obtaining the end and effect of his purchase of redemption that he should rise from the dead; for God the Father had committed the whole affair of redemption, not only the purchasing of it but . . . the bestowment of the blessings purchased, that he should . . . bring about that which he died for."[21] This idea has been expressed in more modern language:

> He died to purchase what He rose again to apply. So it is that in a sense the resurrection of Christ is referred to as the cause of justification. It is doubtlessly true that Paul did not make an abstract separation between Christ's death and His resurrection, as if the death and the resurrection either had different motives or served ends separable from each other. Christ's work is one and its end is one. He both died and was raised for our justification, but the end effect was only through the resurrection.[22]

[20]Charles H. Spurgeon, *Spurgeon's Sermons*, Volume 40, electronic edition, Logos Library System (Albany, OR: Ages Software, 1998), Sermon No 2357.
[21]Jonathan Edwards, *A History of the Work of Redemption*, WJE Online, Vol. 9, 358; http://edwards.yale.edu/archive?path=aHR0cDovL2Vkd2FyZHMueWFsZS5lZHUvY2dpLWJpbi9uZXdwaGlsby9nZXRXb2plLnBsP3VydD0mamplY3QucGcmMTg6MS53am5Vv.
[22]Spiros Zodhiates, *The Complete Word Study Dictionary New Testament*, electronic edition (Chattanooga: AMG Publishers, 2000), G1347.

This reminds us once again that it is foolish to attempt to completely separate the work of Christ into two different parts. It is crazy to try and imagine what would have happened if Christ had not risen from the dead. Since Jesus applies our salvation actively, even if a potential salvation could somehow be purchased by Jesus' death, if he had not been raised there would have been no one able to apply it to us.

How does Jesus apply salvation to us? He prays on our behalf. Edwards comments on Romans 4:25, "That is, delivered for our offenses, and raised again that he might see to the application of his sufferings to our justification, and that he might plead them for our justifying."[23] Jesus is before the throne of God pleading for us, no doubt on the grounds of his death and resurrection. "Who is to condemn? Christ Jesus is the one who died—more than that, who was raised—who is at the right hand of God, who indeed is interceding for us" (Romans 8:34).

SAVED BY THE DEATH *AND* THE RESURRECTION

It is Jesus himself who saves us. We are united with him in both his death and his resurrection and so are saved. Romans 4:25, which we have been examining, seems to be designed to rescue us from two errors. Firstly, we could easily neglect either the death or the resurrection of Jesus and ascribe the work of salvation to only one of them. The verse says, "[He was] delivered up for our trespasses *and* raised for our justification." The second error is clearly explained by two different scholars.

F. F. Bruce: "We must not interpret the two clauses so woodenly as to suggest that his resurrection had nothing to do with the atonement for their sins, and his death had nothing to do with their justification."[24]

Joseph Fitzmyer: "This verse is not to be understood as though Paul meant that human trespasses were removed by Christ's death and that human justification was achieved by his resurrection. They are so formulated in a literary parallelism both effects are to be ascribed to the death and the resurrection."[25]

Justification and forgiveness are entwined, and so too are the cross

---

[23]Jonathan Edwards, *The Miscellanies*, WJE Online, Vol. 13, 189; http://edwards.yale.edu/archive?path=aHR0cDovL2Vkd2FyZHMueWFsZS5lZHUvY2dpLWJpbi9uZXdwaGlsby9nZXRvYmplY3Gw/Yy4xMjo0OjE6NDEud2plbw==.
[24]F. F. Bruce, *The Letter of Paul to the Romans* (Leicester, UK: Inter-Varsity Press, 1985), 113.
[25]Joseph Fitzmyer, "Romans," in *The Anchor Bible* (New York: Doubleday, 1993), 389.

and the resurrection. Fitzmyer goes on to explain that there is an asymmetry to this, however, quoting Augustine:

> He did not say, he was handed over for our justification and rose for the sake of our sins. In his being handed over sin is mentioned; in his resurrection justice is mentioned. Therefore let sin die, and let justice rise.[26]

If we too quickly say it is the combined work of Jesus that saves us, there is a real danger we will make the resurrection a mere auxiliary to the cross. It is helpful to consider the work of the cross and resurrection and what they contribute to our salvation. However, the message we should take away is that it is union with Jesus himself, the one who died and was raised, that saves us.

As one commentator put it, "For Paul, the death and resurrection of Christ belong together, and the former without the latter would be of little significance. Therefore he rarely thinks of one without the other."[27]

Jesus is the one who delivers the verdict himself and declares us not guilty but instead righteous. It is he who grants repentance and forgiveness to us. As we shall explore in the next chapter, because of the risen Jesus we are born again. Thanks be to Jesus for all that he has accomplished for us: "God exalted him at his right hand as Leader and Savior, to give repentance . . . and forgiveness of sins" (Acts 5:31).

---

[26]Ibid., 389.
[27]Tremper Longman and David Garland, eds., *The Expositor's Bible Commentary, Romans-Galatians*, revised edition (Grand Rapids: Zondervan, 2007), 86.

CHAPTER TEN

RESURRECTED WITH JESUS

But God, being rich in mercy, because of the great love with which he loved us, even when we were dead in our trespasses, made us alive together with Christ—by grace you have been saved—and raised us up with him and seated us with him in the heavenly places in Christ Jesus.

EPHESIANS 2:4-6

If we have died with him, we will also live with him.

2 TIMOTHY 2:11

LEX LOIZIDES, AN EVANGELIST who preaches all over the world, describes what happens when we become Christians:

> Conversion is coming to faith in Christ, trusting him for forgiveness through his death and resurrection, repenting of your sinfulness and sins, and humbly asking for forgiveness, while believing that He hears you, and receives you. This trusting in Christ leads to a change of inclination towards following Jesus, and a teachability in the person's posture. You become like a child in that sense, and desire to learn how God wants you to live and seek to follow that, albeit imperfectly.
>
> This is all precipitated by an inward change of desire that causes you to want to be forgiven. So the new birth, as Jesus describes it, is the impartation of a new life—the dynamic, ultimately irrepressible seed of spiritual life—and this continually draws the believer to Christ, in pursuit of holiness, and ever on to fulfill Christ's commission on the earth. This dynamic new life will finally bring the believer home to Christ in eternity.[1]

---

[1] Lex Loizides, personal communication, 2009; see also http://lexloiz.wordpress.com.

We feel that we are choosing to respond to Christ's call, and yet it is God himself who is at work in us, changing us on the inside and causing us to be born again. As Jesus himself said:

> Do not marvel that I said to you, "*You must be born again.*" The wind blows where it wishes, and you hear its sound, but you do not know where it comes from or where it goes. So it is with everyone who is born of the Spirit. (John 3:7–8)

This act of God occurs through the resurrection of Jesus. "Blessed be the God and Father of our Lord Jesus Christ! According to his great mercy, he has caused us to be born again to a living hope through the resurrection of Jesus Christ from the dead" (1 Peter 1:3).

The same event is described in Ephesians 2 as a spiritual resurrection. This is consistent also with Jesus' description of someone who doesn't follow him as "dead" (see Luke 9:60). We who were dead to God are now alive to him. Mark Driscoll explains:

> Jesus' death on the cross paid the penalty for our sin. The result is forgiveness, justification, imputation of righteousness, and our acceptance as children into God's family with Jesus as our Lord and brother. Jesus' resurrection from death brings formerly dead people to life. The result is life, regeneration, and a new heart imparted to us by the power of the Holy Spirit. If the cross were the only work, then we'd be forgiven corpses. But through the resurrection, the very life of God has broken into this world to give us life that is new in character and eternal in duration.[2]

Jesus tells us that "whoever hears my word and believes him who sent me has eternal life. He does not come into judgment, but has passed from death to life" (John 5:24). The Christian is already no longer dead but alive! Thus to revisit the subject of the last chapter, one final way in which Jesus' resurrection is connected to our salvation is that he was resurrected so we could be raised with him. The resurrection of Jesus has life-giving power. Salvation is a miracle caused by the same creative power that conquered the grave.

---

[2]Mark Driscoll and Gerry Breshears, *Vintage Jesus* (Wheaton, IL: Crossway, 2007), 123.

WHY MUST WE BE BORN AGAIN?

In what I believe to be his most important book, *Finally Alive*, John Piper is eager to warn us that not everyone who goes to church is a true Christian. He says:

> [When anyone] uses the term born again to describe American church-goers whose lives are indistinguishable from the world, and who sin as much as the world, and sacrifice for others as little as the world, and embrace injustice as readily as the world, and covet things as greedily as the world, and enjoy God-ignoring entertainment as enthusiastically as the world—when the term born again is used to describe these professing Christians, [people are] making a profound mistake. It is using the biblical term born again in a way that would make it unrecognizable by Jesus and the biblical writers. . . .
>
> Instead of moving from a profession of faith, to the label born again, to the worldliness of these so-called born again people, to the conclusion that the new birth does not radically change people, the New Testament moves in the other direction. It moves from the absolute certainty that the new birth radically changes people, to the observation that many professing Christians are indeed . . . not radically changed, to the conclusion that they are not born again. The New Testament . . . does not defile the new birth with the worldliness of unregenerate, professing Christians.[3]

The frightening prospect that Piper describes is that many churches are full of people who have not actually been born again. To the Bible, the idea that Christians could remain the same as the world is totally alien.

> No one born of God makes a practice of sinning, for God's seed abides in him, and he cannot keep on sinning because he has been born of God. (1 John 3:9)

A divine impulse is implanted in us that works to transform our lives. Without it we are not true Christians. Could anything be worse than a preacher discovering on Judgment Day that many in his congregation were never connected with the resurrection life of Jesus? As my pastor, Tope Koleoso, replied without a moment's hesitation, "Yes, get-

---

[3]John Piper, *Finally Alive* (Ross-shire, Scotland: Christian Focus, 2009), 14–15.

ting there and discovering that he himself was not truly saved either."
Every preacher must begin by ensuring that he himself is saved, and then
focus on his hearers.

> Watch your life and doctrine closely. Persevere in them, because if you
> do, you will save both yourself and your hearers. (1 Timothy 4:16, NIV)

We must consider this subject extremely carefully. Piper lists ten
reasons why we need to experience a spiritual resurrection. Without
this new birth:

1. We are dead in trespasses and sins (Ephesians 2:1–2).
2. We are by nature children of wrath (Ephesians 2:3).
3. We love darkness and hate the light (John 3:19–20).
4. Our hearts are hard like stone (Ezekiel 36:26; Ephesians 4:18).
5. We are unable to submit to God or please God (Romans 8:7–8).
6. We are unable to accept the gospel (Ephesians 4:18; 1 Corinthians 2:14).
7. We are unable to come to Christ or embrace him as Lord (John 6:44, 65; 1 Corinthians 12:3).
8. We are slaves to sin (Romans 6:17).
9. We are slaves of Satan (Ephesians 2:1–2; 2 Timothy 2:24–26).
10. No good thing dwells in us (Romans 7:18).[4]

Regeneration is God's solution to all of these problems. It is God's
work to bring about a spiritual resurrection in us—bringing those who
are dead to him to life.

> But God, being rich in mercy, because of the great love with which
> he loved us, even when we were dead in our trespasses, made us alive
> together with Christ—by grace you have been saved—and raised us
> up with him and seated us with him in the heavenly places in Christ
> Jesus. (Ephesians 2:4–6)

When God declares the change in our status as righteous before
him, he also works in us to change our behavior. We are immediately
justified in status, and our righteous standing leads to our being changed
over time to become righteous in our actions. An inward change does
immediately occur that works within us, causing change that will lead to

---

[4]Ibid., 48–58.

changed behavior. Jesus tells us that this is a work of the Spirit intimately connected to Jesus' own words: "It is the Spirit who gives life; the flesh is no help at all. The words that I have spoken to you are spirit and life" (John 6:63). John Piper explains:

> The new birth is something that happens in us when the Holy Spirit takes our dead hearts and unites us to Christ by faith so that his life becomes our life. So it makes sense that Jesus must be raised from the dead if we are to have new life in union with him.[5]

Regeneration then is brought about by a spiritual connection to the life-giving power of the risen and ascended Christ. No wonder that Jesus said, "I am the resurrection and the life. Whoever believes in me, though he die, yet shall he live, and everyone who lives and believes in me shall never die" (John 11:25–26). It is impossible for such an event to leave us unchanged. Two things happen to us. God promises:

> I will sprinkle clean water on you, and you shall be clean from all your uncleanness, and from all your idols I will cleanse you. And I will give you a new heart, and a new spirit I will put within you. And I will remove the heart of stone from your flesh and give you a heart of flesh. And I will put my Spirit within you, and cause you to walk in my statutes and be careful to obey my rules. (Ezekiel 36:25–27)

Piper explains this: "in other words, the ones who will 'enter the kingdom' are those who have a newness that involves a *cleansing* from the old and a *creation* of the new."[6] He links this to Jesus' requirement in John 3 that we be washed by water and renewed by the Spirit. This new creation or spiritual resurrection is designed to free us from the slave-like compulsion to continue in sin.

> For if we have been united with him in a death like his, we shall certainly be united with him in a resurrection like his. We know that our old self was crucified with him in order that the body of sin might be brought to nothing, so that we would no longer be enslaved to sin. (Romans 6:5–6)

This freedom from sin is not an automatic thing, nor is it instan-

---

[5]Ibid., 83.
[6]Ibid., 40.

taneous. We have a part to play and will be fighting against sin all our earthly lives. That very determination to battle sin and our growing victory as we are transformed from one degree of glory to another (2 Corinthians 3:18) is one clear evidence that we have been born again.

> So you also must consider yourselves dead to sin and alive to God in Christ Jesus. Let not sin therefore reign in your mortal body, to make you obey its passions. Do not present your members to sin as instruments for unrighteousness, but present yourselves to God as those who have been brought from death to life, and your members to God as instruments for righteousness. (Romans 6:11–13)

All Christians have a new life within them. The Scripture tells us simply, "Whoever has the Son has life; whoever does not have the Son of God does not have life" (1 John 5:12). A simple definition of a Christian then is someone who "has" Jesus. Spurgeon takes up this point and explains the hope it gives us that others too can share in this wonderful good news:

> If you have Jesus Christ, you have the resurrection. Oh, that you might now realize what power lies in him who is the resurrection and the life! All the power there is in Christ is there for his people. . . . Christ has a life in himself, and he makes that life to flow into every part of his mystical body . . . you possess as a believer this day that same life which is inherent in the person of your glorious covenant Head. Moreover, our Lord has power to quicken whom he will. . . . If the salvation of souls depended upon the preacher, nobody would be saved; but when the preacher's Master comes with him, however feeble his utterance, the life flashes forth, and the dead are raised. . . . Our risen Redeemer is the Lord and Giver of life. What joy to Christian workers is found in the life-giving power of the resurrection![7]

HOW CAN WE BE SURE WE ARE BORN AGAIN?

A number of different factors contribute to our assurance, and it is wise to examine ourselves to be sure that we are saved. The answer to this vital question is, in one sense, devastatingly simple. We can know that we are born again when we have true faith in Jesus. John 3:16 says, "For

---

[7]C. H. Spurgeon, *Sermon No. 2080*, "The Power of His Resurrection," delivered on April 21, 1889 at the Metropolitan Tabernacle, Newington; http://www.recoverthegospel.com/Old%20Recover%20 the%20Gospel%20Site/Spurgeon/Spurgeon%202001-3000/2080.pdf.

God so loved the world, that he gave his only Son, that *whoever believes in him should not perish but have eternal life.*"

If we truly trust in Jesus to save us and give us eternal life, we can know that we are saved. We come to him, recognizing that salvation itself is his to grant, casting ourselves on his mercy and asking him to save us. We have nothing to offer him, but he will not turn away anyone who genuinely leans on him. The danger is complacency and an assumption that "of course" we have believed. The question, have I really been born again? should not be answered too hastily. Nonetheless, God wants us to experience the joy of being sure that we have been saved. We will return to the vital role of the Holy Spirit in this matter in a later chapter.

RAISED WITH CHRIST, SEATED IN HEAVEN

Raised with Christ is a frequent description of what it means to be a Christian. This phrase obviously implies a state of death from which we were rescued. We were "dead" in our sins (Ephesians 2:1). Since Christ died instead of us, these two concepts can be united to say that Jesus entered our state of spiritual death and invited us to share in his physical death, so that this unity with him would also lead to us entering his resurrection life.

Paul says God has already "raised us up with him and seated us with him in the heavenly places in Christ Jesus" (Ephesians 2:6; see also Colossians 3:1–2). Our salvation is eternally secure. We are, in some mysterious sense, already in heaven and share in Christ's authority. Our spirits right now have access into the holy of holies. It may seem a bit fanciful, but I sometimes like to think of our current life as being a bit like a form of virtual reality. The true reality is, we are already seated in heaven, no matter what is happening to us in this world. This is not to minimize the importance of our current life, just to emphasize that we are already secure in heaven.

When Christ died, we died, and when Christ rose, we rose. "I have been crucified with Christ. It is no longer I who live, but Christ who lives in me" (Galatians 2:20). Those events in the past happened to us without our being aware of them, before we even existed in this world. For this language to make any sense whatsoever we have to believe in a God who is outside of time. At some point we repent and become Christians, and at that point these events are applied to us. We are quite literally re-created or resurrected.

Christians already are spiritual beings. Our glorious new life is currently hidden from view since, as Paul says, "you have died, and your life is hidden with Christ in God. When Christ who is your life appears, then you also will appear with him in glory" (Colossians 3:3–4). The world has no idea that our true identity is veiled from it. It is profitable to meditate on this glorious truth of our being hidden with Christ in God. These words also lead us to grasp one of the most mysterious things in the whole Bible—our union with Jesus.

UNITED WITH CHRIST

Not only are we already spiritually seated in heaven, we are already in union with Christ. This is not the kind of union that means we are swallowed up in God—the route to true freedom and identity is by sharing in Christ's riches. We remain distinct. Paul repeatedly tells us that the blessings of our salvation are found "in Christ Jesus." For example, he said, "Therefore, if anyone is in Christ, he is a new creation" (2 Corinthians 5:17). Jonathan Edwards explains to us that every benefit of salvation can only be ours because of this new relationship we have with Christ himself:

> That justification that believers have at their conversion is as partaking of the justification that Christ had in his resurrection; and so all the benefits that believers [have], their comfort and hope and joy here, and their eternal life hereafter, is as partaking with a risen Savior.[8]

It is this union with Christ that helps us make sense of why God was not unjust in punishing our sins in the crucifixion of Jesus. We are so united with him that what belongs to us belongs to him, and conversely what belongs to him belongs to us. All the blessings and privileges of being a son of God are now ours. "For our sake he made him to be sin who knew no sin, so that *in him* we might become the righteousness of God" (2 Corinthians 5:21).

[8]Jonathan Edwards, *The Miscellanies*, WJE Online, Vol. 18, 534; http://edwards.yale.edu/archive?path=aHR0cDovL2Vkd2FyZHMueWFsZS5lZHUvY2dpLWJpbi9uZXdwaGlsby9nZXRvYmplY3QucGw/Yy4xNzo0OjMyMy53amVv.

The concept of this unity is hard for us to grasp. We don't often think in terms of a federal identity. Perhaps the closest modern analogy is the union we have with the countries in which we live. If you are a citizen of a particular country that is at war, you might not feel enmity against the aggressor country, but that changes nothing in your experience. You are still under attack because you are a member of your country. If, on the other hand, you were able to escape and become an adopted member of another country, your previous attackers would no longer see you as the enemy. Similarly, we are now blessed because we are in Christ: "Blessed be the God and Father of our Lord Jesus Christ, who has blessed us in Christ with every spiritual blessing in the heavenly places" (Ephesians 1:3).

Some things that should have happened to us, like death and punishment, happened instead to Jesus. God considers us as if we really had experienced what Jesus experienced on the cross. Conversely, there are things that happened to him that we did not deserve—like resurrection and receiving the approval of God. Thanks to our union with Christ we share in those benefits.

Jesus suffered the penalty due our sins so that we do not have to. He was raised to life so that we will also experience future resurrection. He is our substitute, and we participate in his blessings. He represents us, and yet we are also in union with him. We are reconciled to our Father. The very judge who is righteously angry with us provides the solution, and we are adopted by the one who is fully justified to hate us for our sin.

Salvation is not merely a case of believing in something that happened thousands of years ago. We are not saved by a belief. We are saved by union with a person. We cannot separate the propitiatory work of Christ from Christ himself. We are saved not only by believing the fact that Christ died for our sins, but by union with the crucified and risen, exalted Savior. Only through union with a living Savior who has in him the virtue of his atoning death do justification, forgiveness, and all the blessings of redemption become ours: "In him we have redemption through his blood" (Ephesians 1:7; cf. Colossians 1:14). We are accepted "in the Beloved" (Ephesians 1:6). "There is therefore now no condemnation for those who are in Christ Jesus" (Romans

8:1). We are united to both his death and resurrection. As one scholar
put it:

> Justification is ours as we are "in Christ" in such living union with him
> that His life becomes identified with ours and ours with His. Because
> of this identification or incorporation, Christ's acts are repeated in us
> so that in His death we die to sin, "crucified with Christ" (Galatians
> 2:20), and in His life we live to righteousness. But it is only by His risen
> life that Christ can come into such living union with men as thus to
> effect their redemption.[9]

All that he is, all his credit, all his life, are imputed to us, and
although we may initially appear to be much the same as we were the
moment before we were declared righteous, a change does happen
within us. We begin a whole new type of life and become an entirely
new kind of being. We spend the rest of our lives becoming what we
now are. As Paul said:

> We were buried therefore with him by baptism into death, in order
> that, just as Christ was raised from the dead by the glory of the Father,
> we too might walk in newness of life. (Romans 6:4)

> For he was crucified in weakness, but lives by the power of God. For
> we also are weak in him, but in dealing with you we will live with him
> by the power of God. (2 Corinthians 13:4)

CONCLUSION

To fully appreciate the wonder of what has happened to us, we must
turn to 2 Corinthians 5:17: "Therefore, if anyone is in Christ, he is a
new creation. The old has passed away; behold, the new has come."

Because of the resurrection, a radical change has happened inside
us. We are made new already. Inside us we are already new creatures
who were made for an eternity with God. The old sinful nature really
has gone. It may not always feel that way, but the Christian truly has
changed inwardly. We are already part of the new creation that is to
come. The renewal of all things has begun in us. We are totally different
from those around us. We form a community of the newly created, and

---

[9]Spiros Zodhiates, *The Complete Word Study Dictionary: New Testament*, electronic edition
(Chattanooga: AMG Publishers, 2000), G1347.

the family of God's people is incomprehensible to those who are not yet spiritually alive. We should not be surprised when people misunderstand us since we are like a different species. When Christians stop being different from the world and instead fall back into their old habits, it is as tragic as finding a royal prince sleeping out on the streets in a gutter, having forgotten he belongs in the palace.

CHAPTER ELEVEN

TRANSFORMED BY THE RESURRECTION

If then you have been raised with Christ, seek the things that are above, where Christ is, seated at the right hand of God. Set your minds on things that are above, not on things that are on earth. For you have died, and your life is hidden with Christ in God. When Christ who is your life appears, then you also will appear with him in glory. Put to death therefore what is earthly in you: sexual immorality, impurity, passion, evil desire, and covetousness, which is idolatry. On account of these the wrath of God is coming. In these you too once walked, when you were living in them. But now you must put them all away: anger, wrath, malice, slander, and obscene talk from your mouth. Do not lie to one another, seeing that you have put off the old self with its practices and have put on the new self, which is being renewed in knowledge after the image of its creator.

COLOSSIANS 3:1-10

I REMEMBER TRYING TO explain grace to a room full of children. Without warning, I took a large chocolate bar and gave it to the child who had been misbehaving the most all morning. The look of surprise and pleasure on the child's face told me he understood that this was far from what he deserved. A chorus of howls from the other children of "That's totally not fair!" told me they had grasped it too. "Exactly," I said. "That's grace!" In response to this the boy immediately began to behave well and continued to do so for the rest of the morning.

When we appreciate the grace that we have received and understand the inward change that has happened to us, it will affect every aspect of our lives. Christians will find their drinking habits, their sex life, their relationships, and their attitudes toward work and authority transformed. In short, every aspect of their behavior will begin to change. We are not passive in this process but work to become what we already are. We have been changed by an encounter with Jesus who is not the long-dead subject of a historical biography but is very much alive today. There are many ways to cooperate with God in our fight against sin. We will briefly consider several of them before honing in on one that is less spoken about.

FREEDOM TO SERVE

We are no longer bound by rules and regulations, which lead to death (see Romans 8:2). Laws teach us that we cannot perfectly obey them in our own strength no matter how hard we try. We are free from the law but are, however, bound to the resurrected Christ. We have promised to follow him.

> Likewise, my brothers, you also have died to the law through the body of Christ, so that you may belong to another, to him who has been raised from the dead, in order that we may bear fruit for God. (Romans 7:4)

LIVE APPROPRIATELY

Knowing that God has declared us righteous, we should not live as we used to.

> I therefore, a prisoner for the Lord, urge you to walk in a manner worthy of the calling to which you have been called. (Ephesians 4:1)

We have already died to sin; so we should consider ourselves free from its grasp and simply walk away from it (Romans 6:1–11).

WORK OUT WHAT GOD WORKS IN

Those whom the Lord declares to be righteous are righteous indeed. He will also ensure that their behavior becomes righteous. While conversion is a work entirely of God's doing, we cooperate in eradicating sin in our lives.

> Work out your own salvation with fear and trembling, for it is God who works in you, both to will and to work for his good pleasure. (Philippians 2:12–13)

There is a world of difference between fighting to live a holy life by the power of the Holy Spirit and a legalistic, fear-filled attempt to please God. God is already pleased with the Christian. We are not working to become worthy to be called his children; we are already considered worthy. As Tim Keller explains, "Religion operates on the principle: I obey, therefore I am accepted. The gospel operates on the principle: I am accepted through Christ, therefore I obey."[1]

CONSIDER CHRIST'S EXAMPLE

Paul urges us in Philippians 2 to carefully consider the work of Jesus on the cross. This will fill us with a sense of the seriousness and weight of our own guilt. It causes us to be humble and to demonstrate our gratitude to Christ by following his example. Our worship consists of offering our bodies to God (Romans 12:1–2).

CONSIDER THE EFFECTS OF SIN

Joseph reminded Potiphar's wife that the sex she wanted them to recklessly enjoy would affect her husband who had been kind to him. This led him to literally run from temptation (see Genesis 39). Many sins require us to be in the wrong place at the wrong time to commit them and can sometimes be avoided by simply removing ourselves from the situation.

STUDY THE SCRIPTURES

God's Word teaches us to be wise and avoid temptation (2 Timothy 3:16–17). We are also told that it is by the power of the Spirit at work in us, linked to the resurrection of Jesus, that we defeat sin.

---

[1] Tim Keller, *Redeemer Vision Paper 1*; http://www.redeemer2.com/visioncampaign/papers/Vision_Paper_1-The_Gospel-The_Key_to_Change.pdf.

SET OUR MINDS ON SPIRITUAL THINGS

"Those who live according to the Spirit set their minds on the things of the Spirit" (Romans 8:5).

As we saw in the verses that opened this chapter, we are urged to be heavenly minded. This is so we can be of earthly use. We focus on the worth of our risen Savior, his many wonderful attributes, and our future resurrection. By gazing on the resurrected Jesus we will be transformed and will find that Jesus himself is at work in us, changing our appetites and desires. Being born again is a radical transformation, as Paul tells us:

> For God, who said, "Let light shine out of darkness," has shone in our hearts to give the light of the knowledge of the glory of God in the face of Jesus Christ. (2 Corinthians 4:6)

In the presence of light, darkness disappears. What is the light? It is the revelation of the nature of God to us through his Son, Jesus. Looking into the depths of this revelation changes us:

> And we all, with unveiled face, beholding the glory of the Lord, are being transformed into the same image from one degree of glory to another. (2 Corinthians 3:18)

Jesus is at work changing every believer to be more like himself. Not every Christian is changed to the same degree. Many Christians lose the wonder of Jesus and forget to gaze on him. Thus often the new Christians are the ones who seem most enthusiastic in their love for God. We almost don't want to spoil them by telling them of the cynicism and settling down that we assume is associated with "maturity." Maybe you know some Christians who have refused to walk this path of early excitement and change followed by a long, slow plateau or even spiritual decline. The longer they have lived, the more they feel they have to thank Jesus for, and their passion only increases. Such older Christians seem to glow with the presence of Jesus. It is not too late. The resurrected Jesus himself is inviting us, calling us, imploring us. He wants us to return to our first love, and if we do, we will find that our love for the things of this world will dim once more, and we will be changed to another degree of glory. May God help more of us to share in the glory that only a lifetime of loving our Savior can produce.

The more we gaze upon the risen, glorified King Jesus, the more we will become like him. The more we see Jesus for who he is, the more we will be made into his image. Our current knowledge is at best partial. "For now we see in a mirror dimly, but then face to face. Now I know in part; then I shall know fully, even as I have been fully known" (1 Corinthians 13:12). Our current partial knowledge of God will be swallowed up and replaced with a full knowledge of him. Ultimately there will be a day when we will see Jesus face-to-face, and in an instant our transformation will be complete.

> Beloved, we are God's children now, and what we will be has not yet appeared; but we know that when he appears we shall be like him, because we shall see him as he is. (1 John 3:2)

In the meantime, even our imperfect knowledge of Christ leads to change. John Piper has written:

> One of the most important principles that guides the way I preach and what I preach . . . is this: true gospel change of a person's character comes from steady gazing at the glory of Jesus. . . . We become like what we treasure enough to spend time focusing on. Some say, "Seeing is believing." This text says, "Seeing is becoming." You become like what you behold.
>
> The implication of this for preaching is that, if I aim for us as a church to be transformed from one degree of glory to another—to become more and more like Jesus—then I should hold up Jesus again and again for you to gaze at. . . . The primary way of gazing on Christ today is through his Word. That is the clear implication of these words in [Revelation 1:11]: "Write in a book what you see and send it to the . . . churches." Why else write in a book what he saw except to transmit to the readers some of that same experience?[2]

GETTING A RIGHT IMAGE OF JESUS

Our biggest problem is that we do not see Jesus as he is. If we could desire him, treasure him, delight in him, be satisfied in him, cherish him, savor him, value him, revere him, esteem and admire him as much as he deserves, we would want to follow him as our Lord in every area of our

---

[2]John Piper, "A Year-End Look at Jesus Christ"; http://www.desiringgod.org/ResourceLibrary/ScriptureIndex/17/822_A_YearEnd_Look_at_Jesus_Christ/.

life, and sin would instantly lose its appeal. One of the most important
ways for us to deal with sin in our lives is to get a clear picture of Jesus
in our minds and hearts. Jesus shares every attribute with God and is
therefore not to be messed around with, argued with, or treated with
contempt. It is as we contemplate Jesus and his resurrection that we will
be changed.

Surely what we have been discussing is related to what Jesus was
referring to when he urged us to abide in him (John 15).

Don't underestimate the potential that simply meditating on the fact
that Jesus rose from the dead has to empower and transform us. I am not
only speaking of the emotional outpouring that often accompanies such
a revelation. I am talking about a deep impact on our soul that weans
us from our sinful desires and thrills us with our Lord in all his glory.

If we only contemplate Jesus experiencing terrible suffering on the
cross, there is a danger that we might even feel sorry for him. Jesus does
not want our pity. He wants our worship, adoration, and celebration
as the rightfully installed King of the universe! Contemplating the resurrection and glorification of Jesus helps us recognize him for who he
really is. Whenever we seek his face, we see glimpses of his glory, and
our transformation into his likeness continues. We are not talking about
merely constructing a mental image of what Jesus looked like as a man.
The Bible does not place much significance on how Jesus looked on
earth. Isaiah prophetically describes Jesus, the incarnate man: "He had
no form or majesty that we should look at him, and no beauty that we
should desire him" (Isaiah 53:2).

The one who eternally was beautiful beyond description laid that
aside. Isaiah also describes what the crucified Jesus looked like. It is not
a pleasant depiction: "His appearance was so marred, beyond human
semblance, and his form beyond that of the children of mankind"
(Isaiah 52:14).

While we are commanded to remember the sacrifice Jesus made for
us on the cross, we are also called to gaze upon his glory, seek his face,
and meditate on him. While on earth, the fullness of his glory was hidden. Now Jesus is reigning in majesty, and his full glory and beauty are
once again on display. This is the accurate picture of Jesus, the Jesus of
eternity, who briefly visited us and made the ultimate sacrifice for us and

who is now seated at the right hand of God. He prayed before he was arrested, "And now, Father, glorify me in your own presence with the glory that I had with you before the world existed" (John 17:5).

It is Jesus who reveals God to us. There are a number of times recorded in the Old Testament when God was revealed to people. However, John tells us, "No one has ever seen God; the only God, who is at the Father's side, he has made him known" (John 1:18). This is consistent with what God said to Moses: "you cannot see my face, for man shall not see me and live" (Exodus 33:20). Who then did the Old Testament saints see?

When discussing the encounter with God in Isaiah 6, John tells us, "Isaiah said these things because he saw his glory and spoke of him" (John 12:41). From the context of John's Gospel it is clear that the word "he" here is referring to Jesus himself. We can conclude that every appearance of God in the Old Testament was actually an appearance of Jesus. As Jesus himself said, "Whoever believes in me, believes not in me but in him who sent me. And whoever sees me sees him who sent me" (John 12:44–45).

When Abraham received promises from God and interceded with him, it was Jesus he saw. When Jacob saw God (Genesis 32:24–30), it was Jesus who wrestled with him. When Moses conversed with God face-to-face, it was Jesus who treated him as a friend, and it was Jesus who was like a devouring fire (Exodus 33:11; 24:17). When Ezekiel saw the cloud of glory, it was Christ himself who shone so brightly (Ezekiel 10:4–5).

JOHN'S REVELATION OF THE GLORIFIED JESUS

John's final book is described as "the revelation of Jesus Christ, which God gave him to show his servants the things that must soon take place" (Revelation 1:1). Jesus, with his glory now unveiled, confronted the disciple whom he loved, who had rested his head on his chest. John recorded for us the following description of what he saw:

> Then I turned to see the voice that was speaking to me, and on turning I saw seven golden lampstands, and in the midst of the lampstands one like a son of man, clothed with a long robe and with a golden sash around his chest. The hairs of his head were white, like white wool, like snow. His eyes were like a flame of fire, his feet were like burnished

bronze, refined in a furnace, and his voice was like the roar of many waters. In his right hand he held seven stars, from his mouth came a sharp two-edged sword, and his face was like the sun shining in full strength. When I saw him, I fell at his feet as though dead. But he laid his right hand on me, saying, "Fear not, I am the first and the last, and the living one. I died, and behold I am alive forevermore, and I have the keys of Death and Hades." (Revelation 1:12–18)

This was Jesus, full of all glory, risen from the dead, ascended on high! The description is graphic and compelling, but its poetic nature means that we can't form a complete picture of what he actually looked like.

Jesus Is Still a Man

Although glorious and 100 percent God, Jesus also remains eternally 100 percent a man and hence dignifies mankind. Not only did God become man, a man is now ruling in heaven as God. Because he took his resurrected body to heaven, the earth was a few pounds lighter when Jesus left. Jesus, the man who is also God, stands before the throne of God forever pleading our case. We ourselves do not enter the Trinity, still less become "gods," but we will obtain a body like his. He is the firstborn of the new creation. Everything about him is glorious. Jesus is the one mediator between man and God—he is *both* the Son of Man and the Ancient of Days.

Jesus' Robe

Jesus is wearing a long robe, which brings to mind the robe of Jesus seen in Isaiah 6 filling the temple. The robe makes us think of kingship and his presence, which fills heaven and earth. The golden sash he is wearing around his waist is an ancient mark of authority.

The Whiteness of His Hair

Jesus' hair is described as white as wool. There are many references in the Bible to the color white. At the Transfiguration, Jesus' "clothes became radiant, intensely white, as no one on earth could bleach them" (Mark 9:3; see also Luke 9:28–35). White symbolizes complete purity. Jesus is entirely holy and without sin. When Jesus saves us and we become Christians, it is as if our clothes become pure white. God sees us as pure and sinless, just like Jesus. Because of Jesus' death and resurrection, the price was paid for our sin, and God now sees us as perfect. By trusting in Jesus and repenting of our sins, God rids us of all traces of guilt.

This is important because many Christians struggle with condemnation and feelings of guilt. Many disqualify themselves from serving because they feel they "are not good enough." They do not want to bless others because they feel they somehow have no right. They feel trapped in anxiety and depression, never fully understanding that God sees them as guiltless, that Christians "have washed their robes and made them white in the blood of the Lamb" (Revelation 7:14). We have been made pure like Jesus. God sees us as sinless and spotless. "Come now, let us reason together, says the LORD: though your sins are like scarlet, they shall be as white as snow; though they are red like crimson, they shall become like wool" (Isaiah 1:18). Paul exclaimed, "There is therefore now no condemnation for those who are in Christ Jesus" (Romans 8:1).

By considering fully the glorious purity of our Lord Jesus in his radiant state and the Scriptures that tell us that God now sees us like he sees his Son, we will be able to grasp our total cleansing from sin. This will transform our lives, removing our guilt.

His Blazing Eyes

Jesus' eyes flash like fire. One glance of some people's eyes can make your knees go to jelly—and I am not referring to a teenage boy when the prettiest girl in the school looks at him! The authoritative look of the judge, the glance of the parent, the disapproving glare of an employer can all make us tremble. Jesus' eye is watching you. He can see everything. He can look through walls. His vision penetrates the heart: "For the LORD sees not as man sees: man looks on the outward appearance, but the LORD looks on the heart" (1 Samuel 16:7).

Those eyes say, "I love you, but do not mess with me." They are confident, authoritative, but also gentle and full of love. Too often we relate to Jesus in our mind's eye as our best friend, a heavenly boyfriend, or a Father Christmas in the sky. We need to see his majesty, glory, authority, power, and wrath against sin. Just one glance from Jesus

would be enough to cause our weak, timid, overly gentle, soft carica-
tures of Jesus to disappear in an instant.

Jesus' Feet

Even Jesus' feet exude strength and authority. For such an important
part of our bodies, our feet can be weak, and pretty ugly at times. They
are also incredibly vulnerable. If just one small stone gets in your shoe,
you may feel like you can't walk another step. Jesus' feet are made
instead of solid bronze. He cannot be crippled or harmed. Heaven is
Jesus' throne, and the earth is his footstool (Isaiah 66:1). He has complete authority over the whole earth and everything in it (Acts 17:24).

Jesus' Voice

The thing that would both terrify you and thrill you most about Jesus
would be his voice. Oh what a voice! It is like thunder, louder than
waves crashing on a beach, dwarfing the roar of Niagara Falls, and
shaking the world. "Let there be light!" he said, and there was. When
he says, "A new heaven and a new earth," the end will come. When he
says "No!" to Satan, the Devil is unable to resist him. What Jesus says
is always done: "So shall my word be that goes out from my mouth; it
shall not return to me empty, but it shall accomplish that which I purpose, and shall succeed in the thing for which I sent it" (Isaiah 55:11).

No one can succeed in challenging him. We need to completely
submit to his will. When he speaks something into being in your life,
it will happen. When he says, "This one is forgiven," you are forgiven.

Not only do Jesus' words make things happen, they are also able to
discern our motives and attitudes. When we read the Bible, we can be
convicted to the very core of our being by the word of God. Our deepest
motives and attitudes are uncovered by the words of Jesus:

> For the word of God is living and active, sharper than any two-edged
> sword, piercing to the division of soul and of spirit, of joints and of
> marrow, and discerning the thoughts and intentions of the heart.
> (Hebrews 4:12)

God's Word is referred to in Ephesians 6:17 as "the sword of the
Spirit," our only offensive weapon. Jesus himself is fighting for us. We

are never alone in our struggles: "For the LORD your God is he who goes with you to fight for you against your enemies, to give you the victory" (Deuteronomy 20:4).

This should encourage us when we undergo trials and persecution. Jesus is the victor. He always wins. As the psalmist says, "Who is this King of glory? The LORD, strong and mighty, the LORD, mighty in battle!" (Psalm 24:8).

Charles Wesley understood this, writing in his great hymn "O for a Thousand Tongues to Sing":

> He speaks, and, listening to His voice,
> New life the dead receive,
> The mournful, broken hearts rejoice,
> The humble poor believe.
>
> Hear him, ye deaf; His praise, ye dumb,
> Your loosened tongues employ;
> Ye blind, behold your Savior come,
> And leap, ye lame, for joy.

Jesus' Face

In biblical Hebrew, a word frequently translated in English as God's presence literally means to "see one's face."[3] Jesus' face is as bright as the sun in full strength. "It was humanly impossible to look Jesus in the face."[4] When Moses met with Jesus, he returned with a shining face so that he had to wear a veil so others could look at him (Exodus 34:35). Jesus' face shining on us represents blessing and favor.

> The LORD make his face to shine upon you and be gracious to you. (Numbers 6:25)
>
> Make your face shine on your servant; save me in your steadfast love! (Psalm 31:16)

As we meditate on Jesus' shining face, our own faces begin to reflect him. We can probably think of Christians who look like this. If we

---

[3]Francis Brown, Samuel Rolles Driver, and Charles Augustus Briggs, *Enhanced Brown-Driver-Briggs Hebrew and English Lexicon*, electronic edition (Bellingham, WA: Logos Research Systems, 2000), 816.
[4]Simon J. Kistemaker and William Hendriksen, *Exposition of the Book of Revelation*, New Testament Commentary, Vol. 20 (Grand Rapids: Baker Book House, 1953–2001), 98.

want to be transformed into the image of Jesus, we need to gaze on and meditate on his face, cry out to him to shine his face upon us, and allow his glory to be reflected in our own. Our inward character change even begins to affect our external appearance.

JESUS THE WARRIOR

John shares a second picture with us of Jesus as a powerful figure:

> Then I saw heaven opened, and behold, a white horse! The one sitting on it is called Faithful and True, and in righteousness he judges and makes war. His eyes are like a flame of fire, and on his head are many diadems, and he has a name written that no one knows but himself. He is clothed in a robe dipped in blood, and the name by which he is called is The Word of God. And the armies of heaven, arrayed in fine linen, white and pure, were following him on white horses. From his mouth comes a sharp sword with which to strike down the nations, and he will rule them with a rod of iron. He will tread the winepress of the fury of the wrath of God the Almighty. On his robe and on his thigh he has a name written, King of kings and Lord of lords. (Revelation 19:11–16)

This describes Jesus as a powerful general riding out to war and striking fear into the hearts of his enemies. It is an image that a man can relate to and worship much more readily than the "gentle Jesus, meek and mild" of many artistic portrayals.

OUR RESPONSE TO THE RISEN JESUS

The only appropriate response to Jesus is similar to that of John. Immediately this Jew who had been schooled in worshipping only the one God fell on his face as though dead in order to worship his best friend. This was the Son of God in all his glory. Who could stand before him? This revelation of the glory and majesty of Jesus had shaken him to his core. The only appropriate reaction was reverence, awe, and wonder.

We must never become casual in our relationship with Jesus. He wants us to know him and to love him and at the same time to have a fear of him. What is this fear of God? It is the respect that comes from knowing and understanding that we are men and he is God. We are the created ones, and he is the Creator. It is understanding that God's ways are best, and our decisions may not always be right. It is believing all of God's promises of love and faithfulness even when our circumstances are difficult. It is not daring to deny God by disbelieving his Word. As the proverb says, "The fear of the LORD is the beginning of wisdom, and the knowledge of the Holy One is insight" (Proverbs 9:10).

We have nothing to give him. We are helpless before him and need his help to even stand. Some foolish people get angry with God and say, "When I get to heaven I will have a few questions for him to answer!" If Jesus were to walk into your room today, you would not be able to remain in your seat. When we see him we too will fall on our faces before Jesus to worship him. His nuclear-hot holiness burns up every trace of sin. We are right to fear him. When the Bible tells us to fear him, it means simply that—*fear him*. Sometimes people say they are afraid of God. We might need to tell some of them that they are not frightened enough.

The passage does not end there. Instead we see that amazing word "but" (Revelation 1:17). Few words are more welcome than *but* in the right place. John is terrified in the presence of the fearsome, risen Christ. He is on his face. He may be thinking, "That's it, I am undone." At that very moment the passage tells us, *"But he laid his right hand on me."* What is Jesus going to do? Is he going to kill him? Is he angry with him? Is he going to scold him for not being good enough? Does he say, "Be afraid, be very afraid"? No; rather he says, "Fear not." The Bible is full of commands to fear God. But when God turns up on the scene, he always seems to say, "Do not be afraid!" The reason for this is that God wants us to fear him but not to be terrified of him. Jesus tells John he has no need to fear. Why? Because of what Jesus has just done for him—he has reached out and touched him. Why? Because he is the one who died for John. He is the one who was raised for John. He is the one who holds the keys of death and hell in his hands. If he says you are one of his, then the Devil can't touch you. If he says, "This one belongs to me," then the door of hell is locked to you and heaven is open wide.

This is the Jesus we come to today—the living one, the fearsome one, and yet the loving one, who delights in reaching his hand out and touching you. When he touches you, amazing things happen. Do you need Jesus to touch you? Do you need your guilt to be removed? He died so you could be forgiven. Do you feel dirty because of your sin or because of the sin someone committed against you? His blood cleanses you from all shame. Do you need healing? He is the healer. Do you need a victory in your personal life? Do you need his help in your relationships or in your work? This Jesus is the triumphant one, and nothing can stop him from acting on your behalf. Even as we wait for the fulfillment of his promises, we can begin to receive some of them right now.

CONCLUSION

Jesus prayed, "Father, I desire that they also, whom you have given me, may be with me where I am, *to see my glory* that you have given me because you loved me before the foundation of the world" (John 17:24). The psalmist also understood the importance of savoring the Lord's glory:

> One thing have I asked of the LORD, that will I seek after: that I may dwell in the house of the LORD all the days of my life, to gaze upon the beauty of the LORD and to inquire in his temple. (Psalm 27:4)

When David wrote the Psalms, he was relishing an experience of God in this life and not only looking forward to the future: "I have looked upon you in the sanctuary, beholding your power and glory" (Psalm 63:2). We may not be able to experience this in its entirety today, but we can see Christ, especially in the pages of the Bible. Paul describes how this transformation occurs:

> We were buried therefore with him by baptism into death, in order that, just as Christ was raised from the dead by the glory of the Father, we too might walk in newness of life. For if we have been united with him in a death like his, we shall certainly be united with him in a resurrection like his. We know that our old self was crucified with him in order that the body of sin might be brought to nothing, so that we would no longer be enslaved to sin. For one who has died has been set free from sin. . . . So you also must consider yourselves dead to sin and alive to God in Christ Jesus. Let not sin therefore reign in your mortal body, to make you obey its passions. Do not present your members to sin as instruments for unrighteousness, but present yourselves to God as those who have been brought from death to life, and your members to God as instruments for righteousness. (Romans 6:4–13)

CHAPTER TWELVE

SEND A RESURRECTION, O LORD!

Will you not revive us again, that your people may rejoice
in you? Show us your steadfast love, O Lord,
and grant us your salvation.

PSALM 85:6-7

A SERIES OF ADVERTISEMENTS on British television move me close to tears every time I see them. They begin with someone crying, hugging a loved one. A voice begins, "When I was diagnosed with cancer . . ." You appreciate immediately the terrible impact of the word "cancer." After a few seconds the patient says, "Today I was told I have my life back." Suddenly you realize that the person is crying for joy, not anguish, and through their tears a smile appears. This commercial reminds us of the power of death and of the precious nature of life. The thread by which we hang on to life is so slender.[1]

We all begin to die the moment we are born. Death is at work in us in many different ways. When we are sick we sometimes say, "I feel half-dead." It is also common to speak of emotional death when bad things happen to us. When a relationship breaks down we might say, "I died on the inside." Is the reason we speak of death in this way because we instinctively realize that it is not God's original purpose for us?

Jesus was our obedience substitute during his life, our punishment substitute in his death, and our rebirth substitute in his resurrection. When we become united with Jesus, his life of obedience, his painful

---

[1]An example of this series of ads appears online at http://www.tellyads.com/show_movie.php?filename=TA2056&advertiser=Cancer%20Research.

death, and his resurrection into glorious power are all credited to us. When someone becomes a Christian, a spiritually dead person is united with a life-giving one. His resurrection produces a resurrection in us. We are connected to the same power that raised Christ from the dead.

Our Christian lives can be a daily experience of sharing in the power of Christ's resurrection. The word *resurrection* comes from the same root as *resurgence* or *rising again*. God is in the business of reviving, restoring, and renewing or, if you like, fixing us. God is an expert in revival, and he wants our lives on this earth to increasingly mirror heaven. On earth we will always live with the tension of the now and the not yet. Even when we are in the midst of difficulties, however, he wants us to learn to live "life . . . to the full" (John 10:10, NIV). This will lead to, among other things, a sense of joy and peace, which will cause many to question why we are so different.

The church today does not always live in the good of what Jesus has done and is in need of widespread revival. History reveals that periods of stability or decline have been punctuated by the sudden, sovereign, and miraculous intervention of God. When this happens, the church seems to be resurrected from a state of near-deadness. Throughout history these revivals have demonstrated the power of God. One motivation behind this book is to encourage a deeper longing for an experience of Christianity that is truly beyond the natural realm. For if there is one thing the resurrection teaches us, it is that God is miraculous. If God can intervene in human history in such a dramatic way, it is a small thing for him to do so in other ways. In revivals the church en masse experiences more fully the change made possible by the resurrection.

WHAT IS REVIVAL?

Today we do not speak much about revival. Many of us are cynical about it. We have heard it all before, and yet there has been no major revival in the English-speaking world during our lifetime. Possibly such cynicism is caused by a misunderstanding of the meaning of revival and our failure to appropriate what I call a personal revival. This experience is available to all Christians individually, even outside of a generalized revival affecting a broad geographical area. This chapter will attempt to define revival and prepare us for subsequent chapters that will outline how we can connect to God's reviving power.

History teaches us that the greatest need of the church today is a revival. Yet there is great confusion about what revival actually is. Revival is nothing more than a wide-scale outworking of Jesus' resurrection power. It is the restoration of life to dead or near-dead beings. A revival could almost be described as a resurrection. Having examined church history, Stuart Piggin defines revival:

> Revival is a sovereign work of God the heavenly Father, manifesting his glory on the earth. It consists of a powerful intensification by Jesus of the Holy Spirit's normal activity of testifying to the Savior, accentuating the doctrines of grace, and convicting, converting, regenerating, and sanctifying large numbers of people at the same time. It is therefore a community experience.
>
> It is occasionally preceded by an expectation that God is about to do something exceptional; it is usually preceded by an extraordinary unity and prayerfulness among Christians; and it is always accompanied by the revitalization of the church, the conversion of large numbers of unbelievers, and the reduction of sinful practices in the community.[2]

The key phrase in this definition is *"a powerful intensification by Jesus of the Holy Spirit's normal activity."* Too often people misunderstand revival as something totally different in its very nature from anything we normally experience. We might ask God to send a revival and expect that the experience will be totally new to us. Actually a revival is something that is only quantitatively different from what we can experience normally rather than something qualitatively unique. It is an escalation of the usual work of the Spirit to connect us directly with the life-giving power of the resurrected Jesus. In other words, the Spirit of revival is always available to us. Thus, when a revival comes, we should recognize it as a greater manifestation of normal Christianity. The writer of Hebrews reminds us, "Jesus Christ is the same yesterday and today and forever" (Hebrews 13:8).

Understanding it in this way protects us from the disappointment

---

[2]Stuart Piggin, "The Lord's Firestorms: God the Holy Trinity and the Experience of Religious Revival in Australia"; http://www.anchist.mq.edu.au/CTE/Documents/BCV%20LECTURE%20ON%20 REVIVAL.doc.

and cynicism that can result if we feel we are not in any way connected to revival. We can learn to recognize when the reviving work of God is going on around or within us and can sometimes identify local moves of God as mini-revivals. It also helps us to realize that we can cooperate with God's reviving work or resist it, and those decisions do have an effect on our experience. We need to stop seeing revival as something "out there" and instead expect to experience what Jesus planned for us through his resurrection. If we experience personal revival and it begins to spread, then, history suggests, church growth will result. Martyn Lloyd-Jones writes:

> If you look back across the history of the Christian church, you immediately find that the story of the church has not been a straight line, a level record of achievement. The history of the church has been a history of ups and downs. It is there to be seen on the very surface. When you read the history of the past you find that there have been periods in the history of the church when she has been full of life, and vigor, and power. The statistics prove that people crowded to the house of God, whole numbers of people who were anxious and eager to belong to the Christian church.
>
> Then the church was filled with life, and she had great power; the Gospel was preached with authority, large numbers of people were converted regularly, day by day, and week by week. Christian people delighted in prayer. You did not have to whip them up to prayer meetings, you could not keep them away. They did not want to go home, they would stay all night praying. The whole church was alive and full of power, and of vigor, and of might. And men and women were able to tell of rich experiences of the grace of God, visitations of his Spirit, a knowledge of the love of God that thrilled them, and moved them, and made them feel that it was more precious than the whole world. And, as a consequence of all that, the whole life of the country was affected and changed.[3]

REVIVAL IN ACTS

Even in the early church God's blessing came in waves, with differing geographical extent and depth. We read how the gospel spread through sudden and successive dramatic outpourings of the Spirit's intensified activity. It is not a story of unmitigated and uninterrupted success. We

---

[3]Martyn Lloyd-Jones, *Revival* (Wheaton, IL: Crossway, 1987), 26.

often forget that the book of Acts is a collection of edited highlights of events that occurred over several years. Because the early church experienced these seasons of revival and other quieter periods, examining their experiences is the best way for us to learn how to identify what revivals look like.

Some people argue that we cannot use narrative sections of Scripture to teach doctrine. But, ironically, this goes directly against a clear doctrinal statement from one of the epistles:

> *All* Scripture is breathed out by God and profitable for *teaching*, for reproof, for correction, and for training in righteousness. (2 Timothy 3:16)

Acts, like all Scripture, must have a role in forming our doctrine and shaping our practice. The book of Acts is unique in the historical books of the Bible in that the mistakes of its heroes are almost never reported. Even when difficulties arose, such as over the applicability of Jewish law and the argument over John Mark, the focus is on how the problems were resolved. Major issues that arose in churches and are addressed by the epistles are not even mentioned. As Luke was a trusted associate of Paul, this is surprising since he certainly would have known all about what had happened. Acts has all the hallmarks of being a model account of how church mission *should* ideally proceed. It is a collection of highlights of the good times experienced by the church, without being in any way misleading.

In Acts 2, we find what is in some ways the archetypal revival. Perhaps we have felt some disappointment that it has been more than one hundred years since the last widespread revival in North America or mainland Britain. Yet the coming of Jesus and the subsequent events of Pentecost occurred after more than four hundred years of silence from God! During that time there was no recorded divine activity.

Suddenly the church was born following the life, death, and resurrection of Christ. In the upper room a few believers gathered to pray; then something dramatic happened, and the transformed Peter began to preach boldly. He had been awakened. He was no longer frightened; he had been *revived*. The result of all this was the addition of three thousand men, plus women and children, to the church in one day.

A pattern that mirrors what happened at Pentecost can be seen in almost every subsequent revival in church history. First the church experienced a period during which there was a new and more intense emphasis on prayer. Following that, something dramatic and God-given occurred—in this case, the descent of the Holy Spirit on the believers. This work of the Spirit was designed to connect believers to the life-giving resurrection power of Christ.

Once the believers had themselves been revived, the gospel was simply but boldly preached. As a result, the life-giving power of the Word of God was unleashed. Once the church herself had been empowered from on high, then large numbers of people were saved. A revival is something that happens to individual Christians first and only subsequently has implications for those on the outside. Once a significant number of God's people are experiencing more of the change that the resurrection brings, a large number of conversions seems almost inevitable. Such "awakened" Christians are infectious in their joy in God, delight in telling people about the love of God for them, and tremble at thinking about the eternal state of the unbeliever.

Because of the clear link between what we read in Acts and what has been described in revivals in church history, my own preferred definition of revival is: *the return of the church to something of the experience of the book of Acts*. It is a "return" because often our experience seems very dissimilar to that recorded in the book of Acts. I deliberately say "something of the experience" to allow for the variations seen in revivals and to include what I call mini-revivals. This approach to revival is helpful as we each seek to be changed by the resurrection of Jesus irrespective of what is happening around us. It is possible for *any* Christian today to return to at least something of the experience of the book of Acts.

REVIVALS IN CHURCH HISTORY

Throughout history many times it was thought that the church would die out, but suddenly God intervened. The church has always grown in fits and starts, with special times of blessing on both a local and more widespread scale. The history of the church shows that the fires of revival are often lit when one man connects with God's reviving power and this power then spreads to others. For example, over his twenty-five years of ministry, Charles Spurgeon experienced a personal revival that affected his own church before, during, and after the more widespread 1859 revival. He learned how to ride the sovereign waves of revival, and when these subsided, his preaching continued to be powerfully anointed. Many were saved, and hundreds of church plants resulted from Spurgeon's connection to God's reviving Spirit. John Piper has published helpful, brief accounts online of the life of Spurgeon and several other individuals who experienced revival.[4]

Another example was John Knox, who lived during the time of the Reformation and said, "God did so multiply our number that it appeared as if men had rained from the clouds." It was said that almost the whole of Scotland turned to Christ in just a few years.[5] Richard Baxter similarly saw almost every family in Kidderminster turn from godlessness to the Christian faith during his ministry. The Wesley brothers, George Whitefield, and Jonathan Edwards were all part of an amazing work of God that stretched from the American colonies to England. Dramatic changes in society are often seen during revivals. During the Welsh revival of 1904, it was said that pit ponies, used in coal mines, would no longer work because their masters had stopped swearing at them.

Possibly the clearest account of God's supernatural power in revival is a description of the Lewis revival of 1949. On our honeymoon, while visiting the Scottish island of Lewis, it was a real delight for my wife and me to speak with a woman who had lived through this revival. The unmistakable sparkle in her eyes when speaking about those events struck me profoundly. Here is how a revival historian describes what happened:

> Duncan Campbell, an evangelist, came to the Island of Lewis in the Hebrides Islands. On the first night of his arrival, he preached in a church building. When he left the building at 11 p.m. he found 600 gathered outside; 100 from the nearby dance hall; the other 500 who had been awakened, got out of bed, and felt compelled to walk to this place. Campbell preached the gospel to them till 4 a.m., at which

---

[4]John Piper, Biographical Messages; http://www.desiringgod.org/ResourceLibrary/Biographies/.
[5]Iain Murray, "The Puritans and Revival Christianity," *Banner of Truth Magazine*, September 1969, No. 72; http://www.puritansermons.com/banner/murray2.htm.

time he was requested to come to the police station where 400 people were gathered, baffled as to why they were there. On his way to the station he came across other people along the road who were crying out to God for mercy! Revival continued for 3 years with 75% of the converts coming to Jesus outside of church buildings.[6]

There have been many similar occurrences in other countries around the world. Studying such accounts produces a hunger in us to see the same thing today. Martyn Lloyd-Jones said:

> [Normal life outside of a revival] can produce a number of converts, thank God for that, and that goes on regularly in evangelical churches every Sunday. But the need today is much too great for that. The need today is for an authentication of God, of the supernatural, of the spiritual, of the eternal, and this can only be answered by God graciously hearing our cry and shedding forth again his Spirit upon us and filling us as he kept filling the early church.
>
> What is needed is some mighty demonstration of the power of God, some enactment of the Almighty, that will compel people to pay attention, and to look, and to listen. And the history of all the revivals of the past indicates so clearly that that is invariably the effect of revival, without any exception at all. That is why I am calling attention to revival. That is why I am urging you to pray for this. When God acts, he can do more in a minute than man with his organizing can do in 50 years.[7]

REVIVAL TODAY

When we hear stories like these, we need not fall into the temptation of feeling nostalgic or becoming discouraged. Today, from a global perspective, we are seeing the largest revival the world has ever seen. The growth of the church in Africa, South America, and across Asia has been phenomenal. God has done great works in the past, and he is continuing to do great works now. If we understand that revival is directly related to our own personal experience, albeit with a greater intensity, such accounts will thrill us and make us long to experience more revival ourselves. As we read about what God has done in the past, we can recognize some similarities with our current Christian experience.

---

[6]Nate Krupp, *The Church Triumphant* (Shippensburg, PA: Destiny Image Publishers, 1988), 26–27.
[7]Lloyd-Jones, *Revival*, 121–122.

Revival is often characterized by protracted seasons of prayer. I personally experienced such a mini-revival as a teenager. When I arrived at a new school at the age of thirteen, a number of the students had been meeting for prayer early every morning before class. These children had decided quite spontaneously to begin to pray. And pray they did! There was an awareness of the presence of God in the room in such a weighty manner that I remember only a handful of other times in my life when God has felt as close as he did then. There was a seriousness, as well as a joy, about it. Students would come to the prayer meetings not quite knowing why, and some would become Christians there and then. There were tears sometimes. There was a sense of God "undoing you" in the room—he revealed himself in his fearful holiness, and boy, did you want to get yourself sorted out. Although there weren't hundreds of conversions, even now I look back on those days and pray, "Do it again, Lord!"

A study of the history of revival will show us what we might expect if, in our day, God sends a sovereign and widespread revival. As in the case of Jesus' first miracle, God seems to save the best wine until last. Many of those who have gone before us, and whom we respect, have predicted great times ahead. Of these, perhaps one of the most famous predictions was given by Latimer before he and his friend were martyred: "Be of good cheer, Ridley, and play the man. We shall this day, by God's grace light up such a candle in England, as I trust will never be put out."[8] Latimer has not been proven wrong yet, although people are now beginning to predict the wholesale demise of the church in my nation. We must pray for God to intervene and meanwhile play our part in re-evangelizing the nation. We cannot afford to wait until preaching the word is "in season" again (see 2 Timothy 4:2).

There is biblical warrant to optimistically expect a global end-time revival before Jesus returns. This view is perhaps best described and defended in Iain Murray's book *The Puritan Hope*. The argument comes from Romans 9–11 that following a period of a hardening of the Jews, large numbers of both Gentiles and Jews will be converted.

Other passages also promise great success to the church, leading

---

[8]John Foxe, *Foxe's Book of Martyrs* (Charleston, SC: Forgotten Books, 2007), 299. First published in 1563.

to large numbers of people becoming Christians. Isaiah 9:7 proclaims, "Of the *increase* of his government and of peace there will be no end." Habakkuk 2:14 states, "For the earth will be filled with the knowledge of the glory of the LORD *as the waters cover the sea.*" Jesus himself promised that "this gospel of the kingdom will be proclaimed *throughout the whole world* as a testimony to all nations, and then the end will come" (Matthew 24:14). Perhaps the most widely quoted of such passages is found in Revelation 7:9–10:

> After this I looked, and behold, *a great multitude that no one could number*, from every nation, from all tribes and peoples and languages, standing before the throne and before the Lamb.

REVIVAL AND ME

The single greatest need of the church today is to connect to the resurrection power of God seen in the book of Acts and mirrored throughout church history in revivals. To state the obvious, the church is made up of individuals. A revival is quite simply a group of those individuals all making a vibrant connection to Christ's resurrection power. This is possible for any individual Christian even outside of revivals.

Both the biblical accounts in Acts and the study of revivals in church history teach us that two things are emphasized whenever a group of people experience a revival—*prayer* and the *Word of God*. It seems reasonable, then, to assume that a focus on such things will also lead to individual renewal. Learning to pray effectively and allowing God's life-changing Word to shape our lives is the only way to diligently seek God. Only by prayer and Bible study can we connect with the life-changing power of God that Jesus obtained for us through his resurrection.

CHAPTER THIRTEEN

REVIVING PRAYER

Where is the LORD, the God of Elijah?

2 KINGS 2:14

WE NOW COME TO what is potentially the most important chapter in this whole book. It is probably the one that, if acted upon, will lead to the most dramatic and immediate changes in the average Christian's experience. Ironically, it is also the one many of us might be tempted to skip over. It is, however, impossible to overestimate the importance of prayer. Down through the centuries countless Christians who have been used by God in remarkable ways have been people who were particularly devoted to prayer. Yet ordinary Christians like you and me often feel guilty at the mere mention of the word. Which of us feels satisfied with our prayer life? Who feels that he or she prays enough and that his or her prayers are as effective as they could be? We offer many reasons, or rather *excuses*, for our prayerlessness. Wayne Grudem has rightly pointed out:

> If we were really convinced that prayer changes the way God acts, and that God does bring about remarkable changes in the world in response to prayer, as Scripture repeatedly teaches that he does, then we would pray much more than we do. If we pray little, it is probably because we do not really believe that prayer accomplishes much at all.[1]

I wish I was more of an expert at prayer and that I prayed more than I do. I do thank God that I am learning. Sadly, however, I recognize myself all too often in that quote. I long to know more about reviving

---

[1]Wayne A. Grudem, *Systematic Theology* (Leicester, UK: Inter-Varsity Press, 1994), 377.

prayer. I know I am far from alone in feeling this way. Like Jesus' disciples, almost all Christians regularly feel the need to come to the Lord and ask that he "teach us to pray" (Luke 11:1).

Prayer is the way in which we communicate with the divine. We must not underestimate this privilege of being able to speak directly to God. Prayer is often intended to change *us* rather than to alter our situation. In other words, it is meant to help us mature spiritually. Prayer is also one way in which we express our faith, and it is a means by which our faith is nourished and developed.

We are invited to direct our prayers to the risen Christ. Jesus said, "If you ask me anything in my name, I will do it" (John 14:14). Paul describes Christians as those who "call upon the name of our Lord Jesus Christ" (1 Corinthians 1:2). Stephen prayed to Christ, saying, "Lord Jesus, receive my spirit" (Acts 7:59).

Because of the resurrection of Jesus we can pray boldly knowing that our God is alive, and because he is capable even of raising the dead, he is definitely able to do whatever we ask him. If he is willing to send his Son to die and rise again for us, why should we doubt that he also now wants to do good for us? We come as a child to a loving father in the sure and certain knowledge that even though we do not always understand, he will only say no if it is for our good.

Historians tell us that every recorded revival started with a prayer meeting.[2] Prayer becomes more intense, and all-night prayer meetings are not uncommon. People even become Christians in the prayer meetings. Perhaps one of the most striking examples of this happened in Coleraine in Northern Ireland in 1859:

> A schoolboy in class became so troubled about his soul that the schoolmaster sent him home. An older boy, a Christian, went with him, and before they had gone far, led him to Christ. Returning at once to school, this new convert testified to his teacher, "Oh, I am so happy. I have the Lord Jesus in my heart." These artless words had an astonishing effect; boy after boy rose and silently left the room. Going outside, the teacher found these boys all on their knees, ranged along the wall of the playground. Very soon their silent prayer became a bitter cry; it was heard by another class inside and pierced their hearts. They fell

---

[2]Roger R. Nicole, "Prayer the Prelude to Revival," *Reformation and Revival*, Vol. 1 (Act 3, formerly Reformation and Revival Ministries, 1997), 25–37.

on their knees, and their cry for mercy was heard in turn by a girls' class above. In a few moments, the whole school was on their knees. Neighbors and passers-by came flocking in, and all as they crossed the threshold came under the same convicting power. Every room was filled with men, women and children seeking God.[3]

Something similar happened the same year in New York when a weekly prayer meeting, which began with just six people, swelled to fill theaters and led directly to one million Americans apparently being converted that year. This amounted to one in thirty of the whole population.

This clear link between revival and prayer has led some to think this is an automatic process—that if you do certain things, a massive revival is always the result. However, God is sovereign, and we cannot force his hand. Of course, we must not stop doing everything else and just pray. A well-known motto is attributed to William Booth, founder of the Salvation Army: "Work as if everything depends on you. Pray as if everything depends on God." When we pray, we passionately ask God to act; and when we have finished praying, we get up and go do the work God has commanded us to do with vigor, trusting him to bless our efforts. We can even do some of the things we would do if revival was already here. For example, it would be a foolish pastor indeed who prayed for God to save souls but never preached an evangelistic sermon.

When Christians repent and pray in a certain way, it's almost as if this is irresistible to God. We can expect him to answer and renew us individually, even if this doesn't lead to a widespread revival. If prayer is one of the catalysts to large-scale revival within the church, certainly prayer can also trigger revival in a local congregation, a small group, or even an individual. A key question then becomes, *what type of prayer will produce this effect?* When we don't confidently know the answer to this question, we too often doubt that our prayers will have any effect. Almost all Christians seem to struggle with prayer and wish they could be more effective in it.

ELIJAH, A MAN JUST LIKE US

One of God's servants who has often inspired me and has taught me much about prayer is the prophet Elijah. He was a man who certainly

---

[3]Winkie Pratney, *Revival* (Cambridge: Huntingdon House, 1994), 24–25.

knew how to pray. Elijah understood the necessity of fervent reviving prayer. The dramatic events of his life are frequently seen as representing revival. When we pray for revival, we say things like "Send the fire!" or "Send the rain!" Elijah saw both sent from heaven quite literally. The New Testament honors Elijah:

> The prayer of a righteous person has great power as it is working. Elijah was a man with a nature like ours, and he prayed fervently that it might not rain, and for three years and six months it did not rain on the earth. Then he prayed again, and heaven gave rain, and the earth bore its fruit. (James 5:16–18)

What exactly is this effective fervent prayer that connects us to God's reviving power? To try to answer that question, we will look at every recorded prayer of Elijah, beginning in 1 Kings 17. Undoubtedly Elijah prayed many more times than the prayers recorded in Scripture. For example, James tells us he prayed that the rain would stop, although that prayer is not specifically mentioned elsewhere. We can be sure that he had already learned many other lessons through his own personal prayer life. These prayers of Elijah are recorded to be examples for us. As we examine his prayers we will discover a series of keys that will help us imitate the prayer life of this man of God.

REVIVING PRAYER RECOGNIZES THE SITUATION WE ARE IN

The prayer that best exemplifies reviving prayer is the first recorded supplication of Elijah in 1 Kings 17. This story concerns a widow who was looking after the prophet during a great drought. When reading this account we might expect that God would give her some kind of reward for doing this. Instead, her son suddenly dies. Elijah's prayer led to the resurrection of the widow's son.

> And he cried to the LORD, "O LORD my God, have you brought calamity even upon the widow with whom I sojourn, by killing her son?" Then he stretched himself upon the child three times and cried to the LORD, "O LORD my God, let this child's life come into him again." (1 Kings 17:20–21)

Elijah was brought into a desperate situation in which there were no clever answers for him to give. It drove him to prayer, and we find that it sometimes takes a similar experience before we are driven to our knees. Faced with the complaint of the boy's mother, as Matthew Henry puts it, "He gave no answer to her expostulation, but brought it to God, and laid the case before him, not knowing what to say to it himself."[4]

This prayer *recognizes the situation* rather than trying to deny it or put a brave face on it. In this regard, it reminds us of the case of Abraham, who "did not weaken in faith when he considered his own body, which was as good as dead (since he was about a hundred years old), or when he considered the barrenness of Sarah's womb" (Romans 4:19). The NIV interprets the idea "considered" here as "faced the fact."

This very honest language is in stark contrast to the way some Christians are taught that to speak the name of a sickness gives it power to harm and that prayer should instead declare that a person is already healed when they clearly are still sick. Elijah told God that the boy was dead. He was merely reminding God of his sovereignty in what initially sounds like an accusation that God had deliberately killed the widow's son. These words were remarkably clear and direct about the facts of the situation facing Elijah. However, like Abraham, he did not only acknowledge the facts. In the midst of this dilemma, he lifted his eyes above the situation, and as a result his faith increased.

REVIVING PRAYER CRIES PASSIONATELY TO GOD

Both Elijah and Abraham faced times when they had to have one eye on their situation and were honest about it, but also had one eye on God. They both knew that despite harsh realities, nothing is impossible with God. As Robert Mounce explains in his commentary on Romans 4:

> From a common sense standpoint, there was not the slightest possibility that she [Sarah] would bear a child. This, however, did not cause Abraham to weaken in his faith. Faith goes beyond human potentiality. It acknowledges the existence of one who is not bound by the limitations of the created order. Conscious of his own utter impotence, Abraham relied simply and completely on the all-sufficient power of God. *Where God is present, there is nothing that lies outside the*

---

[4]Matthew Henry, *Commentary on the Whole Bible* (Peabody, MA: Hendrickson, 1991, 1996).

realm of possibility. The church of Jesus Christ is in desperate need of those who will insist that God is able to bring to pass anything that is consistent with his nature and in concert with his redemptive purposes. *Your God is too small* is a sad epitaph inscribed on all too many ecclesiastical groups who, strange as it may seem, claim to worship the Almighty.[5]

Elijah did not see God as being too small, and he insisted that God was able to perform a remarkable miracle. *He cried out to God.* This prayer had strength about it—it almost challenged God in a way reminiscent of Genesis 32, when Jacob wrestled with God. When Elijah cried out to God passionately, his prayer was answered, and the boy lived. Is our prayer today as fervent and passionate? Of course, passion on its own without biblical roots leaves us prone to excess and error—the contrast between Elijah and the prophets of Baal brings this into sharp focus.

REVIVING PRAYER CALLS ON THE GOD OF HISTORY

Elijah's first recorded prayer had been answered. In the next chapter we find him boldly standing before the whole nation of Israel. He was beside an altar that was soaking wet, facing 450 religious fanatics, the prophets of Baal, who had been cutting themselves with swords, trying to persuade their god to send fire. Elijah stood fearlessly, mocking them. Here is his clear prayer, which led to a dramatic response:

> "O LORD, God of Abraham, Isaac, and Israel, let it be known this day that you are God in Israel, and that I am your servant, and that I have done all these things at your word. Answer me, O LORD, answer me, that this people may know that you, O LORD, are God, and that you have turned their hearts back." Then the fire of the LORD fell and consumed the burnt offering and the wood and the stones and the dust, and licked up the water that was in the trench. And when all the people saw it, they fell on their faces and said, "The LORD, he is God; the LORD, he is God." (1 Kings 18:36–39)

In this prayer, *Elijah called on the God of history*. When we read

---

[5]Robert H. Mounce, *Romans,* in *The New American Commentary,* Vol. 27 (Nashville: Broadman & Holman, 2001), 129.

about what God has done in the past, both through the revivals in church history and in the biblical accounts, it encourages us that the God who acted then can also act today; more than that, he *wants* to act in a similar way today. Why do we often feel it is almost impudent to simply ask him to act in the way he has before? God seems to delight in this type of prayer, which we often see in the Bible. We can remind him of the past and dare to cry out, "Do it again, Lord!"

Habakkuk 3:2 is a good example of this: "O Lord, I have heard the report of you, and your work, O Lord, do I fear. In the midst of the years revive it; in the midst of the years make it known." The niv interprets this as: "Lord, I have heard of your fame; I stand in awe of your deeds, O Lord. Renew them in our day, in our time make them known."

REVIVING PRAYER DESIRES THAT GOD BE HONORED

In this prayer we find that Elijah's motivation was that God might be honored. He prayed that the people would know that God is God. When we pray, we need to examine our hearts and say, "Why am I asking for this? Is it so I can be more comfortable? Or is it so God will be glorified?"

REVIVING PRAYER RECOGNIZES THAT REPENTANCE IS GOD'S WORK

Elijah asked the Lord to turn the hearts of his people back to God. Maybe you have prayed for years for a son or daughter who has wandered far from God or for a friend or relative who has never known him. Understanding that it is *God*, not us, who turns the heart to follow him should encourage us not to give up.

We cannot expect friends or family members to sense their need for God on their own, for "the god of this world has blinded the minds of the unbelievers, to keep them from seeing the light of the gospel of the glory of Christ" (2 Corinthians 4:4). We were all blind once, but God "shone in our hearts to give the light of the knowledge of the glory of God in the face of Jesus Christ" (2 Corinthians 4:6). It takes a resurrection miracle in our heart for any of us to become a Christian.

REVIVING PRAYER BOLDLY ASKS GOD TO ACT

Elijah challenged God, saying, "Answer me!" Too often prayer is simply worrying out loud. We recite our woes to God and then feel a bit better for having done so. Like the early church praying for the release of Peter, we are often shocked when our prayers are actually answered. Imagine Peter standing there knocking at the door while intense prayer is going on inside for his release. This has always seemed humorous to me, especially when the gathered saints in great faith tell the door girl in effect, "Don't be silly; it must be his ghost!" (see Acts 12:15). When we ask God to do something, we should not be surprised when he does it.

Elijah was not surprised when his prayer for fire was answered, and he didn't stop there. He had something else to request.

> And Elijah said to Ahab, "Go up, eat and drink, for there is a sound of the rushing of rain." So Ahab went up to eat and to drink. And Elijah went up to the top of Mount Carmel. And he bowed himself down on the earth and put his face between his knees. And he said to his servant, "Go up now, look toward the sea." And he went up and looked and said, "There is nothing." And he said, "Go again," seven times. And at the seventh time he said, "Behold, a little cloud like a man's hand is rising from the sea." And he said, "Go up, say to Ahab, Prepare your chariot and go down, lest the rain stop you." And in a little while the heavens grew black with clouds and wind, and there was a great rain. And Ahab rode and went to Jezreel. And the hand of the LORD was on Elijah, and he gathered up his garment and ran before Ahab to the entrance of Jezreel. (1 Kings 18:41–46)

REVIVING PRAYER SHAPES IN US A GOD-CENTERED PERSPECTIVE

Elijah then retreated from the hubbub and noise that must have accompanied these events in order to get some perspective. In the Bible, God often meets people in the mountains. Perhaps this is to symbolize how, in prayer, we are called to soar above our circumstances. We need to catch a vision of God himself and of the risen Jesus seated on the throne of heaven.

Praying while walking in a forest, going on a retreat, during a commute, or even just locking ourselves in the bathroom can all be ways of disconnecting from the world and connecting to God.

Elijah's prayer on the mountain may not even have involved words; certainly no words are recorded. Instead, we see *a quiet recognition of God's superiority*. Bowing before God, he recognized that God is the sovereign King. In almost every culture, bowing is seen as being subservient. There are times when it is most appropriate to kneel before God. When things go well for us, as they had for Elijah, that's the time when we most need to humble ourselves before God and to seek his guidance for the next step. No one type of prayer is right all the time, and we must learn how to pray appropriately in each situation.

REVIVING PRAYER IS PERSISTENT IN WAITING ON GOD

Elijah kept praying, sending his servant *seven times* to look for the cloud, and in so doing was *persistent in waiting on God*. He didn't give up as we so often do. Instead he kept coming back to God in prayer despite the lack of any sign that he had been heard. However, his faith was such that when a small cloud finally appeared, he saw that small sign as settling it. Sometimes there comes a point in prayer when we almost feel we don't need to pray any longer. We should not stop praying, but we may suddenly feel a confidence that God has now settled the matter. We might even start to thank him before we have received the answer. This is not something that should be worked up, however. In Elijah's case, it took the report of the small cloud before he knew for certain that the rain was coming and there no longer was any need for him to pray.

REVIVING PRAYER IS HONEST WITH GOD AND ENGAGES WITH HIM

Despite this stream of amazing experiences and answered prayer, even Elijah didn't live on the mountaintop, on a "high" with God, forever. In the next few verses he was down in the valley of despair, and yet in that despair he prayed. You will see that the following two prayers are very different and that there are aspects of them we should not emulate. Yet God honored these prayers with a very rare Old Testament manifestation of his presence—God's "low whisper." Since God obviously did not completely disapprove of Elijah's words, we do have something to learn from them:

> It is enough; now, O LORD, take away my life, for I am no better than my fathers. (1 Kings 19:4)

> I have been very jealous for the LORD, the God of hosts. For the people of Israel have forsaken your covenant, thrown down your altars, and killed your prophets with the sword, and I, even I only, am left, and they seek my life, to take it away. (1 Kings 19:10)

Even when he was desperate, Elijah was still *honest before God and engaged with him*. Although his words were self-centered and exaggerated in a way common to the despairing, it was still a prayer. Elijah recognized his utter dependence on God. The important point of the story seems to be that while God may often bring us to the end of our own strength and we find ourselves crying out to him, he does not want to leave us desperate.

Suddenly Elijah wasn't praying about a dead boy or a wet sacrifice or a cloudless sky. Now he himself needed reviving. We see here that God was still interested in the man, although Elijah was just as weak as we are. When we are in distress and come to God, God is as eager to revive us as he was to revive Elijah.

Prayer is not merely a matter of what words we choose when we pray or even what emotions we feel; it is more a question of understanding whom we are addressing. Elijah approached *the living God*. When the living God meets a man who wants to die, the results can be unexpected. Life instead of death. A new start. A new commission. Perhaps you've been as desperate as Elijah was, and having been faithful to God, you now believe you have reached the end of the road. Maybe you feel you've disqualified yourself. Remember the story of Elijah. God revived the prophet then, and he wants to do just that for you now.

Having followed the prayer life of Elijah, it should perhaps be no surprise that the first recorded prayer of his successor, Elisha, was something to which we can also relate. Elisha cried out, "Where is the LORD, the God of Elijah?" (2 Kings 2:14). We can ask the same thing today: *Where are the miracles? Where are the salvations? Where are the dramatic acts? Where is God?* The answer is, he is still here, he is still in the business of bringing life where there is death, and he still is the One who answers by fire. As churches we can ask him for the fire of revival, as the psalmist did:

> Restore us again, O God of our salvation, and put away your indignation toward us! Will you be angry with us forever? Will you prolong your anger to all generations? Will you not revive us again, that your people may rejoice in you? Show us your steadfast love, O LORD, and grant us your salvation. (Psalm 85:4–7)

CHAPTER FOURTEEN

GOD'S REVIVING WORD

The law of the LORD is perfect, reviving the soul.

PSALM 19:7

WHEN I ASKED ANDRÉE to marry me, I surprised her with a bunch of roses and an engagement ring I had designed. As I was kneeling for what seemed like an eternity, she laughed, then cried, then said, "No." Fortunately, this was said in disbelief rather than as a rejection. I only needed to hear one word—that was all—*one word*. If her answer had really been "no" instead of "yes," I would be a very different man today, and I am sure you would not be reading this book.

We live in a society where the value of words has been greatly diminished. We often talk about "mere words." Actually, words can bring life and death. Words are powerful. They can steal hope away, and they can give it back again. God's Word brings his resurrecting power.

The spoken word was not despised in Bible times. Rather, scholars suggest that ordinary words were highly valued. "In Old Testament times the word was regarded as being alive, and so was portrayed as being sent out of the heart (mind/brain/mouth) of a living person, to leap to the goal at which it was directed. Then, when it arrived, it did the work of the speaker who had sent it forth, for it conveyed the power of the speaker to change the heart or the mind of the hearer of the word."[1]

True Christians place a very high value on words, even if we live in a world that prefers to value image. Apologist Ravi Zacharias is credited with saying, "In the beginning was the Word, not video." Jesus, the Son

---

[1]George Angus Fulton Knight, *Psalms*, Vol. 2, The Daily Study Bible Series (Louisville: Westminster, John Knox Press, 2001), 223.

of God, is described as the Word of God. God could hardly express his high view of words in a stronger way than that. The Bible, so-called "mere words" written down on a page, is what God has left us by which we can know him. The Bible is, of course, not God; we don't worship it. But God's words shape us, and they can save us. They teach us how to live, but more than that, when they are read or listened to and are united with the power of the Spirit who inspired them, they give us life.

In March 2007, John Piper placed the following words on his Website in a post entitled "The Morning I Heard the Voice of God."

> Let me tell you about a most wonderful experience I had early Monday morning, March 19, 2007, a little after six o'clock. God actually spoke to me. There is no doubt that it was God. I heard the words in my head just as clearly as when a memory of a conversation passes across your consciousness. The words were in English, but they had about them an absolutely self-authenticating ring of truth. I know beyond the shadow of a doubt that God still speaks today. . . .
>
> As I prayed and mused, suddenly it happened. God said, "Come and see what I have done." There was not the slightest doubt in my mind that these were the very words of God. In this very moment. At this very place in the twenty-first century, 2007, God was speaking to me with absolute authority and self-evidencing reality. I paused to let this sink in. There was a sweetness about it. Time seemed to matter little. God was near. He had me in his sights. He had something to say to me. When God draws near, hurry ceases. Time slows down.[2]

Very few articles have prompted as many Christian bloggers to comment on them. Fierce discussions ensued on many blogs about exactly what Piper meant. This voice he heard was real and vibrant and full of emotional and spiritual impact. It was directed specifically at him, and since his ears were open, a sense of refreshment and renewed courage resulted. This voice of God was leaping out at Piper through the *words of the Bible*. Words written on a page that had been handed down for thousands of years were producing a restorative, or if you like resurrection, power in a receptive heart.

John Piper's experience illustrates exactly what I mean when I speak of God's reviving Word. In revivals, a hunger for God's Word returns.

---

[2]John Piper, "The Morning I Heard the Voice of God"; http://www.desiringgod.org/ResourceLibrary/TasteAndSee/ByDate/2007/2021_The_Morning_I_Heard_the_Voice_of_God.

Sermons often become longer, sometimes lasting all day. A biblical example of this is found in Nehemiah 8–9, when the first five books of the Bible were preached to people for prolonged periods. Similarly, in revival times throughout church history, people could not hear enough of Holy Scripture, and amazing things happened as they received God's Word.

As we learned earlier, what is true of a multitude of people during a revival may also be true of individuals at other times. I believe God's Word can revitalize us and connect us with revival power for our daily lives. As a result of Jesus' resurrection, the same Spirit who inspired the Bible has been sent to work in our hearts and bring the Bible to life for us. It is through the Word of God that we connect with the power of the risen Christ. A potent proverb says, "Death and life are in the power of the tongue" (Proverbs 18:21). This is true of all words, but it is especially true of the Word of God.

One place in the Bible where God's Word is honored, possibly more than anywhere else, is Psalm 119. Although this psalm talks a lot about God's laws and commands, these words are used interchangeably with the Word of God. The psalmist was a man who loved God, a man after God's own heart (compare 1 Samuel 13:14). He loved God's law because it was God's Word. He loved God's Word because it revealed to him the God he loved. At the time of David, only the Law, Joshua, Judges, and perhaps Job and Ruth would have been written. For us, however, everything the psalmist says here about the law applies to the whole Bible. Psalm 119 richly describes the reviving effects of the Word of God. The key question for us to consider is, how does God's Word come to life and connect us to Christ's resurrection power? As we examine some verses from this psalm, we will identify a number of things that God's Word does to us in order to revive us. Mere words on a page can of course do none of these things. It is necessary for the enlivening power of the Spirit to take God's Truth and apply it to us. Notice how many of the verses discussed below are essentially prayers to God to ask him to do something to us so that the Word can be effective in our lives.

GOD'S WORD BRINGS REVELATION TO US

"Open my eyes, that I may behold wondrous things out of your law" (Psalm 119:18).

God must open our minds so we can understand his Word. David asked God to reveal himself to him in his Word. We need God to shine into our hearts. Like the hymn-writer, the Christian is aware that "I once was blind, but now I see" (compare John 9:25). As Paul said, "For God, who said, 'Let light shine out of darkness,' has shone in our hearts to give the light of the knowledge of the glory of God in the face of Jesus Christ" (2 Corinthians 4:6).

Since we don't actually physically see the face of Jesus today, how then *do* we see him? It is predominantly through the Scriptures that we meet God. As we read and pray over the words of the Bible, we can expect God to go on revealing himself to us throughout our Christian lives.

The revelation mentioned in 2 Corinthians is of the *risen* Jesus. Jesus made this astonishing claim about himself: "You search the Scriptures because you think that in them you have eternal life; and it is they that bear witness about me" (John 5:39). Through the Scriptures, we are meant to hear Jesus' voice. Jesus said, "My sheep hear my voice, and I know them, and they follow me" (John 10:27). As we read the law, even then we see him. He is revealed from the beginning of this Book to its end—it's all about Jesus.

This experience of seeing Jesus, of revelation, is not a once-for-all encounter. I'm sure many of us have known times when we listened to a sermon or read our Bible or a Christian book or had a discussion with a Christian friend, and a light suddenly went on. What we had never understood before unexpectedly became plain, and we could say, "I see it now!" At times we gain from the Bible a sense of being recharged or revived. If God is a reviving God, a resurrecting God, we may expect this to happen often as we read his Word.

William Cowper explains how God's full revelation is not given to us all at once: "If it be asked, seeing David was a regenerate man, and so illumined already, how is it that he prays for the opening of his eyes? The answer is easy: that our regeneration is wrought by degrees. The beginnings of light in his mind made him long for more."[3] We too can ask God to shine his light on us and reveal his truth to us.

Praying for revelation can have certain dangers. We need not ask

---

[3]Cited in C. H. Spurgeon, *Treasury of David*, on Psalm 119:18; http://www.studylight.org/com/tod/view.cgi?book=ps&chapter=119&verse=018.

God for guidance about something already made clear in the Scriptures. For example, we need not ask God whether to be baptized, nor if we should commit adultery; we must simply obey the biblical commands. Spurgeon explains, "The light which they beg is not anything besides the word. When God is said to enlighten us, it is not that we should expect new revelations, but that we may see the wonders in his word, or get a clear sight of what is already revealed."[4]

GOD'S WORD BRINGS RESURRECTION LIFE TO US

"My soul clings to the dust; give me life according to your word!" (Psalm 119:25).

As we recognize our desperate state before a holy God, God in his grace comes to us by his Word and says, "Live!" This is what happens when we become Christians, but it is also an essential part of the ongoing experience of the Christian who immerses himself in the Word of God and prayer. This is mentioned in several other places in the Bible:

> The law of the LORD is perfect, reviving the soul. (Psalm 19:7)

> Man shall not live by bread alone, but by every word that comes from the mouth of God. (Matthew 4:4; Deuteronomy 8:3)

> For the word of God is living and active, sharper than any two-edged sword, piercing to the division of soul and of spirit, of joints and of marrow, and discerning the thoughts and intentions of the heart. (Hebrews 4:12)

Today we are privileged to have so much more of the Bible than was available to David. Like David, the Scriptures can renew our spirits and sustain us even if we are feeling discouraged or in despair. When we feel low in energy and life, well-meaning words of support and comfort may be welcome, but a lifeline from God's Book will do more to energize and revitalize us than anything else our family and friends can say or do.

GOD'S WORD STRENGTHENS US

"My soul melts away for sorrow; strengthen me according to your word" (Psalm 119:28).

---

[4]Ibid.

The life-giving force of the Bible is here described as robust enough for us to lean on when we are feeling weak and lonely and depressed. As earthly food keeps us alive and refreshes us, God's Word sustains our souls, encourages us, and lifts us by focusing our minds and hearts on him.

Even some great men of God like Elijah became depressed. But God's servants learn to feast on his Word; they understand the enormity of its power. The Bible is full of verses that can become a kind of daily spiritual medication we can use, several times a day if necessary, to remind ourselves of God's promises. Spurgeon explains:

> Whatever your particular need may be, you will find some promise in the Bible related to it. Are you faint and feeble because your way is rough and you are weary? Here is the promise—"He gives power to the faint." When you read such a promise, take it back to the great Promiser and ask him to fulfill His own word. Are you seeking for Christ and thirsting for closer communion with him? This promise shines like a star upon you—"Blessed are those who hunger and thirst for righteousness, for they shall be satisfied." Take that promise to the throne continually; do not plead anything else, but go to God over and over again with this—"Lord, You have said it; do as You have said." Are you distressed because of sin and burdened with the heavy load of your iniquities? Listen to these words—"I, I am he who blots out your transgressions for my own sake, and I will not remember your sins." You have no merit of your own to plead why He should pardon you, but plead His written promises and He will perform them. Are you afraid that you might not be able to hold on to the end and that after having thought yourself a child of God you should prove a castaway? If that is your condition, take this word of grace to the throne and plead it: "The mountains may depart and the hills be removed, but my steadfast love shall not depart from you." If you have lost the sweet sense of the Savior's presence and are seeking him with a sorrowful heart, remember the promises: "Return to me . . . and I will return to you." "For a brief moment I deserted you, but with great compassion I will gather you." Feast your faith upon God's own Word, and whatever your fears or wants, take them to the Bank of Faith with your Father's note, which reads, "Remember your word to your servant in which you have made me hope."[5]

---

[5]Charles H. Spurgeon, *Morning and Evening, Revised and Updated by Alistair Begg* (Wheaton, IL: Crossway, 2003), April 28.

GOD'S WORD TEACHES US THE TRUTH

"The sum of your word is truth, and every one of your righteous rules endures forever" (Psalm 119:160).

It is important that we fill our minds and hearts with God's truth and not with lies. If God cannot lie, then neither can his Word. When we focus on God's Word, we inevitably find ourselves focusing on righteousness and not sin. As we read the Scriptures, we find that we can obey Paul's command in Philippians: "Finally, brothers, whatever is true, whatever is honorable, whatever is just, whatever is pure, whatever is lovely, whatever is commendable, if there is any excellence, if there is anything worthy of praise, think about these things" (4:8). As we read the Word, we meet God, and as a result our appetites and desires change, and we become more like Jesus.

God's Word is true. If the Bible is going to revive us, we must be able to trust it and believe that it is completely reliable. Some theologians today claim that to believe Scripture is completely true and without error (inerrant) is a new and therefore incorrect view. But this is very misleading. Berkouwer, contradicting this, says, "There can be no doubt that for a long time during church history certainty of faith was specifically linked to the trustworthiness of Holy Scripture as the Word of God. . . . From its earliest days the church held that Scripture is not an imperfect, humanly untrustworthy book of various religious experiences, but one with a peculiar mystery."[6]

Thankfully, many today still believe the Bible is without error. One such individual is my pastor, Tope Koleoso. Tope has a favorite saying that fits well at this point: "We mustn't stand above the Bible; we must stand under it."

GOD'S WORD GIVES US HOPE

"Remember your word to your servant, in which you have made me hope" (Psalm 119:49). "Those who fear you shall see me and rejoice, because I have hoped in your word" (Psalm 119:74). "My soul longs for your salvation; I hope in your word" (Psalm 119:81).

God's reviving Word gives us hope! If there is one thing that the

---

[6]G. C. Berkouwer, *Holy Scripture, Translation of DeHeilige Schrift*, ed. Jack Bartlett Rogers (Grand Rapids: Eerdmans, 1975), 11.

resurrection is meant to do, it is to give us hope—and that hope goes beyond the grave. Hope is closely related to faith, and we see in the New Testament that it is indeed God's Word that produces such faith in us, since "faith comes from hearing, and hearing through the word of Christ" (Romans 10:17).

Hope is infectious, as is despair. Therefore, we need to surround ourselves with people who will instill hope in us—a hope that is rooted in the Scriptures and not based on a whipped-up delusion. True friends who help us dare to believe the Bible are precious gifts. Scripture, soaked in prayer, ultimately gives us hope, lifts us up, and gives us life. God wants us to be aggressive in how much we place our hope in his Word. Many prayers recorded in the Bible show people reminding God of his promises and almost "suing" him to act. God responds to that kind of prayer—prayer that is mixed with his own Word.

We have examined many ways in which Psalm 119 describes the good that the Bible can do to us. We will now consider several ways in which we can appropriate God's Word.

GOD'S WORD IS WHERE WE CAN SEEK HIM

"With my whole heart I *seek* you; let me not wander from your commandments" (Psalm 119:10).

When we come to the Bible with a humble receptive heart, we may expect to meet the risen Jesus through its pages. We do not come to the Word only to grasp intellectual truth or to get our doctrine right, although those things are important. It is God we seek, and it is him we can encounter. Whether or not we know and understand it fully, he is the desire of our hearts. More than anything, it is God we need.

Many of us attempt to fill our lives with things that are not worthy of such investment as they can only satisfy for a time. This is a path that becomes an unending journey. The child who feels lonely does anything he can to please his classmates. When that fails, he supposes that growing up and leaving school will be the answer. Then he finds himself longing for a girlfriend, and then a wife, a better job, a better car, a better house. For many of us, this pattern only keeps repeating itself. The emptiness never goes away. Why? Because we don't understand that our desires were meant to be *satisfied by God*. We try to replace God with things that have no eternal significance. Even doing things for God can come out of an emptiness or lack of purpose. We must seek God and be satisfied in him before we can begin to reach others. How do we seek God? Primarily we will find him in the Bible. Some say theology is boring, but theology is simply the study of God. Since when was God boring? Rather, he satisfies us and gives us joy!

GOD'S WORD IS TO BE STORED IN OUR HEARTS

"I have *stored up* your word in my heart, that I might not sin against you" (Psalm 119:11).

One purpose of Scripture memorization is to help us defeat sin. David speaks not just of storing Scripture in our minds but also of getting it into our *hearts*. John Wesley explains, "I have laid it up in my mind like a choice treasure, to be ready upon all occasions to counsel, quicken, or caution me."[7] Spurgeon elaborates, "There, laid up in the heart, the word has effect. When young men only read the letter of the Book, the word of promise and instruction is deprived of much of its power. Neither will the laying of it up in the mere memory avail. The word must be known and prized, and laid up in the heart; it must occupy the affection as well as the understanding; the whole mind requires to be impregnated with the word of God."[8]

GOD'S WORD TEACHES US HOW TO LIVE

"Blessed are you, O LORD; *teach* me your statutes!" (Psalm 119:12).

Is it enough to *know* the Word? We may know the Word of God well but find it doesn't affect our daily lives to the extent it should. Theology must not simply remain an academic exercise; we need to allow it to show us how to live. Often evangelical preaching fails to show us how to apply God's Word in practical terms. There is a common belief that once biblical doctrine is preached, its implications will be obvious. But this is often not the case. Preaching should build a bridge from this world to the world of the Bible to allow us to understand the message and meet God, but then it must build a bridge back again to show us how to live.

---

[7]John Wesley, *Wesley's Notes on the Bible* (Grand Rapids: Zondervan, 1987), 219.
[8]Spurgeon, *Treasury of David*, on Psalm 119:11; http://www.studylight.org/com/tod/view.cgi?book= ps&chapter=119&verse=011.

Even if we are fortunate enough to listen to preaching that does work hard to apply the Bible, we may often still fail to understand how to respond personally. We each need mature Christians who know us well and can help us to live out the implications of Jesus' resurrection in our own lives. Christianity was never meant to be a solitary faith. Although ultimately our greatest teacher is God himself, he works through people. God provides us with those whom he has called to help us, and it is up to us to find them and listen to them. Our prayer should be the same as the psalmist in asking God to teach us, but we must not be surprised when he answers us by sending someone to challenge us with his Word. Paul tells us:

> All Scripture is breathed out by God and profitable for teaching, for reproof, for correction, and for training in righteousness, that the man of God may be competent, equipped for every good work. (2 Timothy 3:16–17)

The Scriptures are a powerful weapon that must be wielded with love and specifically applied to us as individuals. We need nothing in addition to the Bible for all matters of doctrine and ethical conduct. Practical wisdom can be acquired elsewhere, even from non-Christians, and many helpful books teach us how to understand the Bible better and how to live in the light of Jesus' resurrection.

There are, however, times when we face choices about which the Bible doesn't seem to speak. For example, we might have to decide between two equally good places to live. At other times, two different biblical principles may both appear relevant to the same situation and seem to have contradictory applications. We might ask whether this is a time to show *perseverance* in a work situation that is difficult or if it is time to show *boldness* and move on into what will ultimately be a better role. The Bible on its own will not be sufficient to help us deal with multiple challenges. We need biblically saturated leaders and friends who can wisely teach us how to apply the Bible's teaching to our specific situations. Such wisdom is a gift from God that is heightened by years of humbly submitting to God's Word. It is imperative to find a church in which there are godly leaders we can follow in this way.

GOD'S WORD IS TO BE DECLARED

"With my lips I *declare* all the rules of your mouth" (Psalm 119:13).

To whom should God's truth be declared? The best person to start with is yourself. We can declare God's Word as we read it. Reading Scripture aloud helps impress a passage on the mind, and often the powerful impact of the words will be made clearer. We can even use it like medicine—perhaps taking it like a pill three times a day.

Often God's Word will suddenly appear new to us, even if we've studied it before. Suddenly we understand it in a fresh way. Reading a verse again several times the same day will help us remember it but, more importantly, will help write it on our hearts.

We can declare God's Word in prayer. God loves it and is glorified when we declare his Word to him. We can also declare God's Word when confronting the enemy of our souls in spiritual warfare.

We are all meant to declare God's Word to others. Our commission is to share God's Word, spreading the good news of the gospel. God wants each of us to teach others at least something from the Bible, even if it is only on a one-to-one basis. To put it simply, God wants us to *learn* the message, *live* the message, and then *give* the message. God intends and indeed commands us to pass along the things he has taught us.

> Declare his glory among the nations, his marvelous works among all the peoples! (Psalm 96:3)

> One generation shall commend your works to another, and shall declare your mighty acts. (Psalm 145:4)

This second verse is an encouragement to all of us who are responsible for teaching children, whether we are parents, family members, pastors, or Sunday school teachers. The word "commend" in that verse implies that something else is necessary when we declare God's Word. Psalm 119:14 tells us what that is: "In the way of your testimonies I *delight* as much as in all riches."

When we commend God's Word to each other or to another generation, it is imperative that we are enthusiastic about it, that it is something we really believe, and that it is something we love and delight in! Do we genuinely *love* the words of the Bible? If we are honest, there are probably times when we don't delight in it the way we should. If that's true, we need to pray and ask God to change us. However, don't wait to feel delight before you begin to feed on God's Word. Instead, read it, study it, memorize it, apply it, and *declare it!* Over time you will find that his words will become more valuable to you, more precious, more reviving than you had expected.

GOD'S WORD IS TO BE MEDITATED UPON

"I will *meditate* on your precepts and fix my eyes on your ways" (Psalm 119:15).

Christian meditation is about filling our minds, not emptying them, and is a discipline that is much easier than many people realize. If you know how to worry, you know how to meditate. If your prayer is deteriorating into worrying aloud, it may be time to direct your mind away from running over the concerns of life again and again and instead to doing the same thing with a Bible verse. Meditation is allowing the words of Scripture to sift through your mind and be thoroughly examined in the same way that you would think about an issue that is worrying you. Allow Bible verses to run through your mind, consciously repeat them, and as you go through the day, let them permeate your thoughts. I love to program my mind with a few verses of Scripture, think on them for a while, and then go about my daily business. Often later that day, if I consciously bring back to my mind the same words, they make more sense. This is one way God's Word shapes our thoughts and becomes part of us.

When we struggle with negative patterns of thought, we can train ourselves to replace those harmful thoughts with an appropriate sentence from the Bible. If, for example, we have a tendency to feel inappropriate guilt for sin that has already been forgiven, when that thought enters our mind, we could develop the habit of replacing it with the words, "as far as the east is from the west, so far does he remove our transgressions from us" (Psalm 103:12).

When we are meditating we can ask all of the following questions: Who? What? Why? When? How? Where? Having asked those questions, we can then ask, So what? That is, what do I need to do, and how can I think or feel differently as a result of this verse? Here's an example of how Christian meditation might proceed.

Let's suppose I just read in the Bible that I have been adopted as God's son. This is how my thoughts might flow: *I am adopted by God. Who has been adopted? I have. By whom? By God! What does adopted mean? It means he chose me. Why has he done this? I suppose because he loves me! When did he do it? Ephesians 1 says, "before the creation of the world"* (NIV). *How did he do it? It was through Christ and his death on the cross as well as his resurrection. So what implications does this have? I suppose I should realize I am special since I am God's adopted child. Yes, but I must remember that I didn't deserve it and it came at a great cost to Jesus. I should be as happy as a child adopted by earthly parents would be. How much more should I be happy if God has adopted me! I should be really grateful, too. You know what? I am grateful! What this day has in store for me doesn't seem quite so bad after all! One last thought: God never changes his mind, so I am safe, I'm secure. He'll never let me go. Wow! Thank you, God! Later on, when my day is getting on top of me, I'm going to remind myself, I have been adopted by God!*

RECEIVING GOD'S WORD

Earlier we saw that God's Word brings revelation, revives, strengthens, and gives hope. We learned ways to connect to the life-giving power of the Bible. Is it any surprise that this Word was so precious to the psalmist? Is it any wonder that because of their diligent attitude toward God's Word the Bereans were honored? "They received the word with all eagerness, examining the Scriptures daily to see if these things were so" (Acts 17:11).

We, too, should receive this reviving Word with all eagerness and in every way allow ourselves to be molded by the gift God has given us in his authoritative Word. It is the only Book that can give life. Through its pages we receive the gift of salvation. It is the only manual for life that reveals the truth about how we should live and who God is. The Bible is incalculable in its value to us. To try to live the Christian life without immersing ourselves in God's Word is like trying to live without food.

If the Bible is like food to us, then prayer is like drink. Prayer connects us to the life-giving Spirit of God, who is often described as being like water. We must learn to feast on God's Word and to drink in his presence through prayer. If we want to be connected to the power made available to us through Jesus' resurrection, God's Word and prayer are the most effective tools we can use to access that power.

If prayer and the study of God's Word have become a chore, I pray that God himself will thrill you again and that he will give you the desire and ability to understand and apply his Word. May he help you pray in such a way that you receive an infusion of his reviving Spirit. Please pray for me too, that I may know the same thing in my life.

We have seen in this chapter and the previous one that prayer and Bible study are critical for experiencing the change that the resurrection brings. It is therefore not surprising that the apostles declared, "We will devote ourselves to prayer and to the ministry of the word" (Acts 6:4). While those words apply particularly to church leaders, we can all put them into practice.

CHAPTER FIFTEEN

A RELATIONSHIP WITH THE RISEN JESUS?

Our fellowship is with the Father and with his Son Jesus Christ.
1 JOHN 1:3

I will not leave you as orphans; I will come to you. . . . If anyone loves me, he will keep my word, and my Father will love him, and we will come to him and make our home with him.
JOHN 14:18-23

I count everything as loss because of the surpassing worth of knowing Christ Jesus my Lord. For his sake I have suffered the loss of all things and count them as rubbish, in order that I may gain Christ and be found in him . . . that I may know him and the power of his resurrection, and may share his sufferings, becoming like him in his death, that by any means possible I may attain the resurrection from the dead.
PHILIPPIANS 3:7-11

THE GREATEST GOAL OF Paul's life was a relationship with the resurrected Jesus. He considered everything else as worthless compared to this one thing. Paul claimed that knowing Jesus is *the* most critical thing, without which we will not be able to be changed by the power of Jesus' resurrection. We share in his sufferings and carry our cross (Mark 8:34), but by so doing, we share in the power of the resurrection, not only in the world to come, but also in this present world. Paul does not have to strive to attain to a future resurrection. That has already been achieved for him. Paul's battle is instead the same as every Christian's, that *in this life* we might experience in increasing measure something of what will be ours in the future. We can enjoy some of the future resurrection's benefits right now.

Jesus also promised that he and the Father would make their home with anyone who loves him. Elsewhere Paul describes this in the words, "Christ in you, the hope of glory" (Colossians 1:27). It is perhaps strange, then, that although some Christians today do talk about a personal relationship with Jesus, those words can somehow sound trite. Many are embarrassed by such a statement and perhaps for fear of being labeled a "crazy charismatic" do not seek such an experience, nor value it if it has happened to them.

Others are too busy seeking the gifts of the Holy Spirit to seek Jesus himself. The extremes that some go to in pursuing subjective experiences repulse many of us. Indeed, much controversy can arise when we speak about the validity of such experiences. We might even conclude that seeking to know God intimately is a sign of immaturity.

Many avoid showing any kind of emotion in response to God and are satisfied with studying God in a purely intellectual manner through Bible reading. We console ourselves with the idea that this is the "mature" approach and look down on those who are full of passion for a Jesus they claim to know. But a man who claimed to love a girl he had never met, but had only read letters she had written, would earn our pity. We were not promised a relationship with a book but with a person. Paul was not immature, and he wasn't foolish. He *was* passionate for his books (see 2 Timothy 4:13), but more so for his relationship with Jesus. There has to be a way for us to pursue a personal knowledge of Jesus without throwing away our biblical anchor. We can love the author of the book he left us, which is intended to reveal the person of Jesus to us.

Unfortunately, over the last few decades the controversy about whether or not the gifts of the Spirit are for today has largely obscured the more fundamental question—*are Christians today able to experience a truly personal relationship with Jesus?* In other words, what exactly did Jesus mean when he promised, "I will never leave you nor forsake you" (Hebrews 13:5) and "I am with you always, to the end of the age" (Matthew 28:20)? As we consider this question, let's leave aside for the moment our opinions on the gifts of the Holy Spirit and focus instead on whether an experience of God is available to believers today.

Paul says in Romans, "God's love has been poured into our hearts through the Holy Spirit who has been given to us" (Romans 5:5). Martyn Lloyd-Jones argues that these words require an experience of God's love:

> Paul says that the love of God is "shed abroad" in great profusion, overwhelmingly, in our hearts. Now that is what we should seek. We believe in God, in the Lord Jesus Christ, in the doctrines of salvation. All right! But the question that confronts us at this particular point is not that of believing, but love! A belief that does not lead to love is a very doubtful belief, it may be nothing but intellectual assent. . . .
>
> Here, then, is the question—to what extent do we know this love of God to us and how do we love God? We are meant to love him with the whole of our being and there is nothing that can make us do so but the love of God shed abroad in our hearts. . . .
>
> New Testament Christianity is not just a formal, polite, correct, and orthodox kind of faith and belief. No! What characterizes it is this element of love and passion, this pneumatic element, this life, this vigor, this abandon, this exuberance—and, as I say, it has ever characterized the life of the church in all periods of revival and of reawakening.[1]

This language of striving to know more of the power of the risen Christ in us sounds strangely alien to modern Christian ears. However, as one theologian argues, "The New Testament does not exhibit Jesus' resurrection as merely a prelude to some distant future. For regenerate believers, the resurrection is a present reality known and anticipatively experienced in daily fellowship with the risen Jesus. From the ascended Christ his followers received the indwelling Spirit outpoured at Pentecost; so too they still receive from him the Spirit's daily filling, and by the Spirit taste even now the powers of the age to come (Hebrews 6:5) and are daily sampling their coming inheritance (Ephesians 1:14)."[2]

Previous generations of Christians spoke warmly about their walk with God. Francis Schaeffer criticized many Christians of his day who had begun to lose this experience of God:

---

[1]Martyn Lloyd-Jones, *Joy Unspeakable* (Eastbourne, UK: Kingsway, 1995), 360–361.
[2]Carl F. H. Henry, *God, Revelation, and Authority*, Vol. 3 (Wheaton, IL: Crossway Books, 1999), 163.

Christianity is not just a mental assent that certain doctrines are true—not even that the right doctrines are true. This is only the beginning. This would be rather like a starving man sitting in front of great heaps of food and saying, "I believe the food exists; I believe it is real," and yet never eating it. It is not enough merely to say, "I am a Christian," and then in practice to live as if present contact with the supernatural were something far off and strange. Many Christians I know seem to act as though they come in contact with the supernatural just twice—once when they are justified and become a Christian, and once when they die. . . .

Some Christians seem to think that when they are born again, they become a self-contained unit like a storage battery. From that time on they have to go on their own pep and their own power until they die. But this is wrong. After we are justified, once for all through faith in Christ, we are to live in supernatural communion with the Lord every moment; we are to be like lights plugged into an electric socket. The Bible makes it plain that our joy and spiritual power depend on a continuing relation to God. If we do not love and draw on the Lord as we should, the plug gets pulled out and the spiritual power and the spiritual joy stop.[3]

The above quote is arguing for an experience of living in resurrection power and is much more consistent with what Christians from previous centuries wrote than what we hear or read today. John Owen, for example, wrote a whole book entitled *Communion with the Triune God*. It is remarkable how infrequently experiences such as those described below are mentioned, either during preaching or in modern Christian books. Unfortunately, many Christians are reluctant to talk about their experience of God. In this we differ greatly from Christians in previous centuries. J. I. Packer said that for the Puritans,

Communion with God was a great thing; to evangelicals today it is a comparatively small thing. The Puritans were concerned about communion with God in a way that we are not. The measure of our unconcern is the little that we say about it. When Christians meet, they talk to each other about their Christian work and Christian interests, their Christian acquaintances, the state of the churches, and the problems of theology—but rarely of their daily experience of God.[4]

---

[3]Francis Schaeffer, *Death in the City*, Chapter 9, in Francis A. Schaeffer, *The Complete Works of Francis A. Schaeffer: A Christian Worldview* (Wheaton, IL: Crossway Books, 1996).
[4]J. I. Packer, *A Quest for Godliness* (Wheaton, IL: Crossway Books, 1994), 215.

HISTORICAL EXPERIENCES OF JESUS

As a challenge to us to consider whether we are missing out, I will share some of the experiences of Christian historical figures. Some speak of an experience of God, but for others it is the risen Christ of whom they are aware. A clear picture emerges of a personal knowledge of Jesus. These personal testimonies are varied, but they share a number of common features.

Charles Spurgeon: "Beloved brethren and sisters in Christ, I think that you and I can say, that to us the surest fact in all the world is that there is a God. No God? I live in him. Tell a fish in the sea there is no water. No God? Tell a man who is breathing that there is no air. No God? I dare not come downstairs without speaking to him. No God? I would not think of closing my eyes in sleep unless I had some sense of his love shed abroad in my heart by the Holy Ghost. 'Oh!' says one, 'I have lived fifty years, and I have never felt anything of God.' Say that you had been dead fifty years; that is nearer to the mark. But if you had been quickened by the Holy Spirit fifty minutes, this would have been the first fact in the front rank of all fact, God is, and he is my Father, and I am his child. Now you become sentient to his frown, his smile, his threat, or his promise. You feel him; his presence is photographed upon your spirit; your very heart trembles with awe of him, and you say with Jacob, 'Surely God is in this place.' That is one result of spiritual life."[5]

John Flavel: "Thus going on his way his thoughts began to swell and rise higher and higher like the waters in Ezekiel's vision till at last they became an overflowing flood. Such was the intention of his mind, such the ravishing tastes of heavenly joys, and such the full assurance of his interest therein, that he utterly lost sight and sense of this world and all the concerns thereof, and for some hours he knew no more where he was than if he had been in a deep sleep upon his bed. Arriving in great exhaustion at a certain spring he sat down and washed, earnestly desiring, if it were God's pleasure, that it might be his parting place from this world. Death had the most amiable face in his eye that ever he beheld, except the face of Jesus Christ which made it so, and he could not remember, though he believed himself dying, that he had

---

[5] C. H. Spurgeon, *Sermon No. 2267*, "Life from the Dead," delivered March 13, 1890 at the Metropolitan Tabernacle, Newington; http://www.spurgeon.org/sermons/2267.htm.

one thought of his dear wife or children or any other earthly concern-
ment. On reaching his Inn the influence still continued, banishing sleep.
Still, still the joy of the Lord overflowed him, and he seemed to be an
inhabitant of the other world. He many years after called that day one
of the days of heaven, and said that he understood more of the light of
heaven by it than by all the books he ever read or discoveries he ever
had entertained about it."[6]

Jonathan Edwards: "I have sometimes had a sense of the excellent
fullness of Christ, and his meetness and suitableness as a savior; whereby
he has appeared to me, far above all, the chief of ten thousands. And his
blood and atonement has appeared sweet, and his righteousness sweet;
which is always accompanied with an ardency of spirit, and inward
strugglings and breathings and groanings, that cannot be uttered, to be
emptied of myself, and swallowed up in Christ.

"Once, as I rid out into the woods for my health . . . and having lit
from my horse in a retired place, as my manner commonly has been,
to walk for divine contemplation and prayer; I had a view, that for me
was extraordinary, of the glory of the Son of God; as mediator between
God and man; and his wonderful, great, full, pure and sweet grace and
love, and meek and gentle condescension. This grace, that appeared to
me so calm and sweet, appeared great above the heavens. The person of
Christ appeared ineffably excellent, with an excellency great enough to
swallow up all thought and conception. Which continued, as near as I
can judge, about an hour; which kept me, the bigger part of the time, in
a flood of tears, and weeping aloud. I felt withal, an ardency of soul to
be, what I know not otherwise how to express, than to be emptied and
annihilated; to lie in the dust, and to be full of Christ alone; to love him
with a holy and pure love; to trust in him; to live upon him; to serve and
follow him, and to be totally wrapt up in the fullness of Christ; and to be
perfectly sanctified and made pure, with a divine and heavenly purity. I
have several other times, had views very much of the same nature, and
that have had the same effects.

"I have many times had a sense of the glory of the third person in
the Trinity, in his office of Sanctifier; in his holy operations communi-

---

[6]David Martyn Lloyd-Jones, *God's Ultimate Purpose: An Exposition of Ephesians 1, 1 to 23* (Edinburgh
and Carlisle, PA: Banner of Truth Trust, 1978), 275.

cating divine light and life to the soul. God in the communications of his Holy Spirit, has appeared as an infinite fountain of divine glory and sweetness; being full and sufficient to fill and satisfy the soul: pouring forth itself in sweet communications, like the sun in its glory, sweetly and pleasantly diffusing light and life."[7]

David Brainerd: "Of late, God has been pleased to keep my soul hungry, almost continually; so that I have been filled with a kind of a pleasing pain: When I really enjoy God, I feel my desires of him the more insatiable, and my thirstings after holiness the more unquenchable; and the Lord will not allow me to feel as though I were fully supplied and satisfied, but keeps me still reaching forward; and I feel barren and empty, as though I could not live without more of God in me; I feel ashamed and guilty before God. Oh, I see 'the Law is spiritual, but I am carnal.' I don't, I can't live to God. Oh, for holiness! Oh, for more of God in my soul! Oh, this pleasing pain! It makes my soul press after God; the language of it is, 'Then shall I be satisfied, when I awake in God's likeness' (Psalms 17:15), but never, never before: and consequently I am engaged to 'press toward the mark,' day by day. Oh, that I may feel this continual hunger, and not be retarded, but rather animated by every 'cluster' from Canaan, to reach forward in the narrow way, for the full enjoyment and possession of the heavenly inheritance. Oh, that I may never loiter in my heavenly journey!"[8]

Howell Harris: "Suddenly I felt my heart melting within me like wax before a fire, and love to God for my Savior. I felt also not only love and peace, but a longing to die and be with Christ. Then there came a cry into my soul within that I had never known before—Abba, Father! I could do nothing but call God my Father. I knew that I was His child, and He loved me and was listening to me. My mind was satisfied and I cried out, Now I am satisfied! Give me strength and I will follow Thee through water and fire."[9]

John Owen: "Christ is our best friend, and ere long will be our only

---

[7]Jonathan Edwards, *Letters and Personal Writings*, WJE Online, Vol. 16, 801; http://edwards.yale.edu/archive?path=aHR0cDovL2Vkd2FyZHMueWFsZS5lZHUvY2dpLWJpbi9uZXdwaGlsby9nZXRvYmplY3QucGw/Yy4xNTo3NDo1LndqZW8=.

[8]Jonathan Edwards, *The Life of David Brainerd*, WJE Online, Vol. 7, 186; http://edwards.yale.edu/archive?path=aHR0cDovL2Vkd2FyZHMueWFsZS5lZHUvY2dpLWJpbi9uZXdwaGlsby9nZXRvYmplY3QucGw/Yy42OjQ6NDowOjUuLndqZW8=.

[9]Cited in D. M. Lloyd-Jones, *The Puritans: Their Origins and Successors* (Edinburgh: The Banner of Truth Trust, 1987), 282–302.

friend. I pray God with all my heart that I may be weary of everything else but converse and communion with him."[10]

These quotations are far from unique in their sentiments. Similar accounts are frequently found in the works of Christian leaders of the past. Some of these experiences happened at conversion, while others occurred later on. Often individuals would say they believed their true conversion occurred only when they had received an experience of God for the first time. Assurance of their salvation became secure only after encountering God *relationally*.

HOW SHOULD WE REACT TO REPORTS OF EXPERIENCES OF JESUS?

After examining the previous quotes, most readers, myself included, will be challenged because their own experience is not so dramatic. Indeed, these experiences are largely missing in modern churches. How can we explain the differences between the reports of Christians of the past and those of many of us today? How should we react when we read such passionate accounts of a vibrant relationship with Jesus?

One possible reaction is to simply advocate a purely intellectual approach to the faith, discounting the validity of such experiences altogether. We might honor the memory of great Christian leaders of the past without pursuing the knowledge of Jesus they enjoyed. Martyn Lloyd-Jones was very blunt in his denunciation of this approach to the Christian life. He referred to it as "dead . . . orthodoxy," and his description still bites today, decades after it was first written:

> There is nothing vital in the religion and in the worship of such people. They expect nothing, and they get nothing, and nothing happens to them. They go to God's house, not with the idea of meeting with God, not with the idea of waiting upon him; it never crosses their minds or enters into their hearts that something may happen in a service. No, we always do this on Sunday morning. It is our custom. It is our habit. It is a right thing to do. But the idea that God may suddenly visit his people and descend upon them, the whole thrill of being in the pres-

---

[10]Peter Toon, *God's Statesman: The Life and Work of John Owen* (Exeter, Devon: Paternoster, 1971), 153. Cited in John Piper, *The Chief Design of My Life: Mortification and Universal Holiness (Reflections on the Life and Thoughts of John Owen)*; available online at http://www.desiringgod.org/ResourceLibrary/Sermons/ByDate/1997/990_Let_Us_Draw_Near_to_God/.

ence of God, and sensing his nearness, and his power, never even enters their imaginations. . . .

Do we go to God's house expecting something to happen? Or do we go just to listen to a sermon, and to sing our hymns, and to meet with one another? How often does this vital idea enter into our minds that we are in the presence of the living God, that the Holy Spirit is in the church, that we may feel the touch of his power? How much do we think in terms of coming together to meet with God, and to worship him, and to stand before him, and to listen to him? Is there not this appalling danger that we are just content because we have correct beliefs? And we have lost the life, the vital thing, the power, the thing that really makes worship worship, which is in Spirit and truth.[11]

This idea of church as a place to encounter God through worship and his word is not emphasized today. There is a tendency to divide on this issue of experience. Both sides have reacted to each other at various points. The two sterotypes, that some Christians are obsessed by the latest fad-like experience, while others are theologically correct but as dry as tinder, are not entirely without foundation. But Don Carson, in this succinct statement, urges us to stop overreacting:

Because some wings of the church have appealed to experience over against revelation, or have talked glibly about ill-defined "spirituality" that is fundamentally divorced from the gospel, some of us have over-reacted and begin to view all mention of experience as suspicious at best, perverse at worst. This overreaction must cease. The Scriptures themselves demand that we allow more place for experience than that.[12]

In an effort to steer a similar middle course, Lloyd-Jones wrote the following about the church's tendency to veer from one extreme to the other:

The trouble has generally been . . . that people have emphasized either experience or doctrine at the expense of the other. . . . This is something that has been happening in the church from almost the very beginning. . . . When the whole emphasis is placed upon one or the other, you either have a tendency to fanaticism and excess or a tendency

[11]Martyn Lloyd-Jones, *Revival* (Wheaton, IL: Crossway, 1987), 68–72.
[12]D. A. Carson, *A Call to Spiritual Reformation* (Grand Rapids: Baker, 1992), 191.

toward a barren intellectualism and a mechanical and a dead kind of orthodoxy. . . .

As you read the stories of Luther and Calvin and other reformation fathers you will find that they began to fight this war on two fronts. They were fighting a dead, mechanical intellectualism on one hand, and they had to fight these other people who were running to excess and riot on the other. Then in the seventeenth century you find the same kind of thing in connection with the Puritan movement. . . . There were three main sections . . . in the middle you had people like the great John Owen and Thomas Goodwin in London, who constantly emphasized what they regarded as the only true scriptural position . . . which emphasizes Spirit and doctrine, experience and definition. You must not say it is either/or; it is both. These, too, had to wage a warfare constantly on the two fronts. They had to fight the dead, barren intellectualism of many in Anglicanism and in the ranks of Puritanism, and the wild excesses of the early Quakers and various others. . . .

As Evangelicals we find ourselves fighting on two fronts. We are obviously critical of a pure intellectualism and of a dead mechanical church which lacks any life . . . the gospel of Jesus Christ is a life-giving gospel. That is one side; but on the other side we see certain tendencies and we see certain excesses and we say, "believe not every spirit, but try the spirits to see whether they are of God." And thus we seem to be opposing everything, and so we receive criticism from all sides. . . .

For myself, as long as I am charged by certain people with being nothing but a Pentecostalist, and on the other hand charged by others with being an intellectual, a man who is always preaching doctrine, as long as the two criticisms come, I am very happy. But if one or the other of the two criticisms should ever cease, then, I say, is the time to be careful and to begin to examine the very foundations. The position of Scripture . . . is one which is facing two extremes. The Spirit is essential, and experience is vital. However, truth and definition and doctrine and dogma are equally vital and essential. And our whole position is one which proclaims that experience which is not based solidly upon truth and doctrine is dangerous.[13]

As Jonathan Edwards, a great Reformed theologian who believed in experiences of God for the believer, explained:

So God glorifies himself towards the creatures also in two ways: (1) by appearing to them, being manifested to their understandings;

---

[13]Martyn Lloyd-Jones, *Life in Christ* (Wheaton, IL: Crossway, 2002), 400–403.

(2) in communicating himself to their hearts, and in their rejoicing and delighting in, and enjoying the manifestations which he makes of himself. . . . God is glorified not only by his glory's being seen, but by its being rejoiced in, when those that see it delight in it: God is more glorified than if they only see it.[14]

John Piper claims that these few words have been the foundation for his entire ministry.[15] Their practical application no doubt explains the passion that is seen in his preaching, which has been described as "God-intoxication." Piper frequently hints that there is more to our savoring and valuing of God than what the typical modern-day shallow walk with God allows. Piper elaborates:

Is it not clear that the experience varies from time to time and from person to person? Otherwise, Paul would not pray for it as often as he does. . . . These are the two things Paul did again and again. He wrote to his people to direct their minds to the truth of God in Christ. And he prayed that the Holy Spirit would give them eyes to see the glory of what he was writing about.[16]

In recent years in many churches there has been a coming together of a love of the Bible and a desire to know God personally. Those of us in this middle camp need to do more than be content to accept the validity of the stories of others. Some have described themselves as "open but cautious," and I can understand the reasons for that perspective. However, if experiences are valid and available, we cannot afford to be *too* cautious, passively waiting for God to perhaps one day overwhelm us. Instead we can and should be pursuing a relationship with God. In this process we must test all such experiences by the Bible and avoid the excesses of becoming driven by a desire for experience for its own sake.

Many Christians, myself included, are aware of some level of intimacy with God, yet still long for an increase in the vitality of this personal relationship with our Savior. We long to be as aware of our Lord Jesus as those I have quoted above were.

Can anyone read those accounts and still be satisfied with a lesser

---

[14]Cited in "The Pastor as Theologian"; http://www.desiringgod.org/ResourceLibrary/Biographies/1458 _The_Pastor_as_Theologian/.
[15]See ibid.
[16]See http://www.desiringgod.org/ResourceLibrary/Sermons/ByDate/1999/1101_God_Demonstrates _His_Love_Toward_Us/.

experience? Or does reading them make you yearn for more of God? If the latter, let me urge you to join me in praying that God will reveal himself personally to us in the way he has done to many others before us. Please pray for me, as I am praying for you, that we might all know Jesus more.

As this chapter ends, we should ask ourselves, do I *really* love Jesus? Am I aware of his love for me in such a way that I have a strong desire to be holy? Am I devoted to Jesus? Do I glory in him and value him in such a way that when someone looks at me they could say, "His life is all about Jesus"? This doesn't only mean that we turn up at church on Sunday morning, although it does include that. It's not simply about listening to worship songs in our car or our own personal time with God. Rather, it means that every moment of every day we actively seek opportunities to give God glory.

CHAPTER SIXTEEN

ASSURED BY THE RESURRECTED CHRIST

And I am sure of this, that he who began a good work in you
will bring it to completion at the day of Jesus Christ.

PHILIPPIANS 1:6

ASSURANCE OF SALVATION is an inner certainty that we are indeed Christians who are destined for heaven. At times many Christians feel uneasy about this. Feelings of guilt and condemnation may give rise to serious doubts about whether they are really Christians.

The Bible tells us, "If you confess with your mouth that Jesus is Lord and believe in your heart that God raised him from the dead, you will be saved" (Romans 10:9).

This verse suggests a straightforward way to answer the question, am I saved? The problem is that simply mouthing the words cannot be enough. John Piper makes this point by asking if a computer could become a Christian. He cites 1 Corinthians 12:3, which says that no one can say Jesus is Lord apart from the help of the Holy Spirit, and says, "Now a computer can say it. It must say it and mean it, that is, have an experiential sense that he is worthy of such an ascription, and heartfelt allegiance to his lordship that is different from the Devil's belief that Jesus is Lord."[1] Clearly a computer could not become a Christian and therefore, by extension, if someone merely mouths these words without actually meaning them, they will not be saved either.

James challenges us that "even the demons believe—and shudder!" (James 2:19). So how can we know if our faith is genuine? First, the

---

[1]John Piper, personal communication, 2009.

words must not be mindlessly repeated. We must be convinced in our mind and heart that Jesus is divine, that he has risen and is now ruling. We must determine that Jesus is *our* Lord and begin to follow him. Our lives must change. Jesus says, "You will recognize them by their fruits" (Matthew 7:20). Thus, when we see that we are growing in the fruit of the Spirit recorded in Galatians 5—"love, joy, peace, patience, kindness, goodness, faithfulness, gentleness, self-control"—our confidence can grow. As is often said, it is faith alone that saves, but the faith that saves is never alone.

We must also learn to value Jesus and to love him. This should affect our emotions and give rise to at least some level of experience. This might be very limited, however, and if we claim that everybody has received everything that is available at conversion, we will settle for a very meager experience indeed.

These evidences, and others, do assure us that we are genuine Christians. But there is an even greater source of assurance to be found in the deeper experiences made available for us through the resurrection. What we need is an *inner assurance of the heart*—that deep-rooted confidence that comes when the Spirit confirms to us that we belong to Jesus. I like to call this direct assurance. Paul describes this:

> You have received the Spirit of adoption as sons, by whom we cry, "Abba! Father!" The Spirit himself bears witness with our spirit that we are children of God. (Romans 8:15–16)

> God's love has been poured into our hearts through the Holy Spirit who has been given to us. (Romans 5:5)

These verses best explain the personal accounts describing experiences of Jesus written in the previous chapter. Each person received a new confidence, which was the direct product of a personal encounter with God. The Puritans and others of the past emphasized "full assurance" as being a work of the Spirit of God meeting with our spirit and telling us that we are God's children. Douglas Moo explains:

> The confidence we have for the day of judgment is not based only on our intellectual recognition of the fact of God's love, or even only on the demonstration of God's love on the cross . . . but on the inner,

subjective certainty that God does love us . . . and it is this internal, subjective, yes, even emotional, sensation within the believer that God does indeed love us—love expressed and made vital in real, concrete actions on our behalf—that gives to us the assurance that "hope will not disappoint us."[2]

John Piper clarifies this with a helpful example:

Let me use an illustration from Martyn Lloyd-Jones. . . . He says it is like a child walking along holding his father's hand. All is well. The child is happy. He feels secure. His father loves him. He believes that his father loves him but there is no unusual urge to talk about this or sing about it. It is true and it is pleasant.

Then suddenly the father startles the child by reaching down and sweeping him up into his arms and hugging him tightly and kissing him on the neck and whispering, "I love you so much!" And then holding the stunned child back so that he can look into his face and saying with all his heart, "I am so glad you are mine." Then hugging him once more with unspeakable warmth and affection. Then he puts the child down and they continue their walk. . . .

The child is simply stunned. He doesn't know whether to cry or shout or fall down or run, he is so happy. The fuses of love are so overloaded they almost blow out. The subconscious doubts—that he wasn't thinking about at the time, but that pop up every now and then—are gone! And in their place is utter and indestructible assurance, so that you know that you know that you know that God is real and that Jesus lives and that you are loved, and that to be saved is the greatest thing in the world. And as you walk on down the street you can scarcely contain yourself, and you want to cry out, "My father loves me! My father loves me! O, what a great father I have! What a father! What a father!"

I think this is basically what happened at Pentecost. And has happened again and again in the life of the church.[3]

These experiences are strongly linked in the Bible to the resurrection of Jesus, and as one popular Reformed Bible encyclopedia claims, "Resurrection is not only a future hope, but a present experience."[4]

---

[2]Douglas Moo, *The Epistle to the Romans* (Grand Rapids, MI: Eerdmans, 1996), 304–305.
[3]John Piper, "You Shall Receive Power Till Jesus Comes"; http://www.desiringgod.org/ResourceLibrary/Sermons/ByDate/1990/727_You_Shall_Receive_Power_Till_Jesus_Comes/.
[4]Donald K. McKim and David F. Wright, *Encyclopedia of the Reformed Faith*, 1st edition (Louisville: John Knox Press, 1992), 320.

THE RISEN JESUS—SENDER OF THE HOLY SPIRIT

"This Jesus God raised up, and of that we all are witnesses. Being therefore exalted at the right hand of God, and having received from the Father the promise of the Holy Spirit, he has poured out this that you yourselves are seeing and hearing" (Acts 2:32–33). "If the Spirit of him who raised Jesus from the dead dwells in you, he who raised Christ Jesus from the dead will also give life to your mortal bodies through his Spirit who dwells in you" (Romans 8:11).

In Paul's letters he often refers to what it is that enables him to keep going. Sometimes he attributes this to the Holy Spirit (e.g., 2 Corinthians 3:6), but on other occasions he credits it to Jesus. For example, in 1 Timothy 1:12 he says, "I thank him who has given me strength, Christ Jesus our Lord." Paul is able to say this because he understood that it is the *risen* Jesus who sends the Holy Spirit to do this work in us. Paul also uses the terms "in Christ" and "in the Spirit" interchangeably.

Christians over the centuries have testified to a sense of peace and calm when facing immense challenges. This peace is a direct gift of the risen Christ. Jesus' promise to his disciples is still true today for all believers: "Peace I leave with you; my peace I give to you. Not as the world gives do I give to you. Let not your hearts be troubled, neither let them be afraid" (John 14:27).

Jesus is introduced in each Gospel as the one who will baptize with the Holy Spirit (Matthew 3:11; Mark 1:8; Luke 3:16; John 1:33). The fact that this sending of the Spirit is the work of Jesus is confirmed by the words he spoke to his disciples:

> I will ask the Father, and he will give you another Helper, to be with you forever, even the Spirit of truth, whom the world cannot receive, because it neither sees him nor knows him. You know him, for he dwells with you and will be in you. (John 14:16–17)

Jesus also said, "I tell you the truth: it is to your advantage that I go away, for if I do not go away, the Helper will not come to you. But if I go, I will send him to you" (John 16:7).

Jesus was providing comfort and reassurance to his disciples, promising that when he left them, something would happen that would be to their advantage. The Holy Spirit was to be even better than if Jesus had remained with them. It must have been hard for the disciples to believe this at the time. Lloyd-Jones drives this point home:

> How can it be expedient for the disciples that He should leave them in the flesh and go away from them in the body? How can that be true if it is not possible for the Christian to know him immediately and directly?
>
> Obviously the supreme blessing is to be with Him, in His presence and in His company. What He is really saying is that after He has gone and has baptized them with the Holy Ghost, He will be more real to them than He was at that moment. And this is what actually happened. They knew Him much better after Pentecost than they knew Him before. He was more real to them, more living to them, more vital to them afterwards than He was in the days of His flesh. His promise was literally fulfilled and verified.[5]

Is Jesus more real to you now than he would be if you could see him and talk to him face-to-face? This perspective on that verse alone confirms to me that there has to be more to the outpouring of the Holy Spirit than I have experienced personally. Jesus himself calls us to actively receive the Spirit, described as "living water":

> On the last day of the feast, the great day, Jesus stood up and cried out, "If anyone thirsts, let him come to me and drink. Whoever believes in me, as the Scripture has said, 'Out of his heart will flow rivers of living water.'" Now this he said about the Spirit, whom those who believed in him were to receive, for as yet the Spirit had not been given, because Jesus was not yet glorified. (John 7:37–39)

The *risen* Jesus gave us the Holy Spirit. The Holy Spirit could only be poured out because of Jesus' resurrection. Prior to the death, resurrection, and glorification of Jesus, the Holy Spirit, although at work in the world, had not yet been sent to do this special work. God's active presence had been largely withdrawn ever since the Fall, with the occasional outbreak of his manifested presence.

Obviously Jesus could not be the one who pours out the Holy Spirit today if he had remained dead. The Spirit's outpouring proves that Jesus is alive. As Bible teacher Terry Virgo often says, "Dead corpses aren't too good at giving the Holy Spirit."

[5]D. M. Lloyd-Jones, *An Exposition of Ephesians 3* (Grand Rapids: Baker, 1979), 247–253.

If we neglect to emphasize the resurrection of Jesus, we may also miss out on knowing God in a more direct sense. This is because the experience of the Spirit referred to by Paul in Ephesians 1, Romans 5, and Romans 8 is strongly connected to his resurrection. We receive the same Spirit who raised Jesus from the dead, and this power seems to be more available when we actually talk about the empty tomb. Nothing is impossible for the same power that can bring a crucified corpse back to life.

Because of his resurrection, Jesus became a life-giving Spirit (1 Corinthians 15:45) and pours out the Holy Spirit on his people to empower them for service and assure them of their own future resurrection. There is a mystery to this union between the Spirit and Jesus:

> As resurrected, Christ is in such total and final possession of the Holy Spirit that the two, without confusion or the obliteration of personal Trinitarian distinction, are one (cf. 2 Corinthians 3:17). In the work of communicating eschatological, resurrection life, the activity of the Spirit in the church is the activity of the resurrected Christ (Romans 8:9–10). Primarily with Pentecost in view, the resurrected Christ tells his disciples, "I am with you always, to the end of the age" (Matthew 28:20).[6]

We have received the same Spirit who raised Christ from the dead! The same power that conquered the grave is at work in us. Without the resurrection, there would be no sending of the Spirit. Without the Spirit, there would be no salvation, no power, and no victory in our struggle against sin. Paul illustrates this using words that should thrill us:

> I do not cease to give thanks for you, remembering you in my prayers . . . that you may know what is the hope to which he has called you, what are the riches of his glorious inheritance in the saints, and what is the immeasurable greatness of his power toward us who believe, *according to the working of his great might that he worked in Christ when he raised him from the dead and seated him at his right hand in the heavenly places.* (Ephesians 1:16–20)

WHEN DO WE GAIN THE HOLY SPIRIT?

There is much debate about how and when this happens. Some believe that we receive everything the Spirit has to give us at the moment of our

---

[6]McKim and Wright, *Encyclopedia of the Reformed Faith*, 320.

conversion. But not every Christian has a powerful emotional encounter with Jesus at the moment he or she is born again. Some argue, therefore, that receiving the Spirit is automatic to becoming a Christian and not something that is tangible or outwardly visible. They say that the Spirit is received by faith, and we know we have him because we have believed. Others, such as Martyn Lloyd-Jones, have argued strongly that it is essential that we allow room for a subsequent experience of the Holy Spirit. Lloyd-Jones argues this should be called baptism with the Spirit:

> There is nothing, I am convinced, that so "quenches" the Spirit as the teaching which identifies the baptism of the Holy Ghost with regeneration. But it is a very commonly held teaching today, indeed it has been the popular view for many years. It is said that the baptism of the Holy Spirit is "non-experimental," that it happens to everyone at regeneration. So we say, "Ah well, I am already baptized with the Spirit; it happened when I was born again, at my conversion; there is nothing for me to seek, I have got it all." Got it all? Well, if you have "got it all," I simply ask in the Name of God, why are you as you are? If you have "got it all," why are you so unlike the Apostles, why are you so unlike the New Testament Christians?
>
> The teaching that I have just mentioned is false. The apostles were regenerate before the day of Pentecost. The baptism of the Holy Ghost is not identical with regeneration; it is something separate. It matters not how long the interval between the two may be, there is a difference; there is an interval, they are not identical. But if you say that they are identical, you do not expect anything further. And if you do not believe that it is possible for you to experience the Spirit of God bearing direct witness with your own spirit that you are a child of God, obviously you are quenching the Spirit. That is why so many Christian people are miserable and unhappy; they do not know anything about crying out, "Abba, Father," or about "the Spirit of adoption." God is a Being away in the far distance; they do not know him as a loving Father.[7]

There is much debate about the correct terminology that we should use to define this experience of God mediated through the Holy Spirit. Some would agree with the concept of pursuing God for a relationship

---

[7]D. Martyn Lloyd-Jones, *An Exposition of Ephesians 6:10 to 13* (Edinburgh: Banner of Truth Trust, 1976), 280.

felt experientially but would disagree that one should use the term *baptism with the Spirit* for that relationship. We probably should not get too preoccupied with terminology here, but in the next section we will consider the biblical terms used to describe the Holy Spirit's work in our lives. I hope we can all agree that whatever we choose to call his work, the Spirit is definitely involved in every believer's life but is also available to us in fuller measure and in ways that often represent sudden dramatic invasions of his activity into our lives.

BAPTISM WITH THE HOLY SPIRIT

For a phrase that has become so controversial in the church, there are remarkably few mentions of it in Scripture. It is mentioned once in each of the Gospels as a future act of Jesus (Matthew 3:11; Mark 1:8; Luke 3:16; John 1:33). In Acts 1:5; 2:38; 11:16 it is revealed as the same phenomenon as Luke's preferred term "receiving the Spirit" (see Acts 10:47), and it is used just once by Paul:

> For in one Spirit we were all baptized into one body—Jews or Greeks, slaves or free—and all were made to drink of one Spirit. (1 Corinthians 12:13)

Much ink has been spilled on whether the verse is referring to the same thing as in Acts and the Gospels. It is debated whether every Christian or just the majority of Christians in the Corinthian church had been baptized in one Spirit. Many argue that the first half of the verse must refer to what happens at conversion, although, even if that is correct, we could conclude that this verse itself teaches a two-stage experience—baptism into Christ followed by a drinking of the Spirit.

John Piper appeals to us to lay aside our arguments about what the words *baptism with the Holy Spirit* signify by focusing on the concept of an ever greater need we have to be overwhelmed by the Spirit:

> Jesus immerses people in the Spirit. That's what the word baptize means. There are pictures in the Bible of the Spirit being poured out. But when the idea of baptism (that is, dipping or immersion) is brought in, the point is that the Spirit is poured over us to such an extent that we are enveloped in him.

The point of this image is that the Spirit becomes profoundly and pervasively influential in our lives. When you are immersed in something, it touches you everywhere. So when John says that Jesus is going to baptize with the Spirit, he means that the day is coming when the lives of God's people will be plunged into the life of the Spirit with profound and pervasive effects. . . .

As I have tried to let John define for us what he means by baptism with the Spirit, it seems to me that the term is a broad, overarching one that includes the whole great saving, sanctifying, and empowering work of the Spirit in this age. I don't think it is a technical term that refers to one part of the Christian life—say conversion, or speaking in tongues, or a bold act of witness. It is the continual, and sometimes extraordinary, outpouring of the Holy Spirit on God's people. It immerses them not just in one or two, but in hundreds of his powerful influences.

In other words, if you are not born again, one way to describe your need is that you need to be baptized with the Spirit. That is, you need to be plunged into God's Spirit with the effect that you will be born again and come to faith in Christ. If you are born again, but you are languishing in a season of weakness and fear and defeat, one way to describe what you need is to be baptized in the Spirit. That is, you need a fresh outpouring of his Christ-revealing, heart-awakening, sin-defeating, boldness-producing power. Every spiritual need that we have before and after conversion is supplied by Christ immersing us in greater and lesser degrees in the Holy Spirit.[8]

A DEPOSIT GUARANTEEING OUR INHERITANCE

"In him you also, when you heard the word of truth, the gospel of your salvation, and believed in him, were sealed with the promised Holy Spirit, who is the guarantee of our inheritance until we acquire possession of it, to the praise of his glory" (Ephesians 1:13–14).

Some argue that faith in God (which from Ephesians 2 we know is itself a work of the Spirit) is a distinct experience from a sealing with the Spirit. Lloyd-Jones spends several chapters on this concept, defining it as "God's action, in which He bears witness that we are His children. . . . It is God's authentication of the fact that we really belong to him."[9]

Lloyd-Jones cites John Wesley's definition of this: "It is something

---

[8]John Piper, "This Is He Who Baptized with the Holy Spirit"; http://www.desiringgod.org/ResourceLibrary/Sermons/ByDate/2008/3418_This_Is_He_Who_Baptizes_with_the_Holy_Spirit/.
[9]David Martyn Lloyd-Jones, *God's Ultimate Purpose: An Exposition of Ephesians 1, 1 to 23* (Edinburgh and Carlisle, PA: Banner of Truth Trust, 1978), 255–256.

immediate and direct, not the result of reflection or argumentation."[10]
He also quotes Thomas Goodwin: "There is a light that cometh and
overpowereth a man's soul and assureth him that God is his and he is
God's, and that God loveth him from everlasting. . . . It is a light beyond
the light of ordinary faith. . . . It is the next thing to heaven; you have no
more, you can have no more, until you come thither."[11]

Other commentators conclude instead that this sealing happens at
conversion, is something more visible to God than to us, and is a defi-
nite mark that we are Christians analogous to the mark of blood placed
above the doorposts during the Passover (Exodus 12). According to this
argument we are either Christians or we are not, and so we either have
the seal or we do not, irrespective of whether we know we have it.

Paul also describes the Spirit as a down payment on our future,
which is to spend eternity in a perfect relationship with Jesus. The
deposit is a person. This foretaste or appetizer must include a relationship with Christ by the Spirit, preparing us for the main course, which
will be ours when Jesus returns. For the Spirit to function as a deposit or
guarantee, we have to know that we have him; we cannot be expected
to simply conclude that because we have believed, we have the whole
benefit of the Spirit's work. If a man wanted to buy my house and simply
told me he had given me a deposit, I would not believe him until I knew
that the money was in my bank account and available for me to use. By
the conscious reality of the Spirit's work in our hearts, we experience
some of our future benefits right now in the present. The Holy Spirit is
a foretaste of heaven (see also 2 Corinthians 5:4–5 and Romans 8:23,
which speak of "the firstfruits of the Spirit"). This can only make sense
if his work is something we are aware of in our lives. The Spirit's desire
is to bring glory to Jesus (John 16:14). So we can judge whether an
experience is from the Spirit in part on the basis of whether it causes us
to desire to worship Jesus more.

We are right to eagerly await pie in the sky when we die, but we can
also have cake on our plate while we wait! The psalmist says, "Oh, taste
and see that the LORD is good!" (Psalm 34:8). God is to be enjoyed and
adored in this life.

---

[10]Ibid., 275.
[11]Ibid.

RECEIVING THE SPIRIT

"Repent and be baptized every one of you in the name of Jesus Christ for the forgiveness of your sins, and you will receive the gift of the Holy Spirit. For the promise is for you and for your children and for all who are far off, everyone whom the Lord our God calls to himself" (Acts 2:38–39).

The book of Acts frequently refers to receiving the Spirit. Here Peter promised that anyone who repents and is baptized can receive the Spirit, implying that this is a distinct event from coming to faith. This promise is available to everyone who repents and believes in Jesus and is baptized. It would be circular logic to interpret Peter's words as meaning "repent and believe, be baptized, and you will receive a work of the Spirit automatically without you being aware of it, the main effect of which is to cause you to believe." There has to be some kind of distinct effects of the Spirit in us so we can conclude we have received him. We are told that we can seek for and consciously *receive* the Holy Spirit. Of course, this is not to deny the activity of the same Spirit in causing the believer to come to faith in Christ; it is simply to say that we can become more *aware* of his activity.

In Acts 8, the Samaritans believed in the gospel and were baptized, but it was only when the apostles came from Jerusalem and laid hands on them that they received the Holy Spirit. What is astonishing is that the magician, Simon, had observed miraculous healings performed by Stephen, but it was only when he witnessed the apostles imparting the Holy Spirit that he offered money to be able to do the same. This experience was obviously tangible and powerful, with dramatic life-changing effects on people.

In Acts 9, Paul repented and believed when he met the risen Jesus. Yet Ananias tells Paul, "Brother Saul, the Lord Jesus who appeared to you on the road by which you came has sent me so that you may regain your sight and be filled with the Holy Spirit" (Acts 9:17). This is another example where believing and receiving the Holy Spirit occur as separate events. Secondly, the specific instructions that are recorded as given to Ananias regarding Paul did not actually include praying for him to receive the Holy Spirit. This could suggest this was so commonly part of the normal practice when helping new believers that when Jesus sent him to Paul, Ananias concluded he had also sent him to impart the Spirit.

In Acts 10, while Peter was proclaiming the gospel to the Gentiles for the first time, the Spirit is described as "falling" and being "poured out." Peter then proclaimed they had received the Spirit as a stamp of God's approval of them as part of his saved people.

In Acts 19, Paul asked a group of people about their experience of the Holy Spirit. He assumed that it is possible for someone to believe without receiving the Spirit. The fact that these disciples may well not have believed *or* received the Spirit is immaterial to the argument. John Piper explains this:

> Paul says, "Did you receive the Holy Spirit when you believed?" We scratch our heads and say, "I don't get it, Paul. If you assume we believed, why don't you assume we received the Holy Spirit? We've been taught that all who believe receive the Holy Spirit. We've been taught to just believe that the Spirit is there whether there are any effects or not. But you talk as if there is a way to know we've received the Holy Spirit different from believing. You talk as if we could point to an experience of the Spirit apart from believing in order to answer your question." And that is in fact the way Paul talks. When he asks, "Did you receive the Spirit when you believed," he expects that a person who has "received the Holy Spirit" knows it, not just because it's an inference from his faith in Christ, but because it is an experience with effects that we can point to. That is what runs all the way through this book of Acts. All the explicit descriptions of receiving the Holy Spirit are experiential (not inferential).[12]

In the book of Acts, receiving the Holy Spirit is not something that we can infer or assume has happened to us. Rather, it is a conscious, real experience that, at least in Acts, is usually accompanied by tongues and/or prophecy. At its core, however, it would seem from the rest of the New Testament that it is an experience of the love of God poured out into the believer's heart by the resurrected Jesus, giving tangible, visible effects.

If we were to ask Paul what the purpose of the gospel is for us in this present world, we might be surprised by his answer. In an often

---

[12]John Piper, "What Does It Mean to Receive the Holy Spirit?"; http://www.desiringgod.org/ResourceLibrary/Sermons/ByDate/1991/758_What_Does_It_Mean_to_Receive_the_Holy_Spirit/.

overlooked phrase he says, "Christ redeemed us from the curse of the law by becoming a curse for us . . . *so that* we might receive the promised Spirit through faith" (Galatians 3:13–14).

Here the Spirit is received by faith. Therefore Paul can't simply be referring to the Spirit's role in bringing us to faith. This extraordinary statement means the goal of the gospel is that we become aware of the Spirit's work in our lives. It only makes real sense when we remember what he is primarily meant to do for us. He is to restore something of the same relational intimacy with God that was enjoyed in the Garden of Eden and that we will share more perfectly in heaven. When we receive the Spirit, we are restored to a conscious fellowship with God, and with even this imperfect knowledge, our love and worship for him can only increase. The meaning of this astonishing emphasis on the pouring out of the Spirit is this: Jesus died in order that we might taste heaven even here on earth. That is the role of the Spirit when we are aware of him at work in our lives. He is a gift, or foretaste, given to believers until the day comes when we are finally reunited fully with Christ. Such knowledge of God brings great peace and settles in our hearts the question of whether or not we are children of God. We now know clearly. It is analogous to falling in love in that mere words become inadequate when attempting to describe the experience.

Elsewhere Paul also tells us that the mystery he has unveiled is "Christ in you, the hope of glory" (Colossians 1:27). This indwelling by Christ through the Spirit must be consciously experienced for it to produce glorious hope. Piper elaborates:

> It is right to stress the experiential reality of receiving the Spirit. When you read the New Testament honestly you can't help but get the impression of a big difference from a lot of contemporary Christian experience. For them, the Holy Spirit was a fact of experience. For many Christians today it is a fact of doctrine. Surely the Charismatic renewal has something to teach us here. In sacramental churches the gift of the Holy Spirit is virtually equated with the event of water baptism. In Protestant evangelicalism it is equated with a subconscious work of God in regeneration which you only know you have because the Bible says you do if you believe. It is easy to imagine a spiritual counselor saying to a new convert today, "Don't expect to notice any difference: just believe you have received the Spirit." But that

is far from what we see in the New Testament. The Pentecostals are right to stress the experience of being baptized in the Spirit. . . . If the Spirit overwhelms you like a baptism you can't imagine him merely sneaking in quietly while you are asleep and taking up inconspicuous residence. . . . In Acts the Holy Spirit is not a silent influence but an experienced power. . . . Christianity is not merely an array of glorious ideas. It is not merely the performance of rituals and sacraments. It is the life-changing experience of the Holy Spirit through faith in Jesus Christ, the Lord of the universe. *We could talk for hours about what that experience is. In fact, most of my messages are just that—descriptions of the experience of the Spirit of God in the life of the believer.*[13]

John Piper argues here that the gift of the Holy Spirit is indeed an experience. In the rest of this sermon, he explains why he believes this is something that is distinct from conversion. Piper does not often talk explicitly about the baptism with the Spirit, nor receiving the Spirit; therefore the final sentence of the quote is most illuminating. To Piper, what we *call* this experience of God is perhaps not the most crucial question. He claims that most of his sermons are all about the experiential relationship that is possible with God's Spirit through Jesus. Piper's preaching is well respected and is seen as having something unique about it. Surely this is the result of a specific and unusual empowering by the Holy Spirit. When Piper encourages us to desire God and savor him, which is what characterizes his preaching more than anything, this quote demonstrates that he is actually speaking about the vital effects of the Holy Spirit's work in our lives.

BEING FILLED WITH THE SPIRIT

The concept of being "filled" with the Spirit is probably the biblical term that most strongly implies that an encounter with God's Spirit is not an all-or-nothing event. Paul challenges us to "be filled with the Spirit" (Ephesians 5:18), and Greek scholars explain that the tense used here is present continuous.[14] This means the verse could easily be translated, "be being filled." The implication is that continual filling is available

---

[13]John Piper, "How to Receive the Gift of the Holy Spirit," emphasis mine; http://www.desiringgod.org/ResourceLibrary/Sermons/ByDate/1984/437_How_to_Receive_the_Gift_of_the_Holy_Spirit/.
[14]See Andrew T. Lincoln, *Ephesians*, Word Biblical Commentary (Nashville: Word, 2002), 344 and Charles F. Pfeiffer and Everett Falconer Harrison, *The Wycliffe Bible Commentary: New Testament* (Chicago: Moody Press, 1962), on Ephesians 5:18.

that can be experienced to greater or lesser degrees. For example, in a church where thousands were Spirit-filled, Philip and Stephen and five others could still be selected as *especially* full of the Spirit (Acts 6:1–6).

Thus, experiences of Christ mediated by the Spirit can differ in intensity and frequency at different points in a believer's life. The direct knowledge of God appears to be more frequent and dramatic during times of general revival, but times of personal refreshing are also available to individuals even outside of a more general move of God's Spirit.

The concept of fullness is related to that of a liquid. We are told to "drink" of the Spirit (1 Corinthians 12:13), who has been "poured out" (Acts 10:45). Thus fullness of the Spirit is something that we should be able to recognize when it happens and for which we are to keep coming back for more. We are to desire and savor the Spirit and yearn for a more conscious awareness of him as a person who is living and active in our lives.

What is the difference between the Spirit-filled believer and the one who has not yet consciously received him? Is it that the Spirit is not working in the latter? Absolutely not. The Spirit is at work in every believer. It is just that when Christians are "full" of the Spirit, have "drunk" of the Spirit, have "received" the Spirit, they have been given a tangible awareness of God's love and empowering presence as a reality in their lives.

Spurgeon also advocated that believers should earnestly seek a clear experience of becoming more full of the Holy Spirit:

> Have ye then received the Spirit since you believed? Beloved, are you now receiving the Spirit? Are you living under his divine influence? Are you filled with his power? Put the question personally. I am afraid some professors [i.e., professing Christians] will have to admit that they hardly know whether there be any Holy Ghost; and others will have to confess that though they have enjoyed a little of his saving work, yet they do not know much of his ennobling and sanctifying influence. We have none of us participated in his operations as we might have done: we have sipped where we might have drunk; we have drunk where we might have bathed; we have bathed up to the ankles where we might have found rivers to swim in. Alas, of many Christians it must be affirmed that they have been naked, and poor, and miserable, when they might in the power of the Holy Spirit have been clad

in golden garments, and have been rich and increased in goods. He waiteth to be gracious, but we linger in indifference. . . .

Does any man know what the Spirit of God can make of him? I believe the greatest, ablest, most faithful, most holy man of God might have been greater, and abler, and more faithful, and more holy, if he had put himself more completely at the Spirit's disposal. Wherever God has done great things by a man he has had power to do more had the man been fit for it. We are straitened in ourselves, not in God. O brothers, the church is weak today because the Holy Spirit is not upon her members as we could desire him to be. You and I are tottering along like feeble babes, whereas, had we more of the Spirit, we might walk without fainting, run without weariness, and even mount up with wings as eagles. Oh, for more of the anointing of the Holy Ghost whom Christ is prepared to give immeasurably unto us if we will but receive him![15]

The most crucial question is not, did I receive the Holy Spirit when I was saved? Nor even is it, have I consciously received the Holy Spirit in a special way at some point in the past subsequent to first getting saved? What we should be asking, more importantly, is, am I being consciously filled by the Spirit today? Am I seeking more of his influences?

Many believers report that their experience of the Spirit comes intermittently and is not constant. This seems to be consistent with Acts 3:20, which speaks of "times of refreshing [that] come from the presence of the Lord." Christians may, however, ask God for more of these outpourings in their own experience. Jesus makes a clear invitation to his followers to actively seek the Holy Spirit when he says, "Come to me and drink" (John 7:37–39).

We are not to underestimate the power of God that has been poured out in us. It is, after all, the very same power that raised Jesus Christ from the dead! As the Christian walks with God, he can become increasingly aware (even in the midst of all his troubles) that he is receiving foretastes of God's ultimate promise to us of eternal life. God's Spirit is not inactive—he demonstrated that in raising Jesus to life. Surely we should expect some clear demonstration of the reality of his work in us. How could the same power that raised Jesus from the dead not make a massive tangible difference if living inside us?

---

[15]C. H Spurgeon, *Sermon No 1790*, "Receiving the Holy Ghost," 1884; quoted at http://www.pilgrim publications.com/intrview.htm.

God designed us for a relationship with him. Today spiritualism and other forms of experiential religions are attractive to many people because they are looking for "gods" who are "real" and who are able to communicate with them and do things. We worship an active, living Jesus who desires to relate to his people and to do things for us.

Do *you* feel him? Does your heart tremble with awe? We should seek an experience of God that is Bible-based. Through the Spirit we can have communion with the entire Trinity. He is with us. He wants us to be in relationship with the whole fullness of God the Father, God the Son, and God the Holy Spirit. It is only as we know him that we can fulfill our chief purpose, which is to glorify God by enjoying him forever.[16]

CONCLUSION

The key question is not so much what we should call the various actions of the Holy Spirit in us. What is more important is that we agree that the Spirit is at work in every believer, but that subsequent experiences of the Spirit, which can be sudden and dramatic, are available to believers today.

Becoming a Christian is actually a secret act of the Spirit in regenerating us and joining us to Christ and imparting faith to us. This is something of which we may not be aware, apart from its effects in us. Many believers feel that the faith they have in Jesus is their own. They may not realize that it has been produced in them by the Spirit, that a rebirth has happened. Some argue that this acquisition of faith should be called "the baptism with the Spirit." However, whatever we call conversion, it would be wrong for us to insist that we have experienced the Spirit in all his fullness automatically. Both biblically and in the experiences of believers down through the centuries, there has been a conscious and tangible outpouring of the Spirit that is often distinct from conversion.

Even here we have a danger, however. Many Christians do not pursue an experience of God because they believe they "got it all" at conversion. But there are also many who have settled into the same attitude because they look back to a "second blessing" and believe that it was then that they "got it all." This attitude means that we miss out

---

[16]See John Piper, *Desiring God* (Sisters, OR: Multnomah, 2003), 17.

on the repeated times of blessing and refreshing that God wants to pour out on us. We won't receive from the Spirit unless we eagerly seek him and ask for his outpourings.

Lloyd-Jones delivers a strong challenge: "Has your heart been ravished? Have you known this overwhelming experience of the love of God? Let every man examine himself."[17]

It is impossible to overemphasize the importance of the Holy Spirit in the life of the Christian. Let's resist becoming sidetracked by our various differences over these matters and instead simply cry out to God for more awareness and evidence in our lives of the power that raised Christ from the dead. Then we will know the joy of living our lives not in our own strength but in God's enabling.

If we are convinced that we need a more conscious awareness of the Holy Spirit's work in our lives and that we long to go on receiving the Spirit and being refreshed by him, what should we do? The answer is that we should pray and ask God to pour out the Spirit on us. As Jesus said, "If you then, who are evil, know how to give good gifts to your children, how much more will the heavenly Father give the Holy Spirit to those who ask him!" (Luke 11:13).

We have to ask for the Holy Spirit to come. Lloyd-Jones elaborates upon this verse:

> You notice that our Lord is referring only to children, the children who ask. Here is something interesting in and of itself. He seems to be taking it for granted that those who are going to ask the Father for the Holy Spirit are those who know that they are children and who address him as their heavenly Father. This suggests that here, once more, we are being told that it is only those who are children who ask for this. It is not something that happens automatically, therefore, at regeneration, but it is the regenerate, the "children," who make this request; nobody else will do so.[18]

Having examined the biblical evidence, I hope you agree that the experiences described earlier are indeed both valid and available for us today. God wants us to be personally refreshed and to have our own times of individual revival when his presence is especially sweet to us.

[17]Lloyd-Jones, *God's Ultimate Purpose: An Exposition of Ephesians 1*, 266–278.
[18]Martyn Lloyd-Jones, *Joy Unspeakable* (Eastbourne, UK: Kingsway, 1995), 320–325.

Jesus is not a dead god made of wood that we have to carry. He is a living God who carries us. He wants us to experience his love.

How easy it is to become reticent about seeking God for such experiences! Why would we not want to connect fully to the reviving power of God's Holy Spirit, which the resurrected Jesus has made available to us? The Spirit can assure us of salvation, empower us to live godly lives, embolden us to be more evangelistic, and remove our guilt and condemnation. This infilling is certainly not seen as an optional extra by the Bible. We are commanded to be filled, which suggests there is something we do to connect to the Spirit. To attempt to soldier on without all the equipping power of the Spirit that Jesus is only too willing to supply is like an army trying to fight without asking headquarters for new supplies of equipment and food!

Having prayed, we can read the Bible, listen to sermons, read Christian books, and continue to trust in God irrespective of what we feel while continuing to earnestly seek the God who loved us so much that he came and died for us and rose again to give us the Spirit. There is a need to receive the Spirit by faith. It is also often very helpful to find someone who has already received a touch from the Spirit to pray for you.

Martyn Lloyd-Jones said so much that promoted an interest in the work of the Holy Spirit, it seems appropriate to allow him to ask these questions:

> Has He whispered to you, has He spoken to you? Pray for His blessing, seek it, be desperate for it, hunger and thirst for it. Keep on praying until your prayer is answered. . . . Be satisfied with nothing less. Has God ever told you that you are His child? Has He spoken to you, not with an audible voice, but, in a sense, in a more real way? Have you known this illumination, this melting quality? Have you known what it is to be lifted up above and beyond yourself? If not, seek it; cry out to him, saying, "Speak, I pray Thee, gentle Jesus," and "Sue him for it."[19]

The Spirit is eager to tell us specifically that we are indeed children of God because of what Jesus has done for us. This will bring us great joy and increased motivation to worship God. The only question is, are

---

[19]Lloyd-Jones, *God's Ultimate Purpose: An Exposition of Ephesians 1*, 289–300.

we listening? Or do we drown out his still, small voice by a theology that minimizes the importance of experiencing a filling with the Holy Spirit? It is only through the Spirit's work in our hearts that we will be changed in response to the resurrection. As Edwards said:

> Christ is not in the heart of a saint, as in a sepulcher, or as a dead Saviour, that does nothing; but as in his temple, and as one that is alive from the dead. For in the heart where Christ savingly is, there he lives, and exerts himself after the power of that endless life, that he received at his resurrection. Thus every saint that is the subject of the benefit of Christ's sufferings, is made to know and experience the power of his resurrection. The spirit of Christ, which is the immediate spring of grace in the heart, is all life, all power, all act.[20]

---

[20]Jonathan Edwards, *Religious Affections*, WJE Online, Vol. 2, 392–393; http://edwards.yale.edu/archive?path=aHR0cDovL2Vkd2FyZHMueWFsZS5lZHUvY2dpLWJpbi9uZXdpaGlsby9nZXRvYmplY3QucGw/Yy4xxOjY6MTIud2plbw==.

CHAPTER SEVENTEEN

OUR MISSION FROM THE RISEN JESUS

As the Father has sent me, even so I am sending you.

JOHN 20:21

JESUS WAS SENT into this world to bring glory to his Father and to bring good news to a needy people. He said, "For the Son of Man came to seek and to save the lost" (Luke 19:10).

Our risen Lord sends us into the world with the same task. We are to bring glory to Jesus through our worship of him, enjoying a personal relationship with him, living holy lives in a world that offers endless opportunities to sin, and sharing our faith with others. Having been formed and empowered by the resurrection, the church exists to declare and demonstrate this same power to a risen world. One of the key implications of the resurrection is that this is wonderful news that simply *must* be shared!

Jesus' power is not merely for our enjoyment, but the Spirit gives us an infectious hope and joy. The wonder of sins forgiven and the wonder that comes from his Spirit being poured into our hearts will compel us to share. We did not accept Jesus to selfishly enjoy all the benefits of salvation. We have a job to do.

We need to be full of God in the sense that someone might be full of their new child, a new spouse, or, if you are a real geek like me, even the latest gadget. When we are genuinely enjoying someone or something, we can't help but tell others. When a football fan watches his team win a game, does he not shout and celebrate? Can anyone stop him from telling all his friends about his victory? When we exalt more in other things than we rejoice in Jesus, we make them our idols. Many of us seem to show by our conversations that we are more excited about the latest iPhone than we are about Jesus. How many people who would never dream of clapping or raising a hand in worship would do both *and* dance at a gig by their favorite band? Why are we not thrilled in an even greater way by Jesus? Martyn Lloyd-Jones explains:

> Once a man has the love of Christ in his heart you need not train him to witness; he will do it. He will know the power, the constraint, the motive; everything is already there. It is a plain lie to suggest that people who regard this knowledge of the love of Christ as the supreme thing are useless, unhealthy mystics. The servants of God who have most adorned the life and the history of the Christian church have always been men who have realized that this is the most important thing of all, and they have spent hours in prayer seeking His face and enjoying His love. The man who knows the love of Christ in his heart can do more in one hour than the busy type of man can do in a century.[1]

As we become excited about Jesus and begin sharing him with others, we will receive still more joy and satisfaction from him. This can be as simple as telling a stranger about the church we attend and leaving him an invite card, or it could be helping someone respond to the gospel.

When we fulfill our twin tasks—to worship Jesus and to share him with others—we will feel satisfied, rewarded, and complete. We will also find that we ourselves will understand the gospel better. As the NIV paraphrases Paul's slightly enigmatic phrase:

> I pray that you may be active in sharing your faith, *so that* you will have a full understanding of every good thing we have in Christ. (Philemon 6)

If you are looking for a purpose in life, you will find it here. If you are looking for joy, there is no greater source. We are caught up in the mission of Jesus himself. Great celebration is ours when we are involved in helping others turn to him.

HIS MISSION

When Jesus sends us into the world, he says in effect, "This is what I did; now you do the same. God was with me; remember, I am always with

---

[1] D. M. Lloyd-Jones, *An Exposition of Ephesians 3* (Grand Rapids: Baker, 1979), 247–253.

you, too." Surprisingly few words spoken by the resurrected Jesus are recorded for us. We should therefore listen carefully to these:

> All authority in heaven and on earth has been given to me. Go therefore and make disciples of all nations, baptizing them in the name of the Father and of the Son and of the Holy Spirit, teaching them to observe all that I have commanded you. And behold, I am with you always, to the end of the age. (Matthew 28:18–20)

This mission belongs to Jesus. He will accomplish it. But he will do it through us. Now he is risen, he has all authority, and he sends us out with a task. This is not an optional extra, nor a suggestion; rather, this is a direct command from the ruler of the universe. We ought to pay attention, and we would be wise to obey. Jesus is the Head of his church, and he will ensure that this task of world evangelization is accomplished: "I will build my church, and the gates of hell shall not prevail against it" (Matthew 16:18).

This important statement made by Jesus two thousand years ago must have a radical impact on the way we do church today. We can be optimistic about the future, even when things look challenging. We should remember the church belongs to Jesus. When called to do so, we can undertake brave projects that are so large, we will need miraculous assistance to complete them. What shall we do that would be impossible if Jesus was not alive?

Too often decisions are made by churches with little or no consideration of how Jesus wants them to proceed. He can become an afterthought or perhaps merely venerated, as if he was a long-dead hero, while the day-to-day business of church life carries on without him. "No!" says Jesus. "Human effort and wisdom won't build the kind of church that can smash hell's gates, but *I can* and *I will*."

As members of this great global enterprise, the church, we must not be in defensive mode, worrying that the Devil will defeat us. Jesus leads us on to plunder the enemy's kingdom, pushing forward in eager anticipation of what God will do through us. Because the tomb is empty and Jesus is on the throne, we will be victorious irrespective of what is happening in today's world. In the end, his purposes *will* prevail in the church of which he is Head (Colossians 1:18). Jesus gives us the joy of partnering with him as he works through us to reach the world. He drives the mission; we simply follow.

HOW TO MAKE DISCIPLES

Our mission is not just to make converts, but to make disciples. A disciple is simply a learner or a follower.[2] In today's individualistic world many people prefer to say, "I did it my way!" That is not the Bible way. Paul urged his readers to "be imitators of me, as I am of Christ" (1 Corinthians 11:1). This underlines the importance of discipleship but also stresses its boundaries. We are only to follow our leaders to the extent that they follow Jesus. In order to make disciples, we must first be disciples. Jesus calls us to live a life that is preoccupied by him: "He died for all, that those who live might no longer live for themselves but for him who for their sake died and was raised" (2 Corinthians 5:15).

Disciples must be taught to obey Jesus. He said, "If you love me, you will keep my commandments" (John 14:15). One of John Piper's books, *What Jesus Demands from the World*, helps us by examining everything Jesus told us to do. If we want to follow Jesus, we *must* do what he says. The challenge is to avoid short-circuiting the process by only teaching people rules, perhaps adding a few of our own. We need to learn how to love Jesus more if we want to follow him. When we love him, his commandments will not seem burdensome but rather the loving instruction of someone who cares for us. Those who are involved in training other Christians need to train them to love Jesus, as well as showing them how to live their lives in light of the resurrection.

A disciple is usually first a friend. If we live lives of isolation that never impact other people, we cannot make disciples. People can sometimes be "won without a word" (1 Peter 3:1), by our lifestyle. But this verse should not be used as an excuse to avoid sharing the message since people *must* hear the good news in order to be saved.[3]

We need to be a people full of grace and joy whose hope is infectious. As I write this, newspapers are reporting that a member of the

---

[2]William Arndt, Frederick W. Danker, and Walter Bauer, *A Greek-English Lexicon of the New Testament and Other Early Christian Literature*, 3rd edition (Chicago: University of Chicago Press, 2000), 609.
[3]Indeed, the context of the verse presupposes that the husbands mentioned have already heard the gospel since it says they do not "obey" it.

British government believes we are in the middle of the worst recession in a hundred years. By the time you read this book, you will know whether he was being unduly pessimistic or accurate. Christians have hope even as their savings disappear before their eyes. Our lives will prompt questions.

> In your hearts honor Christ the Lord as holy, always being prepared to make a defense to anyone who asks you for a reason for the hope that is in you; yet do it with gentleness and respect, having a good conscience, so that, when you are slandered, those who revile your good behavior in Christ may be put to shame. (1 Peter 3:15–16)

Jesus wants us to be ever optimistic about his world: "Look, I tell you, lift up your eyes, and see that the fields are white for harvest" (John 4:35). The eye of faith will recognize that some people are ready to respond if we will just tell them how. Often, however, we don't really look, because we can become easily discouraged when we see that many people prefer their life of spiritual death. While not everyone will respond to the message, Jesus promises us that the harvest is "plentiful" (Luke 10:2). All we need to do is to be willing to obey the command to "go," carrying out the mission to which he has called us.

Jesus urges his disciples to teach others "to observe all that I have commanded you" (Matthew 28:20). This would include this very command to teach others and make disciples. The strategy for building the church is very simple—find people you can train, first, to obey Jesus themselves and then teach them how to teach others to do the same. This makes it clear that this command not only applied to the original disciples but also applies to all disciples throughout the church age. If the disciples are to make disciples, and those disciples are to obey all Jesus' commands, then the very command to make disciples is one of the commands they are to obey.

Jesus also commands that disciples are to be baptized and hence joined to a local church. Often we struggle with the simplicity of Jesus' words and think of all kinds of reasons why we do not want to obey even this simple instruction. But how can we follow him for our whole lives if we fail at the first hurdle? Our baptism is meant to reflect the death, burial, and resurrection of Jesus and to mark the beginning of our new life as members of Christ's church. Christians were "buried with him in baptism, in which you were also raised with him through faith in the powerful working of God, who raised him from the dead" (Colossians 2:12). The symbolism of identifying with the death, burial, and resurrection of Jesus is perhaps especially apparent when the believer is immersed. The Christian enters a watery grave and is rescued from it by the strength of another.

WHAT IS OUR MESSAGE?

The gospel is actually very simple. It is a message that is all about Jesus Christ. It is the proclamation of a person and what he has done for us. In almost every New Testament book we find a summary of this, which we can easily overlook but is remarkable in its consistency. In each case this short statement of the gospel announcement begins with God, who we are either told sent Jesus[4] or raised him from the dead.[5] We are called to respond to God in a way that as a result brings to us the benefits of salvation.[6] In these descriptions only rarely is the cross included, although of course it *is* a key part of the clearest summary of the gospel of all, which is found in 1 Corinthians 15. It is hard to see in any case how we can proclaim a resurrection without also reporting that the person had first died. Without the resurrection the cross is not good news, and without the cross the wonderful good news of the resurrection cannot be fully appreciated.

HASTENING THE LORD'S RETURN

Jesus prophesied that the gospel would be preached in the whole world before he would return (Matthew 24:14). He will ensure that this happens, but he also gives us the joy of being caught up in the mission. We each have a role to play. As we wait for the return of the Lord and perhaps wonder why it is taking so long, we must remember that we have a responsibility in "hastening the coming of the day of God" (2 Peter 3:12).

---

[4]Matthew 10:40–41; Mark 9:37; Luke 1:68–75; John 5:24; Galatians 4:4–7; 1 John 4:7–10.
[5]Acts 5:30–32; 17:27–31; Romans 10:8–9; 2 Corinthians 5:15; Ephesians 2:4–10; Philippians 2:5–11; Colossians 1:15–29; 2:12–13; 1 Thessalonians 1:5–10; 1 Timothy 3:16; 2 Timothy 2:8–15; Hebrews 13:15–16, 20–21; 1 Peter 1:18–21, 25; Revelation 1:1–2, 12–18.
[6]Adapted from Eugene Lemcio, *The Past of Jesus in the Gospels* (Cambridge: Cambridge University Press, 1991), 115–117.

A PEOPLE ON A MISSION

There is not enough space in this book to fully explore the changes that Jesus' resurrection can make to our local churches, but I will address a few of them. We are a people carrying out the mission of Christ. One crucial implication of the resurrection of Jesus is that he now lives on earth through his body, his church. It is only *together* that we can reflect him adequately to the world. Jesus never intended there to be any such thing as "solo Christianity" where believers are not rooted and grounded in a community that is centered around the risen Christ. As Paul said, "Now you are the body of Christ and individually members of it" (1 Corinthians 12:27).

Everything about our church life can be changed by the resurrection. If our focus is always solely on the death of Jesus and our sin, then guilt and sorrow will probably characterize the tone of our meetings. But if we also emphasize the resurrection, great joy will result. This is nowhere clearer than in our sharing the Lord's Supper together. Although we are told to remember the Lord's death, we are also told it is to be done with one eye on his future coming again ("until he comes," 1 Corinthians 11:26). We remember his death, but we are also to celebrate that he is now in heaven, and we partake of his life-giving presence during those precious moments. Thus the Lord's Supper does not always have to be a somber and sad event but can be a joyful occasion. During that time we also discern together that we are the body of Christ on earth. We each have very different roles to play, like the organs of our physical bodies.

We are even described simply as "Christ" by Paul (1 Corinthians 12:12). The church is the only Jesus the world will see until he returns. Together we are to reach out and *be* Jesus to this needy world. Sometimes this can be as simple as a Christian introducing a work colleague to one of his church friends. Jesus said the world will recognize that we are his disciples by the love we show toward other believers (John 13:35). In a world full of loneliness, we can introduce people to God's family. Never underestimate the impact for anyone entering a room full of Christians who are enjoying each other's company with laughter but without the need to be intoxicated by alcohol.

We must not imagine that we can leave the task of evangelism to the "experts." Everybody is called to "do the work of an evangelist"

(2 Timothy 4:5). Prayer support, financial giving, cooking food for evangelistic events, playing instruments, teaching children, pastoral care, and a myriad of other ways to serve all play an important part in fulfilling the Great Commission. Just being God's people in his world and fulfilling whatever job we have for his glory has more impact than we will ever know in this life. Paul said, "Whatever you do, work heartily, as for the Lord and not for men" (Colossians 3:23). Whatever your job is, do it excellently for the sake of Jesus. As Jesus urged, "Freely you have received, freely give" (Matthew 10:8, NIV).

Churches need to be involved in sharing the gospel directly with their communities. We should make sure our meetings are welcoming to outsiders and that the gospel is preached. We need also to reach out, and not rely on them to come to us. After all, Jesus said, "Go into all the world."

We must not forget the works of mercy carried out by our forefathers. The abolition of the slave trade, ministering to alcoholics, feeding the poor, and many similar acts can all be part of fulfilling the Great Commission. The following quote from the late Simon Petitt, previously pastor of Jubilee Church, Cape Town, is a challenging reminder of our mandate to "remember the poor" (Galatians 2:10):

> Whether it's the church in Africa, or in Harrow, we need to get an understanding that when we care for the needy, when we preach good news to the poor, when we seek to develop the God-given creativity of poor people, when we equip people with the skills they need so they can make godly choices for themselves and for their families, when we promote enterprise with financial help, those aren't just the work of aid agencies or the government; that's part of the apostolic calling of the church of Jesus Christ.[7]

There is no doubt that God wants us to help those less fortunate than ourselves in practical ways. John the Baptist said, "Whoever has two tunics is to share with him who has none, and whoever has food is to do likewise" (Luke 3:11). We also need to remember that the biggest act of mercy is to share the good news of salvation. The greatest need people have is to be saved, and it is we, the church, who have the

---

[7]Simon Petitt, "Remember the Poor," Brighton Leadership Conference, November 1998; http://www.newfrontiers.xtn.org/uk/resources/social-action-and-the-poor/remember-the-poor/.

most wonderful task of spreading this good news of salvation. As Paul challenges us:

> How then will they call on him in whom they have not believed? And how are they to believe in him of whom they have never heard? And how are they to hear without someone preaching? And how are they to preach unless they are sent? As it is written, "How beautiful are the feet of those who preach the good news!" (Romans 10:14–15)

As Christians, we can easily become fearful of what others may think about the Christian message. We worry about what reaction we may get from others and act as though we are ashamed of the gospel. It's easy to tell others about anything we are excited about. Why not the good news of Jesus? Paul's example encourages us to act likewise:

> For I am not ashamed of the gospel, for it is the power of God for salvation to everyone who believes. . . . For in it the righteousness of God is revealed from faith for faith, as it is written, "The righteous shall live by faith." (Romans 1:16–17)

HIS PROMISE

It is in the context of our call to be missional that Jesus promises he will be with us to the end of the age. He is with us for a reason, which is to enable us to accomplish a specific goal. Only when we are aware of his power and presence with us can we fulfill the task to which he has called us. Conversely, if we are not fully committed to this work, then it is not surprising that we are not as consciously aware of Jesus' presence as we might be. As my pastor, Tope Koleoso, said, "If you want Jesus to go with you, then go and make disciples."[8]

Because Jesus is with the church, it can be described as having been built by him despite the fact that much of the work is apparently being done by believers. Christians teach and preach, they care for one another, and they plant churches. But as we have already noted, ultimately it is *Jesus* who is building the church.

Jesus provides the power we need to equip us for service. He tells us he is the one who is building his church, not so we can become passive

---

[8]Tope Koleoso, "How to Be Missional Every Day"; http://adrianwarnock.com/2008/07/sermon-how-to-be-missional-every-day-by.htm.

but so that, knowing that we are on his team and under his authority and that he is ultimately responsible for the results, we will be extraordinarily motivated to complete the work. If we are conscious of Jesus' power at work in us, we will be more zealous to see his kingdom come "on earth as it is in heaven" (Matthew 6:10). Paul, being aware of God's grace upon him, was able to say:

> But by the grace of God I am what I am, and his grace toward me was not in vain. On the contrary, I worked harder than any of them, though it was not I, but the grace of God that is with me. (1 Corinthians 15:10)

The most energetic and active workers for the success of the church have always been the ones who are most convinced of the sovereignty of Jesus and his responsibility for the ultimate success of the church. When things are going badly, such people, while obviously examining themselves and their methods to see if there is any way they can improve, will take comfort in the fact that only Jesus can build his church. When things are going well, the lure of pride is less strong for those who know that it is only Jesus who has equipped them and granted them success.

In this chapter we have seen that there is a mandate on our lives. We are called to be witnesses. We obey Jesus because he is our Lord and out of gratitude for what he has done for us. Our gratitude grows into an intense desire to see him glorified by others. We want him to be celebrated, preeminent, and honored as God rather than defamed by having his name used as a swear word. We want others to join us in delighting in him. As Piper says:

> Missions exists because worship doesn't. When this age is over, and the countless millions of the redeemed fall on their faces before the throne of God, missions will be no more. It is a temporary necessity. But worship abides forever. Worship, therefore, is the fuel and the goal of missions.[9]

In other words, because we want to see God glorified more, we are eager to recruit others to praise him too. Thus there is no conflict between the two key things we are called to do as Christians—worship and witness. If we love, honor, and glory in Christ, we will find that we

---

[9]John Piper, *Don't Waste Your Life* (Wheaton, IL: Crossway, 2003), 162.

want to talk about him with others. People like to tell others about their heroes and anything that they value and hold dear.

The risen Jesus gave his disciples a clear commission. Evangelizing the world is a task given and empowered by the resurrected Christ. The church is a resurrection people who are implementing something of the age to come in this present world. I can think of no better way to end this chapter than with this prayer from Ephesians 3:14–21:

> For this reason I bow my knees before the Father, from whom every family in heaven and on earth is named, that according to the riches of his glory he may grant you to be strengthened with power through his Spirit in your inner being, so that Christ may dwell in your hearts through faith—that you, being rooted and grounded in love, may have strength to comprehend with all the saints what is the breadth and length and height and depth, and to know the love of Christ that surpasses knowledge, that you may be filled with all the fullness of God.
>
> Now to him who is able to do far more abundantly than all that we ask or think, according to the power at work within us, to him be glory in the church and in Christ Jesus throughout all generations, forever and ever, Amen.

CHAPTER EIGHTEEN

OUR RESURRECTION BODIES

For since by man came death, by man came also the
resurrection of the dead. For as in Adam all die,
even so in Christ shall all be made alive.

1 CORINTHIANS 15:21–22, KJV

Our citizenship is in heaven, and from it we await a Savior,
the Lord Jesus Christ, who will transform our lowly body
to be like his glorious body, by the power that
enables him even to subject all things to himself.

PHILIPPIANS 3:20–21

And God raised the Lord and will also raise us up by his power.

1 CORINTHIANS 6:14

If in Christ we have hope in this life only,
we are of all people most to be pitied.

1 CORINTHIANS 15:19

I ONCE PURCHASED some new shoes online. When the box arrived, I ripped it open. I was pleased with how they looked and mentally consigned my old pair to the trash. I immediately put the new shoes on and went to pick up my children from school. On my return from what is only a short walk, both of my heels had blisters, one of which had burst. My toes were also rather numb. I looked at the aging shoes this new purchase was designed to replace and thought, *I'm sorry for despising you; you may look old, but at least you are not trying to destroy my feet!*

A friend told me that the shoes were the wrong size. I knew better. Over the next few weeks I wore them, at first for quite literally just a few seconds at a time! Slowly the leather softened and stretched a little, and my shoes became comfortable. The pain had been worth it. The shoes have lasted a lot longer than the agony. They are no longer enemies but friends. Without a clear expectation of the end result of my pain, I would not have tolerated it.

When it comes to the pain we all experience from time to time in this world, we often don't have the same degree of choice. Usually we can't control the difficulties that come our way. Jesus said, "In this world you will have trouble" (John 16:33, NIV). As my mentor Henry Tyler used to love to say when preaching about this verse, "Jesus *always* keeps his promises." Some people simplistically argue that we should "name and claim" God's promises. But I have never heard anyone "claim" this one!

When our life is going well, we are just in an interlude between troubles. There is no happiness that this world can give us that can't be taken away in an instant. A telephone call, a visit to the doctor, a short message can suddenly bring everything crashing down around us. We must be realistic about the world we live in. Jesus never promised to remove all hardships from us. Some people even report that when they became Christians, it almost seemed as if their problems began!

Christians must experience pain in this world. Paul declares, "Through many tribulations we must enter the kingdom of God" (Acts 14:22), and "all who desire to live a godly life in Christ Jesus will be persecuted" (2 Timothy 3:12). Without suffering we cannot enter the glorious resurrection Jesus has for us.

We need to understand this in order to live well and to prepare ourselves to die well. A doctor who works in a hospice told me she has seen Christian children calmly dying full of confidence in their best friend, Jesus. We can face death without fear when we understand what we will gain. Christians can be confident when facing death and need not live in denial, pretending that it's not going to happen. Death itself is the result of sin, so it is not something we should desire. However, for the Christian, death has lost its sting (1 Corinthians 15:55). Christians have at times been almost reckless in the face of death. For example, some have traveled to the mission field despite knowing they would most likely die quickly of tropical diseases, because they were certain they had an eternal future awaiting them.

HOPE BEYOND THE GRAVE

Even in our worldly troubles we need not be dismayed. Jesus said, after promising that we would have trouble, "But take heart; I have overcome the world" (John 16:33). He has promised to be with us and to help us, and we will share in his victory. Our troubles do not evaporate in the presence of Jesus, but we can know God in the midst of them. Our problems become his to resolve. We look forward to the day when all pain will cease, and in the meantime we experience his deliverance even in this life.

After two decades of ministry Paul still expressed the tension that even mature Christians can feel during great suffering and that tempted him to lose hope. Yet he still clung to the belief that God would rescue him:

> For we were so utterly burdened beyond our strength that we despaired of life itself. Indeed, we felt that we had received the sentence of death. But that was to make us rely not on ourselves but on God who raises the dead. He delivered us from such a deadly peril, and he will deliver us. On him we have set our hope that he will deliver us again. (2 Corinthians 1:8–10)

The pain we experience in this world will not seem so severe if we understand that it is only temporary and very necessary for us. It is only through suffering, which can even feel like we are dying on the inside, that we experience the victory Jesus intends for us. Paul argued that Christians are "always carrying in the body the death of Jesus, so that the life of Jesus may also be manifested in our bodies" (2 Corinthians 4:10). Thus, through suffering we connect with the transforming resurrection power of God. God does not intend for Christians to merely feel all right under the circumstances. Since we have been raised with Christ, we are actually over our circumstances! As Paul said, "in all these things we are more than conquerors through him who loved us" (Romans 8:37).

Unless we live with an eternal perspective on the all too frequent troubles of this world, we will not be able to face them with the attitude that Paul models: "For I consider that the sufferings of this present time are not worth comparing with the glory that is to be revealed to us. For the creation waits with eager longing for the revealing of the sons of God" (Romans 8:18–19).

One of the best-loved worship songs written in recent years in the UK is partly based on this Scripture. The words, together with its heart-clenching tune, can sometimes reduce even grown men who love eating steak to tears. It is full of hope:

> There is a day that all creation's waiting for
> A day of liberation and freedom for the earth
> And on that day the Lord will come to meet his bride
> And when we see him, in an instant we'll be changed
>
> The trumpet sounds and the dead will then be raised
> By his power, never to perish again,
> Once only flesh now clothed with immortality
> Death has now been
> Swallowed up in victory
>
> We will meet him in the air
> And then we will be like him
> For we will see him as he is
> O yeah!
>
> Then all hurt and pain will cease
> And we will be with him forever
> And in his Glory we will live
> O yeah! O yeah!
>
> So lift your eyes to the things as yet unseen
> That will remain now for all eternity
> Though trouble's hard, it's only momentary
> And it's achieving our future glory.[1]

Christians have a hope that goes beyond the grave. It is a hope that we will be physically raised, not merely somehow survive as spirits. It is surprising how much confusion there is among Christians about the issue of life after death. We all believe that somehow we will survive death, but there is a lot of uncertainty about what that will look like. Popular Western culture speaks about people who die and become angels, and many Christians associate "going to heaven to be with Jesus when we die" with a disembodied "spiritual" resurrection. Spurgeon believed that people in his day were also confused about this matter:

> There are very few Christians who believe the resurrection of the dead. You may be surprised to hear that, but I should not wonder if I discovered that you yourself have doubts on the subject. By the resurrection of the dead is meant something very different from the immortality of the soul: that, every Christian believes, and therein is only on a level with the heathen, who believes it too. . . .
>
> The doctrine is that this actual body in which I now exist is to live with my soul. . . . The spirit, every one confesses, is eternal; but how many there are who deny that the bodies of men will actually start up from their graves at the great day! Many of you believe you will have a body in heaven, but you think it will be an airy fantastic body, instead of believing that it will be a body like to this—flesh and blood (although not the same kind of flesh, for all flesh is not the same flesh), a solid, substantial body, even such as we have here. . . . If ye were Christians as ye profess to be, ye would believe that every mortal man who ever existed shall not only live by the immortality of his soul, but his body shall live again, that the very flesh in which he now walks the earth is as eternal as the soul, and shall exist for ever. That is the peculiar doctrine of Christianity. The heathens never guessed or imagined such a thing.[2]

Jesus promises us, "I am the resurrection and the life. Whoever believes in me, though he die, yet shall he live, and everyone who lives and believes in me shall never die" (John 11:25–26). Paul is full of courage and assurance that Jesus will be honored in his life, and ultimately in his death: "For none of us lives to himself, and none of us dies to himself. For if we live, we live to the Lord, and if we die, we die to the Lord. So then, whether we live or whether we die, we are the Lord's. For

---

[2]C. H. Spurgeon, *Sermon No. 66,* "The Resurrection of the Dead," delivered on Sabbath Morning, February 17, 1856, at New Park Street Chapel, Southwark; http://www.spurgeon.org/sermons/0066.htm.

to this end Christ died and lived again, that he might be Lord both of the dead and of the living" (Romans 14:7–9). Paul expresses this similarly when he says that "to live is Christ, and to die is gain" (Philippians 1:21). We already live for Christ, knowing that we have been born again (Galatians 2:20), and we walk in the newness of life that Christ has given us (Romans 6:4). So our life will continue for eternity!

Paul's desire is only that he will honor the risen Christ Jesus. We can, like Paul, experience a glorious indifference to our sufferings when we know that they are not meaningless but lead to eternal life, which is knowing God.

IMMEDIATELY WITH JESUS

The Scripture repeatedly speaks of Christians who have died as those who have "fallen asleep." This has led some to speak of "soul sleep" and to assume that the Christian has a period of unconsciousness between death and resurrection. This concept is inconsistent with a number of Scriptures. Jesus promised the thief on the cross, "*Today* you will be with me in Paradise" (Luke 23:43). Paul says that when we die we are "away from the body and at home with the Lord" (2 Corinthians 5:8). Also, John says that the souls of the martyrs are in heaven (Revelation 20:4). In short, for the Christian, it is only the body that sleeps. The soul or spirit remains fully alive.

The Christian therefore experiences at death a kind of spiritual renewal, when we become fully aware of what Paul tells us is already true of us. We have already been spiritually raised with Christ, and our life is already hidden with Christ in God. What this means is that our home is already in heaven. Our spirits are already with Christ in heaven:

[God] raised us up with him and seated us with him in the heavenly places in Christ Jesus. (Ephesians 2:6)

If then you have been raised with Christ, seek the things that are above, where Christ is, seated at the right hand of God . . . your life is hidden with Christ in God. When Christ who is your life appears, then you also will appear with him in glory. (Colossians 3:1–4)

Our spiritual experiences on earth are the result of the curtain being lifted so we can catch a glimpse of what is already eternally true of us. Our souls will never be absorbed into God in some kind of mystical eastern "oneness" with the divinity. We remain distinct, aware beings, but in heaven we still await our eternal destiny of a physical resurrection. When we die we only become aware of what is already true of us. When we were born again we entered into this eternal life (see John 3). However, this new birth is just the foretaste of what is to come. Piper explains:

> So when you think of your new birth, think of it as the first installment of what is coming. Your body and the whole world will one day take part in this regeneration. God's final purpose is not spiritually renewed souls inhabiting decrepit bodies in a disease- and disaster-ravaged world. His purpose is a renewed world with renewed bodies and renewed souls that take all our renewed senses and make them a means of enjoying and praising God.[3]

A BODY MADE NEW

It is vital for us to be very clear about the fate of our bodies. It is not enough that our spirits survive this world. Ladd claimed, "Paul never conceives of the salvation of the soul apart from the body."[4] Paul tells us, "If the Spirit of him who raised Jesus from the dead dwells in you, he who raised Christ Jesus from the dead will also give life to your mortal bodies" (Romans 8:11). We will not simply discard our physical bodies.

Paul also said, "It is my eager expectation and hope that I will not be at all ashamed, but that with full courage now as always Christ will be honored in my body, whether by life or by death" (Philippians 1:20). He says that Christ will *always* be glorified through his body. This really does mean our own physical bodies will survive death. As Jesus promises, "Some of you they will put to death. . . . But *not a hair of your head will perish*" (Luke 21:16–18).

Our resurrection is intimately connected with that of Jesus: "But in fact Christ has been raised from the dead, the firstfruits of those who have fallen asleep" (1 Corinthians 15:20), and "he who raised the Lord

---

[3]John Piper, *Finally Alive* (Rossshire: Christian Focus, 2009), 89.
[4]George Eldon Ladd, *I Believe in the Resurrection of Jesus* (London: Hodder and Stoughton, 1975), 45.

Jesus will raise us also with Jesus and bring us with you into his presence" (2 Corinthians 4:14).

The very same bodies that are placed in our tombs will one day rise again. There is continuity between our resurrection bodies and our current ones. We will, however, be changed from being weak, frail, and mortal into being glorious and eternal. It is like a seed placed in the ground that emerges in some ways the same but is in other ways different (1 Corinthians 15:37–44). Our bodies will be "spiritual" in that they are suitable for heaven, but nonetheless they will still be physical bodies of flesh, as there are different kinds of flesh. Paul makes this even clearer elsewhere:

> For we know that if the tent that is our earthly home is destroyed, we have a building from God, a house not made with hands, eternal in the heavens. For in this tent we groan, longing to put on our heavenly dwelling, if indeed by putting it on we may not be found naked. For while we are still in this tent, we groan, being burdened—not that we would be unclothed, but that we would be further clothed, so that what is mortal may be swallowed up by life. He who has prepared us for this very thing is God, who has given us the Spirit as a guarantee. (2 Corinthians 5:1–5)

Paul argues in 1 Corinthians 15 that the resurrection of the believer is a direct consequence of the resurrection of Jesus. Because he was raised, we can be certain that we too will be raised. He is the firstfruit of the new creation.

We will be like Jesus. "But our citizenship is in heaven, and from it we await a Savior, the Lord Jesus Christ, who will transform our lowly body to be like his glorious body, by the power that enables him even to subject all things to himself" (Philippians 3:20–21).

Since our bodies are to be just like Christ's, then we too will be able to eat and drink, yet pass through walls, and fly into the clouds to meet him (1 Thessalonians 4:17). We will be recognizable, although no longer ugly but the attractive unique individuals God intended us to be. That beauty will certainly not look like our modern distorted images (such as the size zero model) that fashion tries to foist on us. Our bodies will no longer be aged and worn-out. I suppose we will look as though we were a perfect age—some suggest perhaps thirty-three, the age we believe Jesus was when he was crucified.

Some worry about what will happen to bodies lost at sea or burned. God can reassemble the molecules or perhaps simply the structure of our bodies. The actual molecules in our bodies are being replaced all the time; it is how they all relate together to form a structure that defines us. God promised us that not even a single hair of these physical bodies of ours will ultimately perish. I suppose a close modern illustration of what may occur is the fictional transporter of *Star Trek*. Do the actual molecules of Captain Kirk get moved from the surface to the ship, or is the energy signature used to re-create his body in a new location? Does it matter? Not really. The key point for us is that God is more than capable of gathering our dust from the four corners of the earth and reassembling it if necessary.

We will be real people with real bodies and real relationships. We will worship our God, but we will also have real reunions with each other. My wife sometimes reminds me that although she understands I will want to spend some time with people like Spurgeon, and we will no longer be married, she certainly wants me not to forget her. I have assured her I will be delighted to spend at least a millennia or two with her! The joy of worshipping our glorious God will only be intensified by our delight in meeting his wonderful creatures. Such thoughts are worthy of meditation. Paul says:

> But we do not want you to be uninformed, brothers, about those who are asleep, that you may not grieve as others do who have no hope. For since we believe that Jesus died and rose again, even so, through Jesus, God will bring with him those who have fallen asleep. For this we declare to you by a word from the Lord, that we who are alive, who are left until the coming of the Lord, will not precede those who have fallen asleep. For the Lord himself will descend from heaven with a cry of command, with the voice of an archangel, and with the sound of the trumpet of God. And the dead in Christ will rise first. Then we who are alive, who are left, will be caught up together with them in the clouds to meet the Lord in the air, and so we will always be with the Lord. Therefore encourage one another with these words. (1 Thessalonians 4:13–18)

CHAPTER NINETEEN

THE RESURRECTION OF ALL THINGS

Then I saw a new heaven and a new earth, for the first heaven and the first earth had passed away, and the sea was no more. And I saw the holy city, new Jerusalem, coming down out of heaven from God, prepared as a bride adorned for her husband. And I heard a loud voice from the throne saying, "Behold, the dwelling place of God is with man. He will dwell with them, and they will be his people, and God himself will be with them as their God. He will wipe away every tear from their eyes, and death shall be no more, neither shall there be mourning, nor crying, nor pain anymore, for the former things have passed away." And he who was seated on the throne said, "Behold, I am making all things new."

REVELATION 21:1-5

JESUS' RESURRECTION does not only change us by saving our souls, making us holy, and filling us with power to live. The fact that it changes our bodies to be immortal is still not the most glorious aspect of the story of salvation. Often the gospel is spoken of as being a great arc leading from the creation to the Fall to the Incarnation to the death of Jesus and then his resurrection and ascension. But that arc is not yet complete. Jesus will return, and when he does, the resurrection really will change *everything*. The Bible tells us, "He must remain in heaven until the time comes for God to restore everything" (Acts 3:21, NIV). Paul tells us that God has "a plan for the fullness of time, to unite all things in him, things in heaven and things on earth" (Ephesians 1:9–10). There will be no more rebellion. Only then will this tiny rebellious corner of the universe we call earth resound with the praise of Jesus' glory.

> He is before all things, and in him all things hold together. And he is the head of the body, the church. He is the beginning, the firstborn from the dead, that in everything he might be preeminent. For in him all the fullness of God was pleased to dwell, and through him to reconcile to himself all things, whether on earth or in heaven, making peace by the blood of his cross. (Colossians 1:17–20)

A CREATION WITHOUT DEATH

If this regeneration or resurrection of all things means anything, it means the reversal of the effects of death. Death entered the world through mankind: "Sin came into the world through one man, and death through sin, and so death spread to all men because all sinned" (Romans 5:12). As a result of one man's sin, the whole of creation was delivered up to bondage and decay. But all is not lost. This process has begun to be reversed as a result of the actions of one man, Jesus:

> For since by man came death, by man came also the resurrection of the dead. (1 Corinthians 15:21–22, KJV)

> For the creation waits with eager longing for the revealing of the sons of God. For the creation was subjected to futility, not willingly, but because of him who subjected it, in hope that the creation itself will be set free from its bondage to corruption and obtain the freedom of the glory of the children of God. For we know that the whole creation has been groaning together in the pains of childbirth until now. And not only the creation, but we ourselves, who have the firstfruits of the Spirit, groan inwardly as we wait eagerly for adoption as sons, the redemption of our bodies. (Romans 8:19–23)

Astonishingly, in that second passage we see that it is the actual revealing of the resurrected children of God that will be associated with the end of death. It is the unveiling of the glory of God's church that creation waits for. What an incredible privilege for us. This must be because we will reflect God's glory. As in God's original plan for Adam and Eve, we will rule over the new creation. And everything will change as a direct result. Even animals will cease from killing.

> The wolf will live with the lamb, and the leopard shall lie down with the young goat, and the calf and the lion and the fattened calf together; and a little child shall lead them. . . . They shall not hurt or destroy in all my holy mountain; for the earth shall be full of the knowledge of the LORD as the waters cover the sea. (Isaiah 11:6, 9; see Isaiah 65:25)

A UNIVERSE MADE NEW

The return of the Lord will lead to the renewal of all things. We are told repeatedly that the heavens and the earth will pass away. They will be renewed or re-created by fire, and we will live eternally in a new heaven and a new earth.

> Lift up your eyes to the heavens, and look at the earth beneath; for the heavens vanish like smoke, the earth will wear out like a garment, and they who dwell in it will die in like manner; but my salvation will be forever, and my righteousness will never be dismayed. (Isaiah 51:6)

> The heavens will pass away with a roar, and the heavenly bodies will be burned up and dissolved, and the earth and the works that are done on it will be exposed. Since all these things are thus to be dissolved, what sort of people ought you to be in lives of holiness and godliness, waiting for and hastening the coming of the day of God, because of which the heavens will be set on fire and dissolved, and the heavenly bodies will melt as they burn! But according to his promise we are waiting for new heavens and a new earth in which righteousness dwells. (2 Peter 3:10–13)

> Then I saw a new heaven and a new earth, for the first heaven and the first earth had passed away, and the sea was no more. And I saw the holy city, new Jerusalem, coming down out of heaven from God, prepared as a bride adorned for her husband. And I heard a loud voice from the throne saying, "Behold, the dwelling place of God is with man. He will dwell with them, and they will be his people, and God himself will be with them as their God. He will wipe away every tear from their eyes, and death shall be no more, neither shall there be mourning, nor crying, nor pain anymore, for the former things have passed away." And he who was seated on the throne said, "Behold, I am making all things new." (Revelation 21:1–5)

If heaven is where God dwells, then in that sense in the new creation heaven will be a place on earth as the heavenly Jerusalem descends. We will live on earth with renewed bodies, but it seems likely that we will be free to explore both the rest of the universe and the whole of heaven at will. As the whole creation exists for God's glory and reflects his majesty, if we are to know God fully, then that must include understanding the universe he created. The hunger within us to explore the stars, evidenced by the perennial appeal of science fiction and astronomy, may perhaps one day be fulfilled. But if we do explore the stars, they will induce wonder in us not merely in their own beauty but rather in the way in which their beauty causes us to worship the One who flung them into space and designed all their beautiful patterns.

THE JUDGMENT OF THE RISEN CHRIST

At the return of Christ, Jesus will judge the whole world and bring restitution. The terrible wrath and vengeance of the spurned Savior will be unleashed. Every wrong that has been committed that has not been placed on his Son will be put right. No evil will go unpunished. "For we must all appear before the judgment seat of Christ, so that each one may receive what is due for what he has done in the body, whether good or evil" (2 Corinthians 5:10).

This is not something anyone can escape, since "it is appointed for man to die once, and after that comes judgment" (Hebrews 9:27). The Christian's experience of the judgment of Christ will be very different since, as Daniel saw prophetically, "the court sat in judgment, and the books were opened" (Daniel 7:10). We will be confident in the knowledge that our names are written in the Lamb's Book of Life.

Those before Christ's judgment will have bodies: "There will be a resurrection of both the just and the unjust" (Acts 24:15). Jesus confirms this in John 5:28–29, "Do not marvel at this, for an hour is coming when all who are in the tombs will hear his voice and come out, those who have done good to the resurrection of life, and those who have done evil to the resurrection of judgment."

Many passages in the Bible demonstrate that this day is coming. We do not like to think of it. It even makes many Christians feel uncomfortable. Some of us may worry that we will not make it into heaven, others that we may only make it in "by the skin of our teeth." However, it is vital that we do think about judgment day. This is not only to motivate ourselves to live worthily, but also to remember that, for those around us who are not Christians, this is a day that will begin an eternity of terror for them. We must remember that it is only through Christ and his righteousness that we can stand guiltless before God. Paul warns us, "Examine yourselves, to see whether you are in the faith. Test yourselves" (2 Corinthians 13:5). God wants us to be so confident in the righteousness of Christ and his work for us that we can come with boldness, knowing that we are forgiven only because of what he has done.

If we are sure of our salvation, far from inducing fear and dread, judgment day should produce a joyful expectation. We will then be eager to press on and enter heaven as victors having lived our lives for the glory of God. Paul puts it this way: "Do you not know that in a race all the runners run, but only one receives the prize? So run that you may obtain it" (1 Corinthians 9:24). Elsewhere he says, "I press on toward the goal for the prize of the upward call of God in Christ Jesus" (Philippians 3:14).

We are called to persevere in our faith. This becomes especially true when difficulty arises. "And you will be hated by all for my name's sake. But the one who endures to the end will be saved" (Mark 13:13). Hebrews 3:14 tells us that those with true faith will persist in following Christ, "for we have come to share in Christ." This is in the past tense, indicating something that has already happened, but the verse continues to say that we will know for sure this has occurred only "if indeed we hold our original confidence firm to the end." The true Christian does not place his confidence in his ability to persevere, but rather in "him who is able to keep you from stumbling and to present you blameless before the presence of his glory with great joy" (Jude 24). If we are confident that we have evidence of genuine faith in our lives, we can also be confident that the one in whom we have trusted will continue to prove faithful and keep us to that final day. No one can be snatched out of his hand. We cannot be unborn again. If we have been renewed, we cannot ever truly die! Before the judgment seat of Christ three possible verdicts could be declared.

"Away from Me, I Never Knew You"

The most terrifying words in the whole Bible come from the mouth of our Lord Jesus: "On that day many will say to me, 'Lord, Lord, did we not prophesy in your name, and cast out demons in your name, and do many mighty works in your name?' And then will I declare to them, 'I never knew you; depart from me, you workers of lawlessness'" (Matthew 7:22–23).

There will be unbelievers who have been members of churches, even ministers. It is possible for the goats to deceive even sheep (Matthew 25:32–33). It is essential to our spiritual future that we appreciate the full horror of the wrath of God and flee to Jesus. Being cast out from the presence of God is the most horrific thing that could ever happen to us.

Spurgeon explains that the punishment experienced by those who are not Christians will be experienced in physical bodies.

> There is a real fire in hell, as truly as you have now a real body—a fire exactly like that which we have on earth in everything except this—that it will not consume, though it will torture you. . . .
>
> I tell thee, sinner, that those eyes that now look on lust shall look on miseries that shall vex and torment thee. Those ears which now thou lendest to hear the song of blasphemy, shall hear moans, and groans, and horrid sounds, such as only the damned know. That very throat down which thou pourest drink shall be filled with fire. Those very lips and arms of thine will be tortured all at once. . . .
>
> O my hearers! the wrath to come! the wrath to come! the wrath to come. Who among you can dwell with devouring fire? Who among you can dwell with everlasting burnings? Can you, sir? Can you? Can you abide the flame forever? "Oh, no," sayest thou, "what can I do to be saved?" Hear thou what Christ hath to say: "Believe on the Lord Jesus Christ, and thou shalt be saved."[1]

"Saved . . . as through Fire"

"For no one can lay a foundation other than that which is laid, which is Jesus Christ. Now if anyone builds on the foundation with gold, silver, precious stones, wood, hay, straw—each one's work will become manifest, for the Day will disclose it, because it will be revealed by fire, and

---

[1]C. H. Spurgeon, *Sermon No. 66*, "The Resurrection of the Dead," delivered on Sabbath Morning, February 17, 1856, at New Park Street Chapel, Southwark; http://www.spurgeon.org/sermons/0066.htm.

the fire will test what sort of work each one has done. If the work that anyone has built on the foundation survives, he will receive a reward. If anyone's work is burned up, he will suffer loss, though he himself will be saved, but only as through fire" (1 Corinthians 3:11–15).

As these are people in whom the foundation of Christ has been laid, Paul is speaking about Christians. We are warned that we must be careful how we build and that there are consequences to carelessness. People whose works are burned up at Christ's judgment seat will still experience the joy of heaven but also the shame of knowing they failed their Master. By the time we reach our eternal state, that disappointment will have passed as there will be no sorrow in eternity; somehow our sense of failure will be swallowed up. But as there will be degrees of punishment, there will also be degrees of reward. As Jonathan Edwards suggested, "The saints are like so many vessels of different sizes cast into a sea of happiness, where every vessel is full."[2]

It is hard for us to identify exactly who the "as through fire" people are. Can someone be a Christian without any outward change at all? This would seem unlikely as Jesus said, "You will recognize them by their fruits" (Matthew 7:16), and Paul tells us that certain sins indicate that people will not inherit the kingdom of heaven (see Galatians 5:19–21). We might not always be able to tell which people will escape "as through fire" and which people were never Christians at all, but we can be certain that God will have no problem making that determination.

Whenever we meet backslidden Christians who are adamant that they are safe and are not concerned about rewards, we should urge them to consider carefully if they have indeed been born again. No one must simply settle for being one of those who will, as it were, "scrape" into heaven. The Bible deliberately gives us no way of being certain that someone is a Christian at all if he is not living in a way that follows Jesus. There is a temptation toward pride here, or at other times to hopelessness. But no Christian ever earns his or her way into heaven, nor by one's own effort does a person become worthy of a greater reward. Conversely, the believer saved "through fire" is no less saved than the one who receives a rich welcome as a faithful child of God.

---

[2]Jonathan Edwards, *Sermons and Discourses: 1723–1729,* WJE Online, Vol. 14, 338; http://edwards .yale.edu/archive?path=aHR0cDovL2Vkd2FyZHMueWFsZS5lZHUvY2dpLWJpbi9uZXdwaGlsby9b 250ZXh0dWFsaXplBsP3AuMTMud2plby45MjAwMDYuOTIwMDEwLjkyMDAxMw==.

"Well Done, Good and Faithful Servant"

The Scriptures clearly offer rewards to those who persevere and serve their God: "If the work that anyone has built on the foundation survives, he will receive a reward" (1 Corinthians 3:14). "Well done, good and faithful servant. You have been faithful over a little; I will set you over much. Enter into the joy of your master" (Matthew 25:21). "Whoever would draw near to God must believe that he exists and that he rewards those who seek him" (Hebrews 11:6).

We often feel embarrassed about using the prospect of reward and recognition from God as motivation for us to behave as God wants us to. The Bible knows no such reticence. We are urged to understand that as a just judge, God will reward us for how we live. Why do we think that God would be so unjust as to not honor us for what we do?

There will be degrees of reward. We will be surprised at some who will be rewarded most by God. Perhaps the older lady who sits quietly in church in the back row but unknown to anyone intercedes daily with great passion will receive a greater reward than the preacher she listens to every week.

God has given us everything we require to be able to enter heaven with our heads held high. God doesn't want us to be "skin of the teeth" Christians but rather to escape the corruption of the world and bring honor to our Savior's name.

> His divine power has granted to us all things that pertain to life and godliness, through the knowledge of him who called us to his own glory and excellence. . . . For this very reason, make every effort to supplement your faith with virtue, and virtue with knowledge, and knowledge with self-control, and self-control with steadfastness, and steadfastness with godliness, and godliness with brotherly affection, and brotherly affection with love. . . . For whoever lacks these qualities is so nearsighted that he is blind, having forgotten that he was cleansed from his former sins. Therefore, brothers, be all the more diligent to make your calling and election sure, for if you practice these qualities you will never fall. For in this way there will be richly provided for you an entrance into the eternal kingdom of our Lord and Savior Jesus Christ. (2 Peter 1:3–11)

A PUBLIC DISPLAY OF GOD'S GLORY

In God's eternal kingdom, we will be prize exhibits, demonstrating something that cannot be seen without us:

> But God . . . raised us up with him and seated us with him in the heavenly places in Christ Jesus, so that in the coming ages he might show the immeasurable riches of his grace in kindness toward us in Christ Jesus. (Ephesians 2:4–7)

> . . . so that through the church the manifold wisdom of God might now be made known to the rulers and authorities in the heavenly places. (Ephesians 3:10)

Through the people of God the grace and wisdom of God is revealed. This revelation has already begun but will be consummated after Jesus returns. Without a world of foolishness how could anyone have truly appreciated God's wisdom? Without sinful wretches who did not deserve his love, how could God have demonstrated his grace? It is not that grace did not exist before the Fall, since God's love was always unconditional. But when the only creatures who existed were without sin, how would God have then demonstrated the true extent of his grace? When a parent looks at their young teenage child and says, "I will always love you, no matter what you do," the full, gracious nature of that love will not be revealed unless that child later rebels and sins in such a way that they do not deserve their parent's love. It is not that the parent's love has therefore changed; it is just that the love is revealed as unconditional for all to see. The well-behaved child deserves the love that the parents give freely and without expecting anything in return and so that love may not be experienced as grace.

The memories of our lives before knowing Christ must survive to the extent of being able to appreciate the fullness of God's mercy in redeeming us. In eternity we will once more become glorious, lovable creatures. Perhaps we will take turns to tell our testimonies of grace. We do know that God will have removed the sting of those memories because he promises that in those days there will be no more sorrow (see Revelation 21:4).

What a contrast there will be between Christians in their glorified state and the people in hell who will be demonstrating throughout all eternity to the universe the meaning of God's holiness and justice. The knowledge of the stark alternatives before every human being should affect the way we see every person. As C. S. Lewis says:

> Remember that the dullest and most uninteresting person you talk to may one day be a creature which, if you saw it now, you would strongly be tempted to worship, or else a horror and a corruption such as you now meet, if at all, only in a nightmare. All day long we are, in some degree, helping each other to one or other of these destinations. It is in the light of these overwhelming possibilities, it is with the awe and the circumspection proper to them, that we should conduct all our dealings with one another, all friendships, all loves, all play, all politics. There are no ordinary people. You have never talked to a mere mortal.[3]

When we fully appreciate what the people around us will one day become, we will treat everyone we meet with greater honor and importance and will be more aware of our influence. How can you and I help people on their journey to heaven rather than hell?

AN ETERNAL KINGDOM

This kingdom of God will be an eternal one, and there will be no rivals.

> Then the seventh angel blew his trumpet, and there were loud voices in heaven, saying, "The kingdom of the world has become the kingdom of our Lord and of his Christ, and he shall reign forever and ever." (Revelation 11:15)

> For he must reign until he has put all his enemies under his feet. The last enemy to be destroyed is death. For "God has put all things in subjection under his feet." But when it says, "all things are put in subjection," it is plain that he is excepted who put all things in subjection under him. When all things are subjected to him, then the Son himself will also be subjected to him who put all things in subjection under him, that God may be all in all. (1 Corinthians 15:25–28)

God is not building a democracy but a kingdom. When we struggle against authority structures in the world today, we are actually strug-

---

[3] C. S. Lewis, *The Weight of Glory* (New York: HarperOne, 2001), 14–15.

gling with a fundamental principle that goes to the heart of the Trinity. Jesus will always submit to the Father. So why do we struggle so much with submitting to those in authority over us in our homes, churches, workplaces, and nations?

THE KINGDOM NOW

We tend to think of the kingdom of Jesus as a future event. Jesus rarely spoke of the kingdom that was to come; instead he said far more often that it is already here. He repeatedly proclaimed, "The kingdom of God has come upon you" (Matthew 12:28).

The Christian already tastes the future kingdom. By virtue of our spiritual resurrection and our awareness of the Spirit's work in our hearts, we have already entered the age to come and are now representatives of the King. The kingdom is in us, and we are experiencing it in ever-increasing measure.

> Therefore, since we are receiving a kingdom that cannot be shaken, let us be thankful, and so worship God acceptably with reverence and awe, for our "God is a consuming fire." (Hebrews 12:28–29, NIV)

God himself is living inside us! We experience the power and presence of a Jesus who is living, active, and doing things today. In every circumstance of our life the resurrection can make the difference, bringing hope when things are hard and joyful deliverances when the power of the age to come breaks through. The kingdom really is now *and* not yet! We can be absolutely confident that all the blessings of the risen Jesus will be ours in the future. Paul even says we have *already* been blessed "with every spiritual blessing in the heavenly places" (Ephesians 1:3). When, for example, we ask God to heal us, we are not twisting his arm to do something he has not promised to do. Rather, we are asking him to consider doing something for us *now* that we already know he has promised he will do for us in the future. When he sovereignly chooses to bring healing by whatever means in this world, this does not reverse the process of decline that will eventually lead to our death. When he does not heal, and a loved one is taken home to Christ, our grief is lessened by the knowledge that death for the Christian is actually the ultimate healing. We do not belong in this world. We are aliens and strangers here, just passing through. We grieve, but not in the same way as those who do not share the hope we have (see 1 Thessalonians 4:13).

We live as an army in occupied territory. We know our Master. We know he rules. We see that his enemy is still ruining this world. So we pray, "Your kingdom come, your will be done, on earth as it is in heaven" (Matthew 6:10). In our evangelism, we understand that we bring a kingdom message. We also know that an enemy is at work trying to discourage us and destroy our efforts.

> When anyone hears the word of the kingdom and does not understand it, the evil one comes and snatches away what has been sown in his heart. This is what was sown along the path. (Matthew 13:19)

In a world full of pain and hatred and disappointment, we understand that "the good seed" is growing right next to the bad (Matthew 13:24–25, 38). We shouldn't try to withdraw but rather recognize that the work of God looks like a tiny mustard seed but will eventually grow into a mighty tree (Matthew 13:31–32).

The kingdom of heaven may seem to us to be hidden at times, but the joy of the believer is in giving our lives to diligently seeking it and cooperating with God in nurturing its growth. Jesus taught a parable about treasure hidden in a field that could be applied to us but also to Jesus himself. Like him, we can know the joy of laying our life down for the sake of digging it up.

> The kingdom of heaven is like treasure hidden in a field, which a man found and covered up. Then in his joy he goes and sells all that he has and buys that field. (Matthew 13:44)

Jesus said, "The kingdom of God is not coming with signs to be observed, nor will they say, 'Look, here it is!' or 'There!' for behold, the kingdom of God is in the midst of you" (Luke 17:20–21). Knowing that we already share in eternal life that will be ours in all its fullness in the future should thrill us and give us great hope.

> But we have this treasure in jars of clay, to show that the surpassing power belongs to God and not to us. We are afflicted in every way, but not crushed; perplexed, but not driven to despair; persecuted, but not

forsaken; struck down, but not destroyed; always carrying in the body the death of Jesus, so that the life of Jesus may also be manifested in our bodies. For we who live are always being given over to death for Jesus' sake, so that the life of Jesus also may be manifested in our mortal flesh . . . knowing that he who raised the Lord Jesus will raise us also with Jesus and bring us with you into his presence. . . . Though our outer self is wasting away, our inner self is being renewed day by day. For this light momentary affliction is preparing for us an eternal weight of glory beyond all comparison, as we look not to the things that are seen but to the things that are unseen. For the things that are seen are transient, but the things that are unseen are eternal. (2 Corinthians 4:7–18)

We have already been raised with Christ, and yet we are waiting for the final day when our bodies will be resurrected with Christ. As Richard Gaffin said:

An unbreakable bond or unity exists between Christ and Christians in the experience of resurrection. That bond is such that the latter (the resurrection of Christians) has two components—one that has already taken place, at the inception of Christian life when the sinner is united to Christ by faith; and one that is still future, at Christ's return.[4]

When Paul described his ministry, he said that he was "proclaiming the kingdom" (Acts 20:25), and he was clear that this declaration has dynamic effects: "for the kingdom of God does not consist in talk but in power" (1 Corinthians 4:20).

It is sobering that Paul warned us that in the last days there would be people "having the appearance of godliness, but denying its power" (2 Timothy 3:5). I trust that none of us deny the power of Jesus' resurrection to work in our lives and change us. But I hope that as we have been studying this subject, we are now more desperate than ever to see his transforming power at work, changing everything in our lives and in those around us. You can sense something of that hunger to see more of God at work in the following words from Spurgeon:

I wish I could venture further to unveil this secret force, and still more fully reveal to you the power of our Lord's resurrection. It is the power

---

[4]Richard B. Gaffin, "Redemption and Resurrection: An Exercise in Biblical-Systematic Theology," *Themelios,* Vol. 27.2, Spring 2002, 16–31; http://www.beginningwithmoses.org/articles/redemption resurrection.htm.

of the Holy Ghost; it is the energy upon which you must depend when teaching or preaching; it must all be "according to the working of his mighty power, which he wrought in Christ, when he raised him from the dead." I want you to feel that power to-day. I would have you feel eternal life throbbing in your bosoms, filling you with glory and immortality.[5]

CONCLUSION

Christians have the same power that raised Christ Jesus from the dead living inside them. One day that power will complete the work of saving us, but in the meantime the normal Christian life can be one in which we are very aware of the change that the resurrection brings. We are citizens of the age to come, living in a world that is dead to God. But we are not dead to him. We live to him. May God help us live in the light of that fact more each day. One day we will all see that, thanks to the death and resurrection of Jesus, everything really has been changed. The whole creation will have been renewed, and we will be like him.

I can think of no better way to end this book than with Paul's prayer that speaks of the work of the Spirit, of the hope Jesus' resurrection has given us, the power of his resurrection and of the coming kingdom in which he rules. May God answer this prayer in our lives and so help us to truly believe in the physical resurrection of Jesus Christ and live in light of the implications of that event.

> The God of our Lord Jesus Christ, the Father of glory . . . give you a spirit of wisdom and of revelation in the knowledge of him, having the eyes of your hearts enlightened, that you may know what is the hope to which he has called you, what are the riches of his glorious inheritance in the saints, and what is the immeasurable greatness of his power toward us who believe, according to the working of his great might that he worked in Christ when he raised him from the dead and seated him at his right hand in the heavenly places, far above all rule and authority and power and dominion, and above every name that is named, not only in this age but also in the one to come. (Ephesians 1:17–21)

---

[5]C. H. Spurgeon, *Sermon No. 2080*, "The Power of His Resurrection," delivered on April 21, 1889 at the Metropolitan Tabernacle, Newington; http://www.recoverthegospel.com/Old%20Recover%20 the%20Gospel%20Site/Spurgeon/Spurgeon%202001-3000/2080.pdf.

SCRIPTURE INDEX

GENERAL INDEX